# Information Services Design

## Routledge Studies in Organization and Systems

EDITED BY NANDISH V. PATEL, ***Director, Brunel Organization and Systems Design Center [BOSdc], Brunel University***

1 **Information Systems**
Critical Perspectives
*Bernd Stahl*

2 **Information Services Design**
A Design Science Approach for Sustainable Knowledge
*Fons Wijnhoven*

# Information Services Design

## A Design Science Approach for Sustainable Knowledge

**Fons Wijnhoven**

Routledge
Taylor & Francis Group
NEW YORK LONDON

First published 2012
by Routledge
711 Third Avenue, New York, NY 10017

Simultaneously published in the UK
by Routledge
2 Park Square, Milton Park, Abingdon, Oxon OX14 4RN

*Routledge is an imprint of the Taylor & Francis Group, an informa business*



Typeset in Sabon by IBT Global.



*Library of Congress Cataloging-in-Publication Data*

Wijnhoven, Fons.
Information services design : a design science approach for sustainable knowledge / by Fons Wijnhoven.
p. cm. — (Routledge studies in organization and systems ; 2)
Includes bibliographical references and index.
1. Information services. 2. Information resources management.
3. Database management. I. Title.
ZA3157.W56 2011
025.5'2—dc23
2011024178

ISBN: 978-0-415-89985-7 (hbk)
ISBN: 978-0-203-15108-2 (ebk)

**Dedicated to my wife, Carolyn Karthaus, who allowed me to do more than my contract requires.**

# Contents

# Figures

# Tables

# Foreword by Professor John Edwards

Designing information systems is a complicated task. Considerations need to run from business strategy and competitive advantage through to sophisticated issues of information technology. The difficulties have been recognized for more than 40 years, but not resolved. Designing information services is an even more complicated task, as increasingly they are targeted at large and diverse groups of potential users, and delivered using Internet technologies. While this trend is a great benefit for access to information services by the users, whether they are the general public or within an organization, it is an additional problem for those who have to design and support the services provided. Many have said that we live in an information age—perhaps it is now becoming an information services age. Yet the rapid and increasing rate of technological change, as well as bringing exciting new possibilities, further confounds the difficulties of improving design.

It is therefore difficult to maintain the balance between business and technological aspects when writing a book on designing information services. Fons Wijnhoven sets out to give clear guidelines about designing information services, especially to those who want to research the topic. Wijnhoven's emphasis on writing for those interested in researching the field enables him to side-step the business-technological debate completely, and instead structure the coverage in terms of philosophical viewpoints. This leads to a much more holistic treatment than is usually found in textbooks on this topic. At the heart of this holistic treatment is C. West Churchman's inquiring systems approach. This is implemented in the "inquiring" terms of five different philosophers (Leibniz, Kant, Hegel, Singer, Locke). Each of the five had a different worldview, and each of these worldviews or inquiry perspectives brings into focus a different aspect of information services design.

The book therefore spans many areas. Fundamentally it is about design science, in this case as applied to information services. In addition, much of the material sheds useful light on other aspects of design, on information systems more widely, and especially on the field of knowledge management, which remains high on the list of priority topics for both business and academia. This breadth is especially important when one bears in mind that (as we have said) the Internet changes very rapidly, and there is plenty of evidence that people are not good at predicting change or its consequences. Psychological research tells us about anchoring, the tendency of people to stick closely to their pre-conceived ideas and what they are already familiar with. Radical change is hard to foresee from such a standpoint.

A strength of the book is that it combines both product- and process-oriented views of information services design. Nevertheless, the design of the book itself leans more towards being process structured, and quite rightly so, as the processes define and describe both the "what" and the "how" of organizational operations. Literally, these are the ways in which the business and technological aspects are linked.

Another strength is the use of detailed case study examples based on Wijnhoven's own experience of researching in the area. For example, Chapter 3 includes a very detailed discussion of music download business models—an information service that would have been unheard of even 15 years ago, and also one with which any student reader anywhere in the world will be familiar with.

The examples gradually become more specific, following the design philosophy of the book. Quoting from Chapter 5, "an information system design process has design steps corresponding with different design layers; i.e., layers of decomposition from abstract notions of a system (the business model) to its realization in concrete databases, organizational and technical means (the infrastructure)." Several of the examples in Chapters 4 and 5 show how information services are relevant to knowledge management: the KINX portal assisting SMEs with the challenge of knowledge integration; the knowledge portal used by the Dutch Police force; and discussion of how to make use of expertise networks. Indeed, two architectures described in Chapter 5—data aggregation and community building—echo the two fundamental organizational knowledge management strategies of codification and personalization.

There are good general business lessons too—for example, the difference between best practice and good practice, as discussed in the Nestlé case.

By the time the lowest level of decomposition is reached, in Chapter 7, the examples become very detailed indeed. Readers will find the use of ArchiMate very helpful, as it goes all the way from the top level objective of the system to the IT architecture delivering it. Any new information service will only work, and continue to work, if all the levels are good enough.

To sum up, this book will not be an easy read—many information scientists do not feel at home with philosophy and so will find themselves in unfamiliar territory. Nevertheless, it will be a rewarding one. It is not possible to instruct someone step-by-step how design science works, but it is possible to show them very detailed examples of different types of systems, and let them use these to help learn how to design for themselves. This Fons Wijnhoven has done.

John S. Edwards
Professor of Operations and Information Management
Dean
Aston University, Birmingham, UK

# Preface

Information services are business and organizational activities for informing people, i.e., helping them understand the world. Internet technologies have a huge impact on the nature of these services and, consequently, we discuss information services in the context of these technologies. Because Internet technologies for informing are vastly changing, writing a book about it is difficult and such a book may become obsolete too quickly to be worth the effort. Instead, therefore, this book starts with *fundamental* (and therefore enduring) *philosophical notions* of information and design-as-a-science, and aims at presenting material that students will find useful during their lifetime. Because philosophy is a very extensive discipline and the author is not a professional philosopher but a management and information systems scientist, these insights are built on the work of C. W. Churchman (1971), who introduced the major philosophical foundations for the information systems discipline in the beginning of the 1970s. This ambition is a search for *sustainable* insights by reusing Churchman's findings. The first chapter presents fundamental design concepts of information, information markets, and information services, by which we scope the area. These understandings give product characteristics of information services and three aspects: content, use-value, and revenue. Chapter 2 describes how we as practitioners and scientists can cope with these aspects for the development of information services; thus we build a process-oriented design theory. Both the product- and process-oriented insights enable the discussion of information services problems and challenges, information service business concepts and models, information provision processes, information services architectures, and information service exploitation in, respectively, Chapters 3, 4, 5, and 6. Chapter 7, on design science, discusses the nature of theory, methods and techniques, and criteria for good scientific results in this highly dynamic area by three case studies that demonstrate the use of the insights from previous chapters. As such this chapter presents a pragmatic perspective, i.e., using philosophical foundations in a practical way to solve real-world problems. The end of this chapter summarizes key findings of this book and discusses its future research potential.

This book came out of a need for an academic text for master's students in business informatics, economics, and communication sciences to *research* information services. The current books in the field of information services are very useful, but they are sometimes too narrowly focused, i.e., too technical or too organizational-economical, or lack an academic research challenge. Many research-oriented courses, therefore, supply a reader with a collection of academic articles and a guide of how to do design science research. This, however, easily results in fragmented basic knowledge. This book wants to organize, structure, and codify the basic knowledge needed, giving students a quick and coherent start to the topic of information services from a design science perspective. But, of course, this book has limitations as well. For example, it puts the focus on the information concept and not the technical systems. It has a design science focus and definitely is limited from a behavioral science perspective. It also reuses a lot of existing knowledge from the disciplines of economics, business, strategy, and information systems, and thus it is not new in everything, but its story is new and, as far as the author knows, is greatly needed.

While I have been teaching an information services course in the last three years, experiences accumulated and some of the best conceptual, theoretical, and methodological insights could be gradually selected. At the same time, my research delivered several insights that are sometimes useful for students willing to learn about researching the design and exploitation of information services. This book therefore combines several teaching notes and several research papers (see the acknowledgments).

This book can serve several audiences and purposes:

1. Its prime aim is to give insights about *information services as an economic entity* in need of sustainability by serving an information market well. This purpose is a useful part of modern curricula of management, communication science, and information systems.
2. Because of its design science approach, it may be a useful book for training people in *design science and its methodologies.* This is especially useful for master's and PhD students in engineering and helps them to contribute to the scientific body of knowledge while aiming at designing innovations. Such a course on design science may also be useful for modern programs in management and social sciences as an addition to the predominantly behavioral (descriptive and explanatory) orientation of most of its research methodology courses.

This explains why this book is useful for students while finishing their bachelor's programs, master's programs, and some PhD programs in a broad area of teaching (management, social sciences, communication science, information systems, and knowledge engineering).

Because this book is a *first* attempt to codify these insights, many improvements are possible and, consequently, suggestions for improving this text are most welcome.

Fons Wijnhoven
Enschede, September 2011.

# Acknowledgments

Chapter 1 is based on my book on information management (Routledge 2009) but extends it so that it grounds a design science approach to information services. Some of the basic concepts of a service have been developed with colleagues from the CTIT/ASSIST group on service science at the University of Twente in the Netherlands.

Chapter 2 uses Walls et al.'s (1992) paper for explaining the concept of design theory. I also use Hevner et al. (2004) for explaining the concept of design science.

Chapter 3 reuses parts of Wijnhoven and Meyer's non-published work on newspaper business models. I reused substantial parts of Koen Voermans work on the Dutch music download market for explaining the concept of business model validation.

Chapter 4 reuses parts of Elorrieta, Lopez, and Wijnhoven (2005) with respect to the description of the KINX portal. KINX was an EU-sponsored research project, resulting in substantial insights on using portals for knowledge exchange. I also acknowledge the European Commission for sponsoring this research via grant GIRD-CT-2002–00700.

For Chapter 5, I reused the Wijnhoven and Kraaijenbrink (2008) paper. I acknowledge the good collaboration with Jeroen Kraaijenbrink on this paper. This chapter also uses Lankhorst et al.'s (2009) work on information systems architecture, which resulted in their ArchiMate language. I also thank Frank Timmer for his collaboration on the case of the Dutch Police to illustrate the use of relevant design methods and techniques.

For the case on Nestlé Waters and the description of action research-oriented information service exploitation, I would like to mention the collaboration of Wieteke Meijer for her intensive fact-finding efforts, Dr. Tanya Bondarouk for the case analysis, and Marit Sollaart and Stephanie Cuynet from Nestlé Paris for facilitating and hosting us.

For Chapter 7, I would like to thank all the students who participated in the Information and Knowledge Exchange Services course. The case of GBA was developed by students Arjan Krukkert, Kelvin Divendal, Ronald Damhuis, and Tycho Bom. The case of WIKIpedia was developed by students Koen Klein Tank, Tom Hendrixen, and Sjoerd van der Spoel. The case of TSi was developed by students Chaithany Karanth, Martin Haitsma, Renske Vermolen, and Laurens Vliegen.

Most parts of this book have been written during my sabbatical stay at the information systems department of the University of Muenster. Students in the information systems program used a draft version of the book and supplied me with important feedback, which is incorporated in this book. I would like to thank Professors Jörg Becker and Stefan Klein for this unique opportunity. I also thank Professor John Edwards for the useful foreword.

The book has been completed while working as an associate professor of knowledge management and information systems at the University of Twente in Enschede in the Department of Information Systems and Change Management. I especially appreciate the intellectual space and freedom offered to me to write this book. For this I would like to particularly thank the head of the department, Jos van Hillegersberg. Finally, I also want to thank Geert van der Molen, who is a knowledge management entrepreneur but also a real thinker and provider of many comments on several drafts of the manuscript. I also thank him for his encouragement and hope that he will be able to exploit this text in the best way possible.

All the responsibility for this text is, of course, with the author.

# 1 Information Service Foundations and Design Science

This chapter discusses the following questions to define the subject and scope of this book:

- What is informing about?
- What does the information concept imply for information service design?
- How does an information service differ from an information system?
- What are the implications of a design science approach to information services management?

The answers to these questions explain the rest of the structure of this book.

## 1.1 INFORMATION

Information is meaningful data or meaningful representations (Floridi, 2005). Something with economic value for a customer is called a good and an *information good* is a meaningful representation with an informing value for an information customer. This informing value implies that the semantic (meaningful) content must be true. Therefore, incorrect and misleading data is indeed semantic content, but it is not information (Floridi, 2005). A lot of semantic content has an entertainment value, and thus its main purpose is not *informing*. This content is also called infotainment. Sometimes "information goods" are defined as all digital representations, including motion pictures and recorded music, without regard to their informative content (e.g., Bhargava & Choudhury, 2001: 91). We, however, reserve the term digital good for this, and recognize that some digital goods do not have an explicit informative objective. While the borderline between informing and entertaining might be difficult to establish, particularly for "infotainment", this book focuses on those goods of which their *informing* role is most important. With informing, here, we mean the process of enabling people to understand

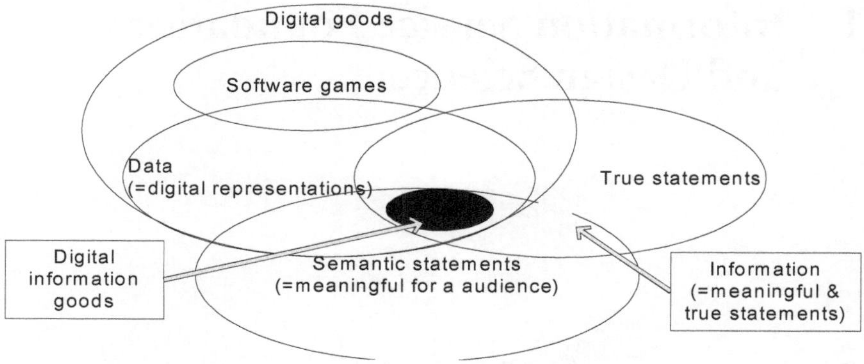


*Figure 1.1* Information and digital information goods.

any phenomenon, object, or event of the world. Some authors, like Meyer and Zack (1996), include different media (printed or digital) as part of their concept of information goods. This book restricts the definition of information goods to *informing digital goods* (Bhargava & Choudhury, 2001). Figure 1.1 gives a Venn diagram of the basic concepts here.

*Information services* deliver information goods that can be bought, selected, created, distributed, or modified by information customers (Womack, 2002). As common in economics, a good has some level of tangibility (for digital information goods, the tangible part is mostly of an binary electronic nature, sometimes materialized on DVDs or burned on chips, or stored by a magnetic pattern on another less permanent data carrier). Information services also deliver information-related value of an intangible nature, for example, by enabling people to interact with content, to build relationships with experts or colleagues, or help people to distribute their ideas, what is mostly the purpose of so-called social media. Like with most services, information services require specific client-service-provider interactions, and organizational and information technological means to realize these (business) processes.

To avoid confusions on the concept of information and digital goods, we describe a few related concepts: (1) signs, (2) data, and (3) knowledge.

## 1.1.1 Representations and Signs

First of all, electronic media are not the only carriers of data as we may have data also in the form of *signs* (like paintings and pictures) and speech and sound, also called *oral* and *auditive* data, but electronic media have an unprecedented level of reproduction and distribution efficiency (Jonscher, 1994). The reason for this efficiency is the extremely high *commonality* of electronic data and electronic data processing equipment, which are able to codify all data as binary units, i.e., + or—on magnetic data storage devices and 1 or 0 in code processing units, flash memory, and computer internal memory units (Jonscher, 1994). This high commonality also explains to a large extent the empirical correctness of Moore's law (i.e., the number of transitors that can be placed on a circuit inexpensively doubles every two years, which seems to be true for the last 50 years). This high commonality also may explain the 50% speed increase of high-end communication connections per year, although these developments are far from technical alone. Jonscher (1994) identifies a mutual reinforcement of user needs and the decline of information technological production costs (i.e., a quite strong learning curve). Information is a key resource for strategic and operational processes in organizations, and data carrying and processing machines are able to hugely reduce information collection, storage, manipulation, and distribution costs. In fact, the marginal reproduction and distribution costs of digital information goods (data) are nearly zero (Shapiro & Varian, 1999). The real costs are the creation of the first copy. On a world scale, though, the energy costs are very substantial, and data centers, which provide Internet hosting services, have to fight for extra bits of electricity at reasonable prices. I am not saying here that any Internet use or information service use (for business or personal needs) should be avoided, but I do say that it has "carbon costs". Besides, Internet usage has large hidden or difficult to measure time, emotional, and ethical costs. We have to be aware of these facts, and next start using the Internet and computers most intelligently. Information services should be there to help you with wise use of information technological resources for informing.

### 1.1.2 Data

Second, although data is technically a very uniform phenomenon, from a user perspective it is very diverse. At least four types of data can be identified (Floridi, 2005):

1. *Primary* data , which are the principal data stored in a database and which information services can deliver to a user
2. *Metadata*, which enable a database management system to fulfill its tasks by describing essential properties of the primary data, like its origin, its format, availability, and copyrights

3. *Operational* data, which are data regarding the usage of the primary data by which the owners of information services can improve and customize data goods to user needs
4. *Derivative* data, which can be created on the basis of the first three types—for instance, stock exchange systems can deliver statistical data and statistical analysis. The primary data of a stock exchange consists of data on the price of stocks of different companies and the people who have offered and bought them on a certain day. The metadata of a stock exchange database may consist of availability rights of these data. For instance, traders may have online access to the data and access to a system to offer and buy stocks. The general public may have only the right to see that database after a certain time has passed and may have access to the general statistics of a day. The managers of the stock exchange service need information on its performance to guarantee the quality of access and potentially intervene when certain transaction volumes seem to become alarming. Stock exchange analysts may be interested in derivative data products that analyze the performance of their buying and sales policies, so that they advise on certain tactics in selling and buying of stocks.

Managers of information services often analyze derivative data extensively to improve the value of the service for their clients and to help customizing services (Albert et al., 2004). Operational data for information service managers may consist of so-called web tracking, which mines users' IP addresses, any other data from users, and what the users do on the manager's site. Metadata for an information service manager consists of, for example, information access and use rights, usage time-slots, and contracts of use. Information service *users* are mostly interested in the primary and derivative data. The primary data may be the data that users submit and exchange with each other, and many information services managers may be "blind" with respect to this content for the sake of the users' own privacy and freedom of speech. Only in cases of the obstruction of key laws, values, and norms (e.g., child porn, racist and terrorist information), information service managers may have to exercise their responsibilities by removing such information or removing the submitters and users of such information from their client base. Derivative information is mostly produced under the responsibility of information service managers to deliver higher-valued content (e.g., regular standard reports) to their clients, but often clients are given tools to create their own derivative data (e.g., statistical and data mining tools).

An interesting case of derivative information is the credit rating information of Moody's Investors Service, Standard & Poor, and Fitch. These companies give information to their customers on investment risks they take. At the Dutch parliament hearings on the credit crisis of 2008 and

2009, it was stated by several bankers and financial service experts that the Dutch banks leaned too much on information from these three rating institutes when buying mortgage packages from US banks in 2008. At that time, insufficient knowledge existed concerning how to reliably rate these investment risks and billions of losses in the European financial sector were the result (source Volkskrant 30–1-2010).

### 1.1.3 Meaningful Data and Information

Third, the actual *contribution of data to knowledge about the world* is complex. We can, for instance, easily calculate the number of data available on our hard disk by looking how many kilo-, mega-, or gigabytes are occupied by our documents, but this does not say much about our understanding of the world. Sometimes even less is better. The foregoing example of the stock exchange and interbank mortgage trade also pointed at the need for creating *reliable* derivative data for making wise decisions. So the key point with information management is not just data management, because *data are carriers of content and not the informing content itself.* But what is informative content? Floridi (2005) mentions at least two criteria for meaningful data to be informative and we add a third in the list here:

1. The data must be *meaningful*, i.e., *people* should be able to understand the message in the language they use. This seems to be an obvious criterion but many data in information systems may be incorrectly understood. An example here is personnel information systems, where sometimes the number of people contracted are taken as the number of employees. But many contracted people may not have an employee contract and are hired via their consulting firm to help in a project. This problem of matching the meanings (*semantics* of users and information systems is in practice more complex but a key prerequisite for any successful information system. This can be achieved by standardizing meanings of terms in a community through the identification of homonyms, synonyms, classes, and subclasses, which together build a so-called ontology (Gruber, 1993).
2. The data must be *true*. Indeed incorrect data do not help in understanding the world, and in fact complicate the realization of understanding. Sometimes, as stated before, incorrect information is the result of unintentional behavior (called mis-"information"), but sometimes information is intentionally incorrect and is created and supplied to confuse the competition or enemy (called dis-"information") (Wijnhoven et al., 2010). This thus requires methods to systematically and critically evaluate the correctness of information goods.

3. The data must be *relevant* for decision-making and problem-solving, which is also called the *pragmatic* (Stamper, 1973) function of information. Having much meaningful and true information does not always mean that this information is relevant for the specific needs and context of its owner. In fact, sometimes too much meaningful and true information may result in information overload, which implies that the receiver of this information is not able to see the trees through the forest (Landau, 1969). This implies methods to collect and relevantly connect information with problems, tasks, and solutions.

Five paradigms to the *nature of knowledge* have developed and have been codified by epistemological (i.e., knowledge theory) traditions (Churchman, 1971), which discuss meaning, truth, and usefulness of information differently. These paradigms are as follows:

1. *Empiricism* (based on the philosophy of Locke) is a theory of knowledge emphasizing the role of experience, especially sensory perception, in the formation of ideas, while discounting the notion of innate ideas. According to this paradigm, knowledge is an intersubjective true representation of the world and believed to be "objectively" true by the community of its owners. This community also agrees on the meaning of observations by sharing an ontology on the subject (i.e., a classification of subjects, definitions, relations, and related formulas, if needed). A good example here is the classifications of animals used by biologists and the periodic table of elements used in chemistry.
2. *Rationalism* (partially based on the philosophy of Leibniz) is any view appealing to reason as a source of knowledge or justification. In more technical terms it is a method or a theory in which the criterion of truth is not sensory but intellectual and deductive. According to Leibniz, real information is incorporated in the models by which we reason about the reality.
3. *Kantian idealism* emphasizes the need of different perspectives to realize a complete picture of a phenomenon. This requires ways of integrating and consolidating sometimes conflicting perspectives. In this perspective, there are many competing ways of looking at reality sometimes resulting in useful complementary insights and requiring both data and models.
4. *Hegelian dialectics* is an exchange of propositions (theses) and counterpropositions (antitheses) resulting in a synthesis of the opposing assertions, or at least a qualitative transformation during the dialogue. Dialectics has been introduced by Kant before as a way of consolidating different perspectives. Theses and anti-theses, though, are carried by different people, who may have antagonistic interests, which

is a key issue in Hegelian epistemology. In this Hegelian approach, informing becomes part of the political and competitive scene and serves the interests of a content supplier (i.e., an information master) to successfully influence an information consumer (i.e., an information slave).

5. *Singerian pragmatism* is an epistemology and ethical theory stating that the value of knowledge should be expressed in terms of how the knowledge improves the human condition and, although people have to strive for truth, they will never reach the ultimate truth and progress is even more important than truth itself. Here information is a pragmatic tool, but the focus is on the interests of the content consumer, who needs information to solve a problem.

### 1.1.4 From Representation to Knowledge

To summarize this discussion of signs, data, and information, we provide a taxonomy of concepts related to information goods in Figure 1.2. In this taxonomy, we specify the focus on electronic digital representations, leaving verbal data and signs out of our study, although when these verbal data and signs have been transformed to an electronic digital nature, they may be of interest in this book. Additionally, meaningless data are excluded, by which we mean not humanly interpretable data. These meaningless data, however, may be important parts of technical and biological systems, which are not part of this book on information services. Also hedonic data are excluded when they do not inform, but we also acknowledge that most hedonic data (like music, video, and games) may have some informative value, and thus it is sometimes difficult if not impossible to exclude them from a study of information services. Misinformation and disinformation are excluded from the concept of information, but because they can be influential for motivating human behavior and cannot easily be distinguished from information, they cannot be excluded from a study of information services, but require a discussion of methods for assessing truth as part of information services.

Note that this book aims at a more fundamental understanding of the concept of information than is common in the information systems field, where information is often equated with knowledge *derived* from data, *processed* data, or data presented in a meaningful context (e.g., Kroenke, 2008: 24). This would imply that knowledge is "something" produced from data, but, for example, according to the Leibnizian approach, knowledge can be derived directly from good human thinking, so no data processing is needed. Also, data can have a value by themselves, as stated by Locke, and sometimes data are intentional (i.e., pragmatic) mechanisms of influencing the world (Hegel). The Hegelian view emphasizes the supply side of information services, i.e., content suppliers and sponsors who use information services to influence customers

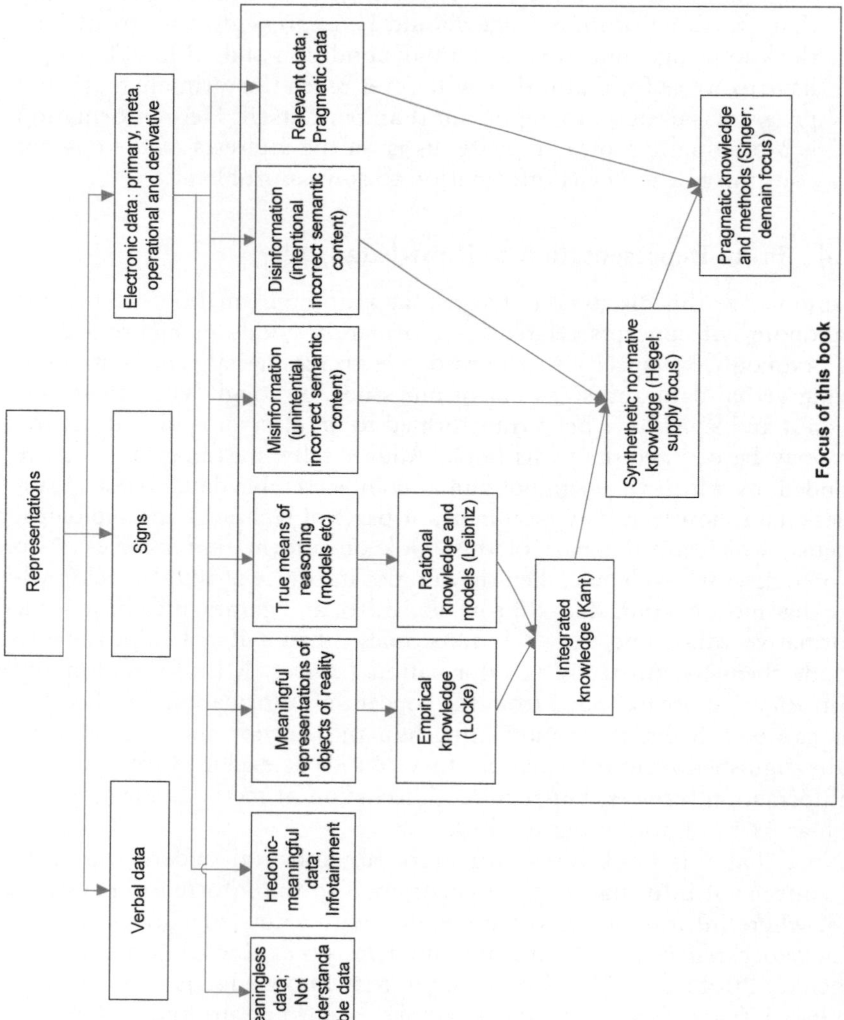


*Figure 1.2* A taxonomy of information goods from representation to knowledge.

and information services and their actor networks to gain certain profit or revenue. The Singerian perspective, on the other hand, emphasizes the revenues of information services from the customer side, i.e., the utility of these services to augment people's understanding and to help them improve their situation.

## 1.2 INFORMATION SERVICES

A service is defined by Kotler (1988: 477) as "... any act or performance that one party can offer to another that is essentially intangible and does not result in the ownership of anything". Services are a very heterogeneous collection of economic activities for helping people. An ad hoc list of services is given here:

1. Personal services (e.g., porters, hairstylists)
2. Professional services (e.g., health care services, lawyers, teachers, accountants, business consulting)
3. Services that provide equipment for intangible values (e.g., theatre, museum, sports training facilities, car rental)
4. Services that handle money (e.g., insurance, banking, credit card processors)
5. Services that handle data (e.g., telecom services, data processing services, data search and retrieval services)
6. Industrial services (e.g., warehousing, logistics, project management)
7. Trade services (e.g., auctions, brokers and contractors, marketers)
8. Information and knowledge services (e.g., publishers, media firms, content brokers, business intelligence firms)
9. Software and systems services (e.g., IBM)

Information goods stored in databases can easily become irrelevant and meaningless. Information services facilitate the *exchange* of these information goods through time (also called organizational memory systems (Wijnhoven, 1999)) and space (like knowledge sharing systems and virtual communities of practice) *with or without transforming* these goods. Information services perform these exchanges to help people understand the world by delivering, making accessible, or sharing relevant and useful information. A key result of using an information service is having meaningful data (this is what Kotler (1988: 477) names "*a major service with accompanying minor goods*"; the major service is "informing" and the minor good is "data and information technology").

An information service is sometimes defined as an independent economic entity performing its activities (information acquisition, processing, and dissemination) on behalf of other agents' information needs (Womack, 2002). This definition is similar to an information intermediary (e.g., a library service or a search engine), although an information service is not always an intermediary, because it also may be the owner of the content it provides to its clients (e.g., a publisher or a company that supplies information about its products). An information service also may be an "independent, profit maximizing economic information processing system performing its activities (. . .) on behalf of other agents' information needs" (Rose, 1999), but depending on the economic context of the service this profit maximizing ambition may be possible or impossible, useful or not useful, but in all cases some kind of revenue collection is needed to cover at least the cost of the service via payments, sponsorships, or donations. An information service is an independent economic entity, because as a company, organization, network, or organizational unit it will have to maintain its existence on the basis of its value for the market, community, or organization it serves, i.e., it will cease to exist when key stakeholders (for example, content suppliers) do not sufficiently recognize its value. To enable an efficient running of its content deliveries, it may use an infrastructure of information and communication technologies.

In the information systems discipline a service is often defined as ". . . a unit of functionality that some entity (e.g., a system, organization, or department) makes available to its environment, and which has some value for certain entities in the environment (typically the "service users")" (Lankhorst, 2009: 85–86). This broad description of a service is applicable to all kind of services, such as people-based services (like professional services, skilled labor services, and unskilled labor services) and equipment-based services (like automated services, equipment services operated by relatively unskilled people, and equipment services operated by skilled people) (Kotler, 1988: 478). Before the extensive use of computers for informing, information services like libraries and newspapers were mainly people-based and mostly professional services. With the growing use of computers, however, information services have mainly become *equipment-based.* Yet, there is still a need for professionals to design, configure, and operate information services skillfully. Related to information services are *web services*. Such services aim at delivering software applications from different supplier locations that match the use context needs (Moseley, 2007; W3C, 2002), whereas *information* services aim at informing. Web services, though, can also deliver useful applications to support informing processes of information services.

When discussing IT support of informing processes, this book uses a more restricted concept of *information system* than is common by many information scientists. It is frequently stated that an information system is ". . . a group of components that interact to produce information" (Kroenke, 2008: 6). While identifying these components, they mention at least hardware, software, data, procedures, and people. This definition is problematic, because it nearly includes everything of what we could call an organization, and thus has insufficient focus. Therefore this book restricts the notion of information systems to software and databases used for information processing. Hardware and data communication facilities are part of the information service infrastructure, and people and procedures are important parts of the organizational and human infrastructure. Following this definition of an information system, *an information system is not an information service* but it will be a part of its infrastructure.

From the preceding, we may conclude that an information service requires the active involvement of different stakeholders (also called web actors; Al-Debei & Avision, 2010), who supply different resources for an information service. These actors have different roles as supplier of content and use-value features (models, etc.), as sponsors, as clients, and as members of the service's infrastructure (see Figure 1.3).

Most existing information services deliver diverse content and use-features. The digital nature of information goods has enabled traditional information services to innovate with the help of computers and the Internet. The Internet has brought both producers and consumers of information an increased range of opportunities for distributing and accessing information. However, this has resulted in at least three types of *problems*. Firstly, people experience information overloads because of the massive volumes of content on the Internet. This results in huge information search and selection problems (Lawrence & Giles, 1999; Poston & Speier, 2005). Secondly, the Internet does not supply sufficient means to establish the use-value of information available on the Internet (Choo et al., 2000; Grote et al., 2002; Vishik & Whinston, 1999). Finally, suppliers of information goods are often unsure about how they can get

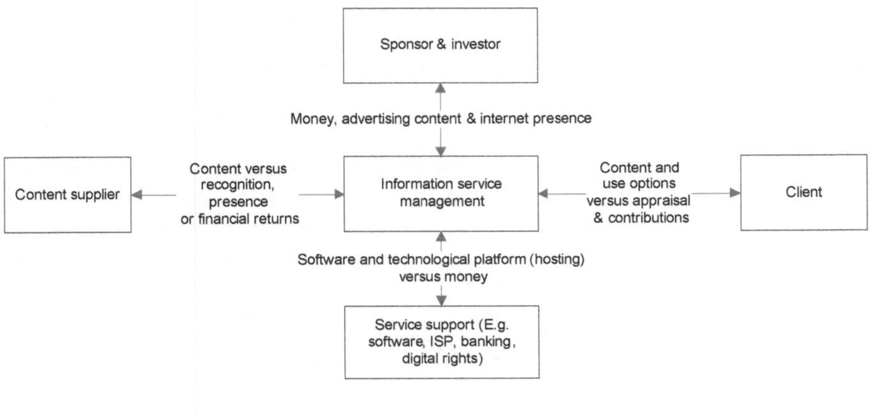


*Figure 1.3* Information service actor web.

revenues back for their efforts (Gallaugher et al., 2001; Kankanhalli et al., 2005; Shapiro & Varian, 1999) and consequently, content owners are sometimes reluctant to share their most valuable content. Therefore, actor webs of information services have three types of exchanges: content, use options, and revenues (financial or immaterial).

The concept of "information service" is not just an academic construct, but numerous information services—also called information brokers, infomediaries, or information intermediaries—have been established to intermediate between producers and consumers of information (Womack, 2002). Some of these services are established firms, like LexisNexis, EBSCO, and Reuters; others serve communities of practice in a non-profit way, like www.aisnet.org, and still others are means for organizations to bundle their content and improve communications internally and externally, like www. vatican.va. We identify four classes of information services on two dimensions, i.e., the *pragmatic* purpose (which we name revenue further on and may be supplier- versus user-focused to identify the difference of the Hegelian and Singerian perspectives on information), and the *delivery* focus (which may be content versus use options to highlight the difference of a Lockean and Leibnizian approach); see Table 1.1.

*Table 1.1* A Classification of Information Services along Delivery and Revenue Dimensions

| | | *Revenue focus* | |
|---|---|---|---|
| | | *Service manager (Hegel; supply)* | *Service user (Singer; demand)* |
| Delivery focus | Content (Locke) | 1. Corporate website; e.g., archives sites; blogs; personal home pages; school sites; political party sites; company sites | 2. Content aggregator (portal); e.g., affiliate content distribution site; content sites; database site; development/ expertise site; employment sites; news site; web portals |
| | Use (Leibniz) | 4. Data and work integrators: advisory site (e.g., a book advisory service); agent-based planning & decision site; auction sites; data mining and warehousing service; dating and matching site; ontology-based expertise site; rating site; review site; weather site | 3. Community builder (social media): e.g., city site; community site; discussion sites and fora; expert search site; fan site; voting sites; wiki site |

1. *Corporate websites* help to communicate certain messages to an audience, while keeping full control over its content and the content property rights. This implies that the website owner collects and creates the content and publishes it to certain content customer groups. Such websites may be customer support websites or intranet sites for company internal communication and information use. Often these websites are combined with e-business purposes (see Lee et al., 2002).
2. *Content aggregators* enable content customers to find and compose their own information goods. This is often the case when the information service wants to help specific groups with similar interests, which are often difficult to specify in advance. An example is the website of the British Horn Society (http://www.british-horn.org/), which has only some little bit of information about itself, but next has a large collection of links for French horn enthusiasts (amateurs, professionals, and general audience) to find more information about, for example, French horn producers, composers, education and training, and orchestras. Such a service thus is a portal to other information resources.
3. *Community builders or social media* aim at providing ways of interacting by content such that it enables community building. Examples here are www.YouTube.com and www.facebook.com, which allow members of the community to share oral and visual representation or anything they like to represent about themselves with others. These services also provide several tools like tagging, filtering, organizing, and commenting to develop communities of people with common interests or expertise and help others to develop their interests.
4. *Data integrators* aim at the consolidation of data from different sources by a common data standard or ontology. A well-known variant of this is the data warehouse (Kimball & Merz, 2000), which integrates data from different resources. Such data integration is much more difficult when more text-based or multimedia data have to be integrated via the Internet. For this purpose the semantic web community tries to realize solutions (Berners-Lee et al., 2001; W3C, 2002), but realizing these solutions is complex (McIlraith et al., 2004), although some interesting options exist by applying text and data mining tools.

## 1.3 INFORMATION SERVICE ASPECTS

Information services thus have content and use aspects. Information services also have a revenue dimension for the content supplier as well as for the user. These content, use, and revenue aspects have a direct correspondence with the reasons for existence of information services and the philosophies of informing. This is shortly summarized in Figure 1.4.

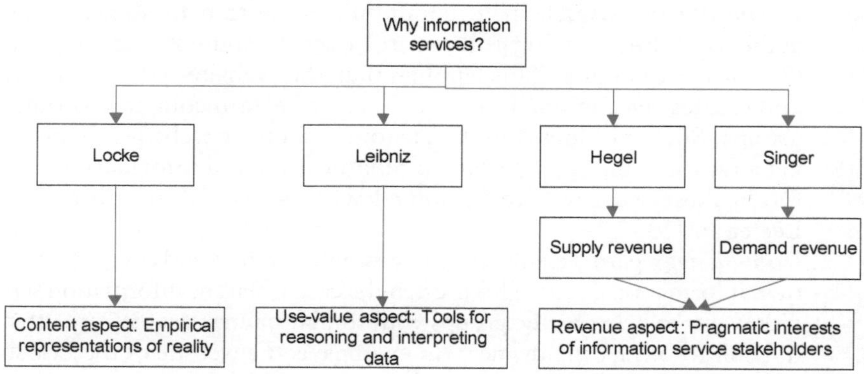


*Figure 1.4* Information service aspects.

### 1.3.1 The Content Aspect: Taking Care of Primary Data

Ogden and Richards (1946; Sowa, 2000) distinguish two dimensions of *content*: *representation* and *conceptualization*, which in this book are sometimes called codification and abstraction.

*Representations* signify objects and events in reality by codes and media, for instance, by words in a language or artifact. Representations are necessarily incomplete and often (partially) incorrect. Because of time priorities, many audiences will not be interested in a full story of an event or will experience information overload if all data are presented. Therefore, selectivity of the content creator and information service, although also a potential source of bias, may be a valuable service for a content consumer. Besides incompleteness, incorrectness, and selectivity, any representation is necessarily ambiguous for its potential users (Poston & Speier, 2005; Weick, 1979). Some creators of representations may even intentionally submit incomplete, incorrect, selective, and ambiguous content. For instance, a press release of a politician may be selective to avoid unwanted interpretations and to invoke actions needed to realize certain policies. Examples here are the selective communications of ministries of finance and central banks during the credit crisis in 2008–2010. The communications were not allowed to increase feelings of uncertainty to avoid bank runs or negatively influencing the reputation of certain banks. At the same time, however, the ministries of finance had to develop a sense of urgency that could allow actions of governments to secure the continuity of the banking industry by substantial government loans and taking over of bank properties. In any representation also a specific type of medium, coding, and possible natural language(s) will be used that possibly fit with the intended audience and purposes. To continue our example, a communication during the credit crisis aimed at the larger audience needs media and language other than that of one aimed at bankers or political decision makers.

*Conceptualization* determines the level of understanding and generalization of the information goods delivered to the service's customers. A low level of conceptualization gives blunt representations of reality, i.e., facts and figures. Such representations consist of labels that have a shared meaning for a certain group. High levels of conceptualization give explanations, predictions, and methodologies, jointly also called epistemological knowledge (Mingers, 2008). Conceptualization thus gives a theoretical or linguistic meaning to representations and may use classes and constructs to describe objects more generally (Sowa, 2000).

Given the different levels of representation and conceptualization, several information goods can be identified from the perspective of the information goods receiver or buyer (see Table 1.2).

Information services need to deliver information goods with appropriate levels of representation and conceptualization, which may vary over different customer groups. For example, academics may appreciate information goods with high levels of conceptualization whereas operational practitioners need low levels of conceptualization. Or, whereas decision makers may need low levels of representation (only specifically relevant data), analysts often need high levels of representation to develop a broader view (e.g., large detailed data sets).

*Table 1.2* A Classification and Examples of Information Goods from a Content Perspective

| | | *Level of representation/codification* | |
|---|---|---|---|
| | | *Low* | *High* |
| Level of conceptualization/abstraction | Low | Qualitative observations & reports; business intelligence reports; skills descriptions | Data deliveries; news; data sets & databases; shared resources for (professional or academic) communities |
| | High | Theories; formalized organizational routines & norms (informal routines are not codified); scientific articles (always need depth and focus) | Paradigms; patents; business process models; management reports, data resources, and overviews |

### 1.3.2 The Use-Value Aspect: Metadata Use and Derivative Data Production

Although a specification of content at appropriate levels of representation and conceptualization is important for the user's *value* experience, it is not enough for user information satisfaction. At least four additional dimensions can be distinguished (Doll & Torkzadeh, 1988): accuracy, format, ease of use, and timeliness. These dimensions each set specific challenges for information services:

1. An information service can handle accuracy, for instance, by rating the certainty of evidences and insights (e.g., by asking a panel or past users to rate it), by certification through an expert in the field, or by giving the user opportunities to check the evidence and conclusions (Poston & Speier, 2005).
2. An information service can handle formats by using different technical and/or natural languages, codes, or visualizations. For instance, for an online mobile stock exchange data service, the data have to be transformed to the technical languages and formats that are compatible with the screen layouts of the clients' mobile devices. Translation services also may be beneficial for people who read messages in a foreign language. An information service may offer software that translates different technical languages and provide interpretations for translation software.
3. An information service can supply different usability options (Choi et al., 1997; Dix et al., 1997; Loebbecke, 1999). *Interactiveness options* enable customers to manipulate the information good, to add features, or to remove items. *Use intensity and use duration options* supply the information good for single-use or multiple-use or for a specific time slot. *Operational use options* may deliver content as a single set of data, but also may include executable codes. *Externalities* may be facilitated by an information service through broadcasting the content to a larger audience so that it can become a standard insight or common knowledge that eases collaboration among its members (Lin et al., 2005). An information service also may supply *intellectual property rights* (IPR) management by excluding access and user rights to the content. When the content owner needs financial returns for staying in business, the right of selling, modifying, applying in products, and copying of the good is mostly exclusive to the content creator or the intermediating information service.
4. Most goods, but especially information goods, can have a very strong declining value through time and space. This applies particularly to stock exchange data, which even depreciate in seconds.

Some other information goods are not that sensitive to depreciation (e.g., archival data and dictionaries). Also, much information is of value only when at specific locations, for example, traffic congestion information. Information services thus need to be tuned well to time and space dimensions, which is also called being context-aware (Hong et al., 2009).

### 1.3.3 The Revenue Aspect: Operational Data Exploitation

Information services may deliver much content with high use-value, but this does not necessarily imply that the service will cover its costs, and insufficient *revenue* may put continuity at risk (Warr, 1994). Gallaugher et al. state that "providers of digital information goods are unsure how to price, package, and market their products and are struggling with determining the appropriate revenue model mix" (2001: 476). Some reasons for this fact are given here.

Digital information goods have very low distribution costs. Therefore, increasing economies of scale may result in excess increases of gross profit for information good suppliers. Consequently, supply easily becomes over-abundant, leaving the customer with large search costs. Quality certificates and branding may be important to generate credence for the customers. However, competition among sellers of commodity information pushes the prices to zero, because there is no natural floor to the price except the cost of producing and distributing another piece of information (Shapiro & Varian, 1999). This causes a big problem for information goods producers, as they mostly have to carry high costs of creating the first copy, whereas their opportunities of generating incomes may be small. This is what Shapiro and Varian (1999) name the "*first copy cost principle*". In many cases, though, information services do not deliver commodity information, but also may deliver more abstract/conceptual and customized information goods. This is particularly the case in professional and academic communities of practice (Davenport & Prusak, 1997; McLure Wasko & Faraj, 2005; Van Baalen et al., 2005). In these communities the information goods that are delivered and exchanged are hard to price, and owners of content may be caught in a prisoner's dilemma when they perceive that the information value they deliver to others is not equivalent to the value others deliver in return (Wijnhoven et al., 2010). In such situations, the information service is solely a facilitator of possible exchanges between members of a community, and the service is valued not so much by the content it delivers but more by the exchanges it enables, i.e. a major service with accompanying minor information goods (Kotler, 1988).

## 1.4 DESIGN SCIENCE AND THE STRUCTURE OF THIS BOOK

As many information services have cost coverage problems or poor levels of content maintenance, or ceased to exist soon after an initial success, it is apparent that it is not self-explanatory how an information service should cope with its business challenges (Ma & Agarwal, 2007; Picard, 2000; Womack, 2002). For instance, many electronic communities have problems of attracting enough members (Ma & Agarwal, 2007), and many have turned into "cyber ghost towns" (Preece, 2001). The large number of design options and the lack of theory for information services exploitation make information services design challenging.

In this book, the reader is invited to actively work on the design, re-design, construction, and exploitation of information services. The reader will learn the kernel ideas of design-oriented research and apply them to the design of an information service. The reader will also learn about the consequences of his or her design efforts, by building information services prototypes and considering how these services may be successfully exploited. Through reflective challenges after each chapter, the reader develops an experiential insight on information services development. Proper decisions in this design and exploitation process should avoid design failures and achieve the objectives of an information service. These objectives are related to the three aspects (content, use, and revenue) that set specific requirements for each stage in the development process. In classic presentations of problem-solving, the following steps are mentioned: problem definition and project agenda, (business and process) requirements description, selection of solution means and configuration of them into a solution architecture, putting into practice and monitoring the performance of the solution (also called exploitation and evaluation). Figure 1.5 summarizes each of these objectives and possible design failure consequences.

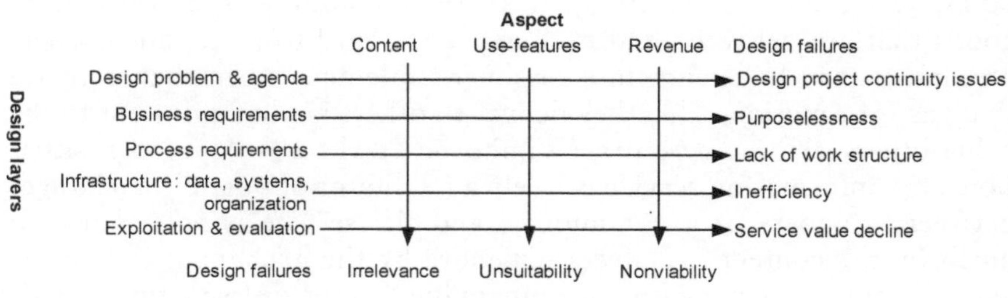


*Figure 1.5* Development space and performance criteria for information services (Wijnhoven & Kraaijenbrink, 2008)

The focus of this book is on learning to design information services, which implies a purposeful shaping and reshaping of services on the basis of insights in the problems that have to be solved by using existing knowledge, i.e., design kernel theories (Walls et al., 1992). Therefore, we take a design science approach, which is distinct from engineering and behavioral science. The last aims at descriptive and explanatory theory for problem understanding, whereas the first aims at making working solutions for a problem. Design science adopts both, but adds that as scientists our problem-solving ambitions should result in not only solutions, but also new theory (Walls et al., 1992; Hevner et al., 2004). Developing information services can best be approached from a design science effort, i.e., it should be done by a proper combination of academic insights and practical needs, and the results should consist of relevant solutions and scientific insights. Design science research aims at improving concepts, theories, methods, and techniques that can be used in the practice of design. This implies that design science develops an interaction between concrete business practice and its challenges and theoretical bodies of knowledge in the design process, for the purpose of improving this body of knowledge (Hevner et al., 2004). Figure 1.6 gives the different steps in building information services and related chapters with theories and methods of this book.

The methods for each layer of Figure 1.6 are explained here.

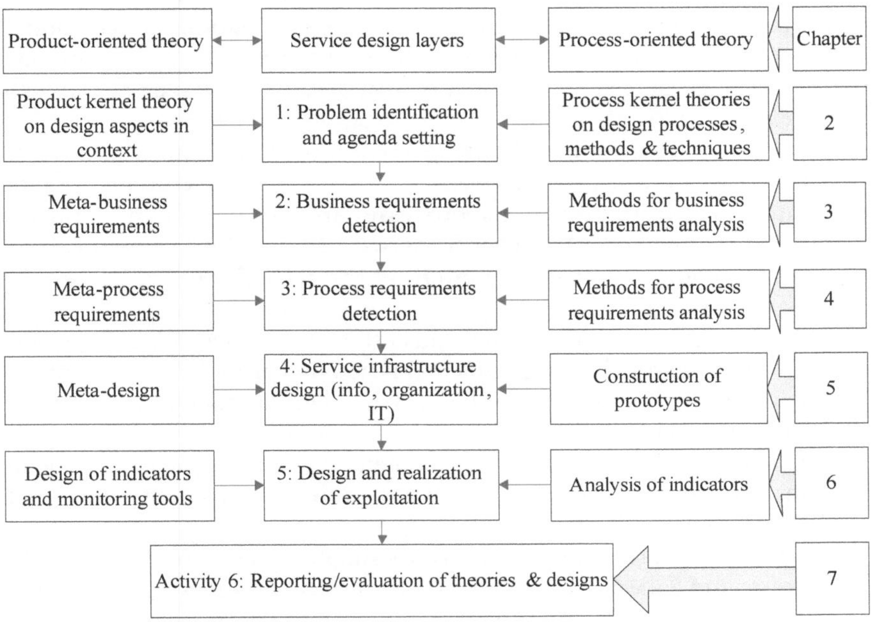


*Figure 1.6* Structure of this book.

*Layer 1: Problem analysis and agenda setting.* A well-known lesson of all information systems development projects is that before a project starts it must be clear that the project has sufficient support from key stakeholders. This implies that a *stakeholder* identification is required and that each stakeholder's needs must be well analyzed, i.e., it should become clear that a sufficient large collection of stakeholders has similar positive opinions about the project so that they will supply the resources needed for the project. The problems and challenges of these stakeholders may be very different depending on the business context they are in (e.g., commercial or non-profit) and different kernel theories may focus on different problems and issues. Chapter 2 will discuss these kernel theories for problem detection and project management.

*Layer 2: Business requirements specification.* Because information services are intermediaries between stakeholders (i.e., suppliers, users, sponsors, and support providers), the existence of an information service depends on its ability to enable value exchanges between these stakeholders, which result in sufficient satisfaction for all to be members of the business network. The *business requirements* can be represented in a business model, which is a (explicit or tacit) business proposal for all actors involved in an information service (Al-Debei & Avison, 2010). Some actors deliver or collect content, user features, and revenues, and some of these are required and others are optional for a successful service. Thus, a viable information service must have a business model that specifies which stakeholders have to deliver what in return for what, and this business model must realize sufficient means to (at least) cover the costs of the information service (Dodd, 1996). Chapter 3 will discuss how a business architecture and business model can be developed for information services, and how such models can be validated.

*Layer 3: Process requirements specification.* Regarding the *process requirements*, an information service delivers content, facilitates content use, and collects revenues. These processes are interlinking mechanisms between the actor web (Al-Debei & Avison, 2010) members of the business model. Four core processes interlink the activities of the actors:

- Account creation, subscribing, and customer relationship management
- Ordering and delivering, which can be content-logistic (using metadata but without changing the primary data) or content transformation (producing derivative information goods)
- Use facilitation via delivering content interaction means or meta-information (e.g., quality indicators) about the content (Vishik & Whinston, 1999)
- Transaction processing compensates suppliers and external use facilitators and collects funds to cover the service's costs by applying rules concerning quality demands and performance (Strens et al., 1998). For

this they process operational data and the business rules developed in the business modeling effort.

- Depending on the type of content and context, business processes should be modeled using different kernel theories.

These business processes are further explained in Chapter 4.

*Layer 4: Service infrastructure design.* For the infrastructure layer, knowing the process activities will facilitate the determination of the informational, human, and technical *means*. For the design aspect (content, value, and revenue), different models are needed. For content, we have to describe the data precisely in data models. For content interactions, we need to specify interfaces, which intersect content and use. For the use aspect, we need activity diagrams as further elaborations of use cases, which next can be used to denote relevant IT applications. The constellation of processes, data, information technologies, and human means can be organized in a so-called architecture of the infrastructure. For revenue we need to formalize the pay-out rules, and we need data collection mechanisms to find out if certain pay-out rules should be activated. This architecture next can be used in the construction stage, where the content aspect is covered by a database system, and the use aspect consists of use and user support applications, acquisition and filing software, and websites. For the data management and publishing part of the service, content management systems can be important. The organizational requirements are further realized by hiring people and task allocations. Finally the revenue aspect is realized by payment systems and by logging/measuring systems. The service infrastructure design of an information service is further explained in Chapter 5.

*Layer 5: Information service exploitation.* Information services are mostly made accessible to their audience via websites. Once published, the webmaster may use a variety of techniques to increase the traffic, or hits, that the website receives. This may include submitting the website to a search engine such as Google or Yahoo, exchanging links with other websites, and creating affiliations with similar websites. Such a design activity involves the definition of performance indicators, the specification of methods and tools for the analysis of performance data, and the specification of ways by which the resulting *behavioral* insights can be used for feedback. With respect to indicators, the use of log data may be essential. Any kind of market research, for instance, gives too superficial and expensive feedback to the designers (Albert et al., 2004). To be effective here, a log information collection and organization mechanism is needed, called the log information architecture (Albert et al., 2004). The current literature on informative web-performance has delivered a few interesting performance measures as well. For instance, Palmer (2002) has developed and validated the following measures: download delay, organization/navigation, information/content, interactivity, and responsiveness. Yang et al. (2005) identify and validate five measures, i.e., usability, usefulness of content, adequacy of information, accessibility, and interaction. Exploitation is further discussed in Chapter 6.

Finally, Chapter 7 summarizes what we have learned about designing information services by integrating the insights per philosophical kernel theory into a pragmatic scheme and method to solve practical problems. The pragmatic use of kernel theories is demonstrated in Chapter 7 by three cases that have all used the elements of this theory. Some key points for further research and thinking are extracted from these cases at the end.

## 1.5 CONCLUSIONS

### 1.5.1 Summarizing Conclusions

This chapter started with three basic questions:

1. What is informing about?
2. What does the information concept imply for information service design?
3. How does an information service differ from an information system?
4. What are the implications of a design science approach to information services?

Question 1 is answered by pointing at the multitude of information types, having roots in different philosophies, but each with a value on its own.

Question 2 is answered by pointing at different views on information and that these result in different requirements for design (the design aspects of information services) and probably different methods and processes for information services. The consequences will be further discussed in the next chapter on kernel theories and information service project approaches. We also introduced the design layers of information services design.

Question 3 is answered by describing information services as service providers on information markets. Four types of information services are identified on the basis of their deliver focus and their revenue focus (i.e., corporate websites, content aggregators (portals), community builders (social media), and data integrators). Information systems (as databases and software) are important means of making information services efficient, but information service infrastructures also requires organization, data, and data communication–related facilities.

Question 4 is answered by explaining the different parts of an information service on the basis of each theory, and the need to combine all these parts in a pragmatic way to a full service. These kernel theories also have high impact on methodologies and processes of information services design. Chapter 2 will discuss in more detail the product and process implications of the kernel theories for information service design.

### 1.5.2 Reflective Exercise

To give the reader a chance to reflect on the basic concepts we introduced here, we provide an exercise on EBSCO, one of the largest information service–providing firms in the world. EBSCO is an example of a very well-developed and extensive information service (www.ebsco.com). This company provides huge databases of articles and informative material for all kinds of industries worldwide. Go to its website and try to answer the following questions:

- What types of information and knowledge products does EBSCO provide?
- Are these products different for different industries?
- What kind of use services does EBSCO provide (you may want to try answering this for only one industry and by looking at a demo)?
- What priorities does EBSCO give on content and use-features, and how is that related to its revenue model?
- What kind of product-oriented theory may be behind EBSCO's development efforts? Specify your answer for the kernel theory, meta-requirements, meta-design, construction, and monitoring.
- Checking the EBSCO case, how would you describe the difference between an information service and an information system?
- Checking the EBSCO case, how would you describe the difference between an information service and a website?
- Describe how you think EBSCO (or an EBSCO-like service) should be managed and designed differently given its context (network, market, or hierarchy)?

## 1.6 FURTHER READING ON INFORMATION AND INFORMATION SERVICES

Floridi, L. (2005). Semantic conceptions of information. In E. Zalta (Ed.), *Stanford Encyclopedia of Philosophy*. Retrieved from http://plato.stanford.edu/archives/

Jonscher, C. (1994). An economic study of the information technology. In T. Allen, M. Scott Morton (Eds.), *Information Technology and the Corporation of the 1990s* (pp. 5–42). New York, NY: Oxford University Press.

Hevner, A., March, S., Park, J., & Ram, R. (2004). Design science in information systems research. *Management information systems quarterly*, *28*(1), 75–105.

Kankanhalli, A., Tan, B., & Wie, K.-K. (2005). Contributing knowledge to electronic knowledge repositories: An empirical investigation. *Management Information Systems Quarterly*, *29*(1), 113–143.

Van Baalen, P., Bloemhof-Ruwaard, J., & Van Heck, E. (2005). Knowledge sharing in an emerging network of practice: The role of a knowledge portal. *European Management Journal*, *23*(3), 300–314.

Womack, R. (2002). Information intermediaries and optimal information distribution. *Library & Information Science Research*, *24*, 129–155.

# 2 Design Science Foundations and Information Service Problem Analysis

This chapter further describes kernel theories for design science. Such kernel theories define the basic assumptions in the design process. The first layer of information service design involves problem identification and project planning on the basis of the basic product (solution of the problem) assumptions and process (realization of the project plan) assumptions for a project. Design kernel theories may be empirical (i.e., descriptive, explanatory, and predictive), normative, ethical, or analytic theories that ground product and process design decisions. *Product-oriented design theories* prescribe user requirements and generic solutions (designs) in specific contexts. *Process-oriented design theories* prescribe development practices, methods, and techniques for certain requirements and enabling environments (Walls et al., 1992; Markus et al., 2002). This chapter reviews kernel theories for product-oriented and process-oriented views on information services. As kernel theories we take Churchman's "inquiring systems", which present different modes of creating knowledge from different conceptualizations of the nature of knowledge, as presented in Chapter 1. Following Churchman, the pragmatist (Singerian) inquiring system is an umbrella to make each presented inquiring system useful in the broader context of improving the informative reality of information producers and consumers. Key elements of this Churchmanian view are explained in the following section, after which the different product-oriented and process-oriented kernel theories are described. The end of this chapter reviews the strong and weak elements of each theory and its implications for the rest of this book.

## 2.1 KERNEL THEORIES FOR DESIGN SCIENCE

This section describes the product-oriented and process-oriented consequences of the inquiring systems for information services by discussing Churchman's Leibnizian, Lockean, Kantian, Hegelian, and Singerian inquiring systems.

The Lockean inquiring system is based on John Locke (1632–1704),[1] who postulated in his first book of *An Essay Concerning Human*

*Understanding* that there are no innate ideas that form our understanding of the world. In book II, he states that the mind is a "blank slate" or "tabula rasa"; that is, contrary to Cartesian or Christian philosophy, Locke maintained that people are born without innate ideas. In book III, he states that language is a key element in forming and codifying understandings, and that we need to share common meanings to make knowledge sharing feasible. Locke recognizes that ordinary people are the chief makers of language and that scientists have the task of checking if the connections made between properties in reality in this language are actually true or not. In book IV Locke states that man should try to use reason, i.e., a combination of observation, experience, and rationality in finding truth. But, man has limitations in reasoning, because many issues are too complex (for the time being), and in such cases it is reasonable to *believe*. Belief is defined by Locke as faith and original revelation through a communication with God and traditions. So revelation comes in where reason cannot reach (Uzgalis, 2007: 25). Consequently, Locke's theories are mainly *descriptive* accounts of regularities and the *predictions* people (i.e., a community of experts) share. In this view, as far as regularities and theories can be developed, they are developed on the basis of induction, i.e., based on observations as far as possible, with an understanding that these observations can never be complete and instances can be found later on that in fact refute the found insights. Thus human capabilities of "explanation *and* prediction" are regarded as quite limited.

Gottfried Wilhelm Leibniz(also *Leibnitz*) (1646–1716)[2] was, along with René Descartes and Baruch Spinoza, one of the three great 17th-century rationalists. Rationalism is any view appealing to reason as a source of knowledge or justification. It is a method or a theory in which the criterion of truth is not sensory but intellectual and deductive. Different degrees of emphasis on this method or theory lead to a range of rationalist standpoints, from the moderate position that reason has precedence over other ways of acquiring knowledge to the radical position that reason is the unique path to knowledge. Leibniz argued that starting with foundational basic principles, like the axioms of geometry, one could in principle deductively derive the rest of all possible knowledge, but he also observed that this was not possible *in practice* and observations and data are important as well. In this view, the creation of knowledge is not based on the development of consensus in a group of experts, but that any person with the proper kind of logical reasoning capabilities may be able to discover knowledge and models of reality on his or her own. In contrast to Locke, it is not the community, but rather rationality that is supposed to determine truth.

Leibniz states in his "principles of sufficient reason" that nothing is without a reason and there is no effect without a cause (Look, 2008: 8). Although it may sometimes be difficult, people are able to discover these reasons and effects by their innate capability of correct analysis of necessities and contingencies. In this people are rational animals. Whereas dogs, for example, observe *phenomena* and react automatically on their appearance (e.g., seeing a cat may result in the willingness to chase it), people are able to identify substances that compose reality, and more importantly people are even able to identify the "soul", also called nomads of a substance. By knowing this soul, people are able to understand the forces of these substances. The soul and its striving to final causes are the result of the work of the perfect engineer or "architect of the world", obviously, according to Leibniz, God. Although some ideas, e.g., those related to the soul and God, may be regarded as quite controversial nowadays, Leibniz's ideal of finding causal *explanatory and predictive* theories is important. Causal thinking has been a common and useful method in many contexts of thinking (Axelrod, 1976; Weick, 1979).

Immanuel Kant (1724–1804)[3] defined the Enlightenment as an age shaped by the motto, "Dare to know". This involved thinking autonomously, free of the dictates of external authority. Kant's work served as a bridge between the rationalist and empiricist traditions of the 17th and 18th century. The foundations of what Kant called his "*critical philosophy*" place the active, rational human subject at the center of the cognitive and moral worlds. With regard to knowledge, Kant argued that the rational order of the world as known by science could never be accounted for merely by the fortuitous accumulation of sense perceptions, i.e., Locke's empiricism. To be able to understand anything, people also need "*categories* of the understanding" operating on the perceptual manifold within space and time. These categories are not concepts, but forms of sensibility that are *a prioris* necessary conditions for any possible experience. Space and time are two of these fundamental a prioris for natural sciences (but possibly for most other sciences as well). Here we see how Kant expressed the need for *analytic* theories for being able to sensefully describe phenomena, but Kant's ambitions involved more. He aimed at ways of *integrating partial explanations* into larger theoretical bodies (i.e., nomological networks) and using empirical data to eliminate bad theories. As such Kant integrates Locke's empiricism and Leibniz's rationalism and adds the need to integrate the views and insights of multiple people into one knowledge network.

Georg Wilhelm Friedrich Hegel[4] (1770–1831) introduced a system for understanding the history of philosophy and the world itself, often described as a *progression in which each successive movement emerges as a solution to the contradictions inherent in the preceding movement.* For example, the French Revolution for Hegel constitutes the introduction of individual political freedom into European societies for the first time in recorded history (at least according to his view). But precisely because of its absolute novelty, it is also absolutely radical: on the one hand the upsurge of violence required to carry out the revolution cannot cease to be on itself, while on the other hand, it has already consumed its opponent. The revolution, therefore, has nowhere to turn but onto its own result: the hard-won freedom is consumed by a brutal reign of terror. History, however, progresses by learning from its mistakes: only after and precisely because of this experience can one posit the existence of a constitutional state of free citizens, embodying both the benevolent organizing power of rational government and the revolutionary ideals of freedom and equality. Marxism interpreted dialectics as an inevitable law of history resulting in an ultimate synthesis: the socialist society. This was probably not Hegel's personal view of history, and Hegel regarded dialectics more as a human, inherent (and therefore never-ending) progression of personal and collective self-consciousness (Sinnerbrink, 2007). As such Hegelian dialectics gives concepts for interpreting human behavior and critically looking at the status quo, and as such is a foundation for interpretive (Klein & Myers, 1999) and critical (Walsham & Sahay, 1999) *explanatory* theories.

The Lockean, Leibnizian, and Kantian inquiring systems all aim at finding some *ultimate* truth. The Hegelian approach, however, regards truth as part of historical and social reality and as arguments in favor of certain ideals and as dialogically developing. The Singerian inquiring system as described by Churchman (1971) on the basis of the work of Edgar Singer (1873–1954), in contrast, proposes that the continuous search for new and improved insights is important, but valuable only as far as it results in human *progress*. Consequently, Singer places the Lockean, Leibnizian, and Kantian approaches in the context of Hegel's dialectics *and* search for human progress. This is consistent with design science (Hevner et al., 2004), which aims at understanding the problems of an individual or organization, and next selects appropriate theories and methods to possibly solve the problems in a *learning project*. Here we see a difference between Hegel and Singer. Whereas knowledge in the Hegelian inquiring system is part of a political and historical process, and thus services the interests of specific stakeholders, the Singerian inquiring system proposes the opportunities of learning. This learning project has information from the problem context and relevant design theories as input for the construction of a solution, which is next tested. After the testing, the conclusions are drawn by delivering advice to the problem context and possibly amending the theories available. This cycle of solution finding and scientific progress has been illustrated by Hevner et al. (2004) in Figure 2.1.

The Singerian approach is an umbrella for the design and exploitation of information services. The other inquiring systems (Lockean, Leibnizian, Kantian, and Hegelian) are useful foundations for identifying specific constructs and methods that all, although each partially, present a useful building block for designing and exploiting information services. Each of these inquiring systems, however, has strong and weak points, and some care has to be taken to not overvalue each of them separately.

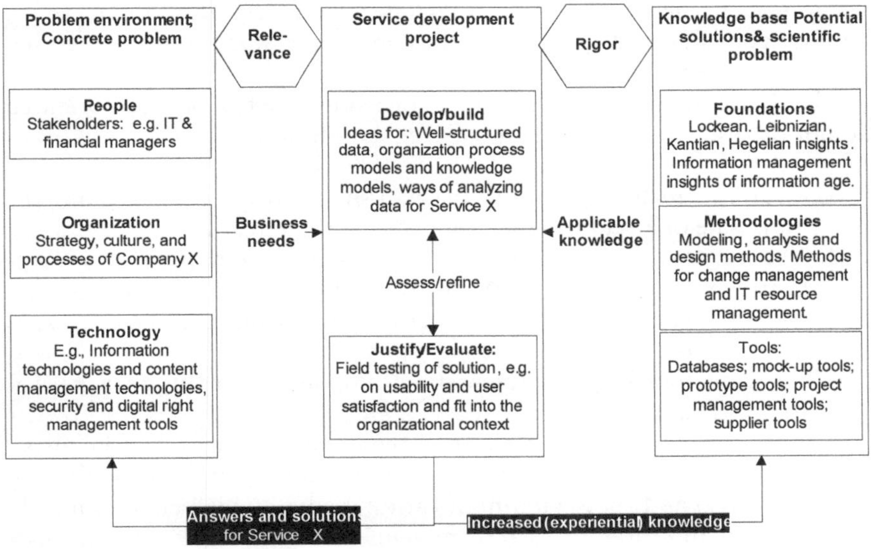


*Figure 2.1* A scheme of the pragmatic-design science cycle (based on Hevner et al., 204).

## 2.2 PRODUCT-ORIENTED KERNEL THEORIES FOR INFORMATION SERVICES

### 2.2.1 Locke's Empiricism and Data Management

Empiricism (Locke's approach) emphasizes true facts about reality as the key to understanding the world. Our senses are a data collection mechanism, and the data we collect are more or less directly understandable and can be shared with other people to develop a collective understanding. Data collection and knowledge creation, though, cannot be fully automated and require substantial organizational efforts and work of the mind. The mind, for instance, will have to develop interests in specific areas (trying to collect all data about everything is obviously impossible) related to specific challenges and goals of the person. These interests and goals thus delimit the boundaries of the universe of discourse, which in turn specifies the data needed and the sensory mechanisms by which these data can be efficiently and effectively acquired. These data need interpretation and analysis to create relevant information for decision-making and problem-solving, but an important bias is already created by the scope definition (i.e., the universe of discourse taken) and the nature of the sensory mechanism itself. Making a universe of discourse description is not only a matter of choosing a proper scope of phenomena to incorporate (and to exclude what is regarded as irrelevant), but also choosing and agreeing on the coding and words for representing these phenomena.

The Lockean inquiring system's consequences for product-oriented design theories thus can be summarized as follows:

1. Data are created by sensory mechanisms, which we could name the input side of an information repository or database.
2. The sensory mechanism has a focused human interest in certain aspects or areas of the world, which is the universe of discourse, i.e., the area that is under consideration, and thus excludes other areas.
3. The data are labeled-representations of objects in reality that the sensory mechanism has acquired.
4. The labels have to fit with an agreed (consensual) set of labels so that data can be meaningfully shared among people through time (archives) and space (communication media), which enables jointly making interpretations (create semantics) out of reality through discussion. In this labeling, synonyms (different labels meaning the same) and homonyms (labels that mean multiple things) have to be handled so that semantic ambiguities are resolved.
5. The labels can be integrated into a *model* of the universe of discourse (see further, e.g., Nijssen & Halpin, 1989), which consists of entities about which data will be collected, and their logical relations, which when well understood ease the maintenance of consistency of data and ease the creation of information outputs from the data.

Several methods for data and information product specification exist consisting of entity-relationship models and representation modes. Many descriptions of *data modeling* and *database design* exist (e.g., Hoffer et al., 2002, and Nijssen and Halpin, 1989). Taylor et al. (2003) adds the need for normalization as an instrument to increase information retrieval of information services. Less literature exists on *information representation modes*. Representation modes are important for high-quality information services and focus more on the layout and usability of content than its formal structure. Therefore, we distinguish *content-structuring* and *content presentation* challenges. Sahlin and Snell (2007: 49) mention the following practical rules for content structuring:

- Break large amounts of text into several pages.
- Intersperse images with the text to break up the content.
- Break up large amounts of text with headlines that visitors can use to ascertain whether they want to read the content.

- Create a newspaper-style page where the information is presented in columns.
- Create a home page that contains links to the information you need to present.
- Create a site map.

The information structure is used to develop a document or visual diagram like a site map. Site maps contain a visual of how the web pages will be interconnected, which helps in deciding what content will be placed on what pages. There are three main ways of diagramming the website structure:

- Linear Website Diagrams will allow the users to move in a predetermined sequence.
- Hierarchical structures (or Tree Design Website Diagrams) provide more than one path for users to take to their destination.
- Branch Design Website Diagrams allow for many interconnections (i.e., a network) between web pages such as hyperlinks within sentences.

To be able to structure content, it is mostly advisable to first structure the content from a substantive and semantic perspective. This implies that the relevant main concepts and areas are identified and related to each other in a meaningful way. For this, concept maps, also called knowledge maps, are useful, especially when large amounts of knowledge have to be communicated. For the theory and techniques of concept mapping we refer to Novak and Canas (2008). An example of a concept map for the agro and food industry is given in Figure 2.2.

In planning the structure, the layout and interface of individual pages may be planned using a storyboard. In the process of storyboarding, a record is made of the description, purpose, and title of each page in the site, and they are linked together according to the most effective and logical diagram type.

Sahlin and Snell (2007) also have some practical rules for content *presentation*:

- Break major ideas into bullet points.
- Arrange the page so that the information has a logical flow.
- Break up text with pictures.
- Don't use color combinations that are hard to read.
- Don't use small fonts.
- When you are designing your site, make sure you view it using the desktop size of your intended audience.
- If you are using a newsletter style with multiple columns for your web page, make the columns different widths.
- Don't use nonstandard font faces when designing your pages.

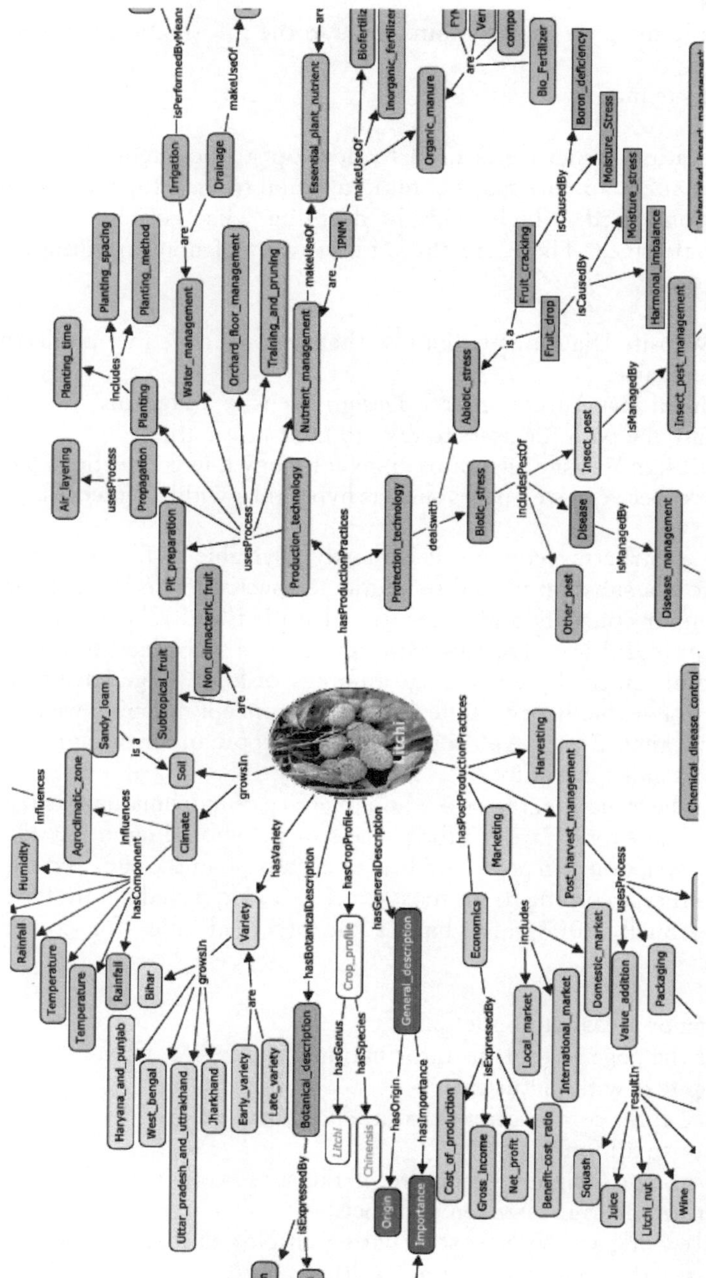


*Figure 2.2* Part of the semantic concept map for the "litchi" from the Indian Institute of Technology, Kanpur, India (Retrieved from http://agropedia.iitk.ac.in; accessed October 18, 2010)

*Note:* The concept map as far as presented here has a hierarchic structure.

But most important of all, select relevant information for your audience and customize content when you serve multiple audiences.

The challenges of empirical product-oriented kernel theories are related to the mentioned issues of scoping (universe of discourse demarcation), data structuring, data presentation, and data acquisition and collection. These challenges have mutually reinforcing relations and when poorly done have several side effects.

### 2.2.2 Leibnizian Rationalism, Models, and Information Use-Value

Rationalism (Leibniz's approach) is a method or a theory in which the criterion of truth is not sensory but intellectual and deductive, and key information in this tradition consists of models of reality and logic.

It is good to know that although rationalism is appealing to a key capability of people (reasoning), even this philosophical approach sees value in experience, sensing, and data. But, of course, what is data and experience without reasoning? The Leibnizian consequences of product-oriented design theories are as follows:

1. Computers cannot make useful logic operations without people who structure reality and provide the computer with correct representations of reality. For databases we need data models and data definitions, not only data. Similarly for reasoning, computers need a causal model. Such a model thus identifies the key "substances" and their dispositions.
2. It is not necessary for the model to be large, but it must have sufficient explanatory power. Because the world consists of huge numbers of substances, people will have to cut down the number of substances and relations they want to include in their models to make the complexity manageable. Although people have innate reasoning capabilities, these reasoning capacities are limited. Consequently, while aiming to serve users, information services must be well-focused to the specific and limited scope of its users.
3. The knowledge gained can be represented by models that include causal relations by which one can emulate logical reasoning about the world. The *model* must have a "calculation" mechanism (which may include calculus or formal logic like if-then statements and operators like "not", "and", "or", and "equality") to infer impacts of states of substances on the states of other substances. These states of substances can be measured and as such they are independent variables. The choice for these variables is based on reasoning, not on sensation. The resulting empirical models thus may emulate expected and predicted behavior (see further, e.g., Turban, 1995).
4. Most *models* can be implemented in computer software systems like spreadsheets, decision support systems, and serious gaming systems,

and thus computers can emulate expected and predicted behavior by simulation of the world (e.g., by "what-if-analysis").

Two simple reasoning mechanisms are the causal diagram and the decision tree. In operations research, specifically in decision analysis, a decision tree(or tree diagram) is a decision support tool that uses a graph or model of decisions and their possible consequences, including chance event outcomes, resource costs, and utility. A decision tree is used to identify the strategy most likely to reach a goal. Another use of trees is as a descriptive means for calculating conditional probabilities. Decision trees are formulated as "if . . . then" statements, i.e., the checking of a condition, which may be true or false, and based on this conclusion a consequence is drawn.

Causal diagrams are very useful in developing theories of action (see, for example, Axelrod (1976) and Weick (1979)) and are widely used for making predictions about the impact of certain policies (e.g., the impact of tax on economic growth and employment). They, however, have to meet logical and empirical correctness requirements (Faran, 2011) and they should be practically usable. A causal model with high empirical correctness can quickly become over-complex and unusable. The complexity of such models explains the need to apply Occam's razor, i.e., well-developed models should be as parsimonious as possible and therefore must fit the reasoning capabilities of the people who have to use it.

The challenges of going from rational ideals to concrete use tools concern the selection of a clear focus again, the development of decision models, emulation of reasoning, and decision tools.

## 2.2 KANTIANISM AND KNOWLEDGE MANAGEMENT SYSTEMS

Kantianism proposes the need of different perspectives that have to be taken to realize a complete picture of a phenomenon. This requires ways of integrating and consolidating complementary perspectives. Knowledge integration in such organizations happens in several ways. One is the definition and communication of policies and priorities, which may be internalized by organization members and, as such, influence their behavior. The other way is to analyze and externalize the existing knowledge, and make it reusable (as explicit knowledge) and as such also standard for the rest of the organization (e.g., method bases at Ernst & Young; cf. Hansen et al., 1999). The third way is to combine explicit knowledge, by defining links between documents and information systems and defining index and search structures for knowledge-containing systems. The fourth way is to identify knowledge sources (without fully externalizing their contents) and to link these sources with search means (e.g., skill databases). Finally, nothing of knowledge description may be done at all, but nevertheless organization members may be given easy search and communication means to exchange ideas and problems and as such build up their expertise networks (thus the knowledge remains tacit). All these features of a shared knowledge and information space are put together under the term of knowledge-based systems (cf. Stein & Zwass, 1995). Besides social software services like Google, there are also more specialist packages to facilitate IT-based integration in this context like OpenText's Livelink, and MS SharePoint.

The number of applications and infrastructures needed for knowledge-based systems (KBS) is very diverse. This is so because KBSs integrate the Lockean and Leibnizian perspectives, i.e. databases-related and model-oriented systems, and because KBSs may be dispersed over many user groups and in fact often aim at group integration through space and time. An overview of the related applications and infrastructures for KBSs is given by Binney (2001) and listed here.

- In a *transactional* KBS, the knowledge is pre-packaged and provided to the user in the course of interacting with the system in a transaction to assist in addressing a customer problem. Examples of transactional knowledge management include help desk, customer service, order entry, and field support applications.
- *Analytical* knowledge-based systems provide interpretations of, or create new knowledge from vast amounts of disparate sources of material. In an analytical KBS, large amounts of data or information are used to derive trends and patterns. Traditional analytical KBSs such as management information systems and data warehousing often focus on customer-related information to assist marketing or product development functions. They are being joined by a range of competitive or business intelligence applications that incorporate external sources of knowledge or information.
- *Asset* management KBS applications focus on processes associated with the management of knowledge assets. This involves one of two things: (1) the management of codified knowledge assets and (2) the management of intellectual property (IP) and the processes surrounding the identification, exploitation, and protection of IP. Once captured, the assets are made available to people to use as they see fit. This is analogous to a library, with the knowledge assets being catalogued in various ways and made available for unstructured access and use.
- *Process*-based KBS applications cover the codification and improvement of processes, also referred to as work-practices, procedures, or methodology. The knowledge assets produced in this category are also known as "engineered assets" in that they often involve third parties or specialists working with practitioners or subject matter experts to

document these best practices in standard formats. Process knowledge assets are often improved through internal lessons, learned sessions, formal engineering of processes by internal best practice selection, and codification and external benchmarking.

- *Developmental* KBS applications focus on increasing the competencies or capabilities of an organization's knowledge workers. The applications cover the transfer of explicit knowledge via training interventions, or the planned development of tacit knowledge through developmental interventions such as experiential assignments. Communities where people can exchange ideas and learn from each other are an emerging form of tacit knowledge development.
- *Innovation* and creation-based KBS applications focus on providing an environment in which knowledge workers, often from differing disciplines, can come together in teams to collaborate in the creation of new knowledge.

There is a phenomenal growth of technologies that make it easier to implement a KBS. These technologies continue to evolve rapidly, especially in the areas of collaboration and search engines. These "enabling" technologies underpin most of today's knowledge management applications and cannot be primarily assigned to only one element of the spectrum. They include Internet/intranet technologies and generic web elements such as portals (also called Web 1.0) and social media (also called Web 2.0).

Whereas traditional organizations group people together at one and the same physical location, several IT variables enable an office to be replaced by electronic mail, video conferencing, and other Internet-based groupware. They also allow for more organizational flexibility, because everyone with an Internet connection may be allowed by electronic access codes and software to share and create knowledge with people with whom they never had face-to-face interaction before. Knowledge management leads to new managerial challenges, because it may be hard to have the shared understanding needed for effective knowledge sharing when people have never met face-to-face before.

### 2.2.4 Hegelianism and Content Owner-Based Revenues

Churchman (1971) describes Hegel's dialectics as a three-step process of "thesis, antithesis, synthesis", namely, that a "thesis" (e.g., the French Revolution) would cause the creation of its "antithesis" (e.g., the Reign of Terror that followed), and would eventually result in a "synthesis" (e.g., the constitutional state of free citizens). Churchman (1971) takes Hegel's view on thesis and anti-thesis as two different views about a single phenomenon, based on different interests and views (Weltanschauungen) people may have. To find truth in such cases is difficult, but there are two ways of solving the resulting conflicts (i.e., realizing a synthesis). One way is to appoint a master who decides like a referee; the other is finding a joint resolution. An example here is a court case, in which the lawyer will selectively use the available data to find arguments in favor of his client. This may easily result in a biased view and even in a distorted view of reality. In contrast, the public prosecutor will try to show the errors and distortions the lawyer presents, and may also selectively use other data to demonstrate that the accused must be penalized. In some cases, the judge will not be requested to make a verdict when the two parties are able to settle the dispute (synthesis by resolution). But when this is hard to realize, the judge (or jury) will have to decide (synthesis by the master).

There are two ways of handling the problem of conflicting views; one is the detection and adoption of a master, which we could give the task of saying what is true. The other way is to empower the information consumer (slave), not by making her/him an expert or master himself (this is mostly infeasible and against the value of specialization in our society) but by giving her/him means to pose critical questions to potential masters.

Information masters can have four functions: making available data, making available meaningful data, making available true data, and making available relevant data.

- *Making available data*: Search engines automatically index files submitted to an Internet location and enable user-friendly information searching. Meta-search engines aim at improving precision and recall using results of multiple search engines. Also specialized search engines are offered on the Internet to improve recall and precision in specific areas, like (1) searching on topics (e.g., sports or social sciences), (2) searching on region (e.g., limited to Dutch or French resources), and (3) searching on medium (e.g., music files or jpeg). Probably only 1% of the total Internet can be searched by public sources like Google (http://searchenginewatch.com/2156481). This means that 99% of the Internet is invisible or that one can see only the front page of a site. This publicly unreachable or not-indexed data are called the deep web.
- *Making available meaningful data*: Internet *guides* index and structure data by human editors. This means that the content and structure of the guide is based on a human meaning of relevance. Although this may be useful, it results in structures that are nearly never complete and these structures will be more selective than the structures that are automatically generated by a search engine (the last we name "technical intermediation").

- *Making available true data*: A number of expert services are available via the Internet that can help people find the right kind of information, like: www.loc.gov/rr/askalib (a free service from the US Library of Congress); www.allexperts.com; www.askanexpert.com; answers.google.com (in contrast to the previous expert services, this service helps to find an expert (not a librarian) who gives an answer, though this service is not free); www.mediaresource.org/request.shtml (focuses on questions of journalists with regard to scientific issues); and www.madsci.org/submit.html, for questions aimed at scientists. Professional associations and non-commercial research institutes also publish certified content. Most newspapers that want to differentiate themselves by quality have teams of scientific journalists who deliver content according to scientific research rules and methods.
- *Making available relevant data*: Recommender systems and discussion forums allow customers to deliver problems. In the case of recommender systems a dialogue between the customer and the service aims at a clearer problem definition and a potential match with a solution (direction). Some consulting firms use these tools to acquire implementation projects. Discussion forums allow the participation of multiple experts and multiple problem owners to engage in a discussion for the further analysis and possible solution of (complex) problems. Many organizational and medical problems nowadays have a multi-disciplinary nature and thus its solution requires the involvement of multiple experts. This is also true with problem analysis and consequently sharing of experiences between problem owners can be very valuable.

What masters mostly do not do is to help information consumers to build their own opinion on the basis of conflicting information sources. For this purpose, we propose critical information triangulation. Denzin (2009) was the first to propose triangulation as a research strategy and he outlined four types of triangulation, namely data triangulation, investigator triangulation, theory triangulation, and methodological triangulation. Triangulation aims at confirming the truth of possibly true statements by comparing the results of different data, investigators, theories, and methods. In contrast, we apply triangulation to falsify presumed true statements from information masters. As such we aim at a critical use of triangulation.

Data triangulation has been defined by Denzin as the affirmative use of different data sources. It is not affirmation that we seek, but criticism and the detection of bias. Consequently, data triangulation serves criticism of data. These data can be criticized by searching for comparable material in different places in time and space. Triangulation of this kind can be done in two ways. One way is to give the information searcher evidence through alternative media, like photos, movies, data, and text, so that the evidence can be compared and checked for (in)consistency. The other way consists of giving the information searcher opportunities to track and trace evidence through space and time, so that original sources can be checked. A plagiarism detector can do both at the same time for a document received from a presumed master. One of them is Viper (http://www.scanmyessay.com/viper-plagiarism-scanner.php), and www.plagiarism.org provides several descriptions and references to other detection tools.

Investigator triangulation is the involving of other investigators in the research. Investigator triangulation on online news can be realized by including articles from different investigators (journalists and correspondents). By "different", we mean people with different affiliations and backgrounds. There are two ways of detecting the background of "investigators":

1. Check the identity and background of investigators via their social network presentations in tools like LinkedIn and Facebook.
2. Check the background of a site owning organization via the "who is" tool.

Theory triangulation (also called theoretical triangulation) involves using multiple perspectives or theories to interpret a single set of data. Theory triangulation of information on the Internet can be done by defining the perspectives you want for theory triangulation. This could be economic, human, cultural, political, or technical. Key economic terms are, for instance, income, profit, economic growth. Human terms are, for instance, aid, birth, death, population, happiness, sadness. Cultural terms are, for instance, music, literature, dance, and art. Political terms are, for instance, power, election, government, state, and army. Technical terms are, for instance, speed, efficiency, invention, and science. Via a word cloud application, one can detect if certain issues and approaches are more dominant in a message than others are. Via this one can detect the theoretical bias of a document. One can systematically search for alternative documents by adding lacking keywords to another query and check the word cloud again. A useful word cloud tool is www.wordle.net.

Methodological triangulation (also called method triangulation) refers to the use of different methods to examine a phenomenon. Research methodologists have widely discussed the different types of evidence that can be collected and the different conclusions that can be drawn on the basis of this (Mingers, 2001; Yin, 2003). These methodologies may be:

1. *Empirical*: Focusing on the collection of data or measurements

2. *Interpretive*: Focusing on what people think and have in their minds, which can be found by personal interviews and in-depth interviews; these data can be found in newspapers, especially background articles.
3. *Historical*: This involves finding evidence to explain people's so-called "genuine because motives", which are often not what they say about why they do certain things but joint histories and shared beliefs. These data are often provided by historians and political scientists.
4. *Critical*: Focusing on finding opinions and ideas for change; this can be collected by document research (e.g., political party programs and public statements of politicians and chief executives).

Any document found on the Internet can be analyzed on the presence or absence of these four data modes via a visual inspection of the documents. Additionally, documents' validity can be checked by assessing indicators of scientific rigor, like propositions, measurements, tests, and replications.

We implement the mentioned critical triangulation methods in successive steps to realize the Hegelian dialectics as follows:

1. First formulate a thesis and on the basis of this create a query.
2. Data triangulation: Insert a document (e.g., the highest ranked) found via the query under scrutiny with a plagiarism detector, such as Viper. Check if other sources say the same. Check the shared background of the sources.
3. Investigator triangulation: Check personal home pages of the author, and network sites, such as LinkedIn and Facebook, and the owner of the publishing site via "who is". Any links from the document may also indicate affiliations. Are the investigator and the site linked to specific ethical communities?
4. Theory triangulation: Create a word cloud of the document, for example with www.wordle.net (based on word count). What are the main issues and to what extent is there a bias?
5. Methodology triangulation: Assess the document on empirical evidence, interpretive grounding, historical grounding, critical view, and scientific rigor (measurements, propositions, testing, replications).
6. If the document seems to survive the four critical triangulations, maintain it as a thesis. If not, modify the thesis and triangulate again, or reject the thesis and stop further dialectic analysis.
7. When a thesis is maintained, formulate an anti-thesis, create a query, and perform the triangulation of a found document.
8. If the anti-thesis cannot survive critical triangulation, reject it or modify it and triangulate again. If the anti-thesis survives critical triangulation, compare the thesis and anti-thesis and formulate a synthesis.

This process is described in more detail in Figure 2.3.

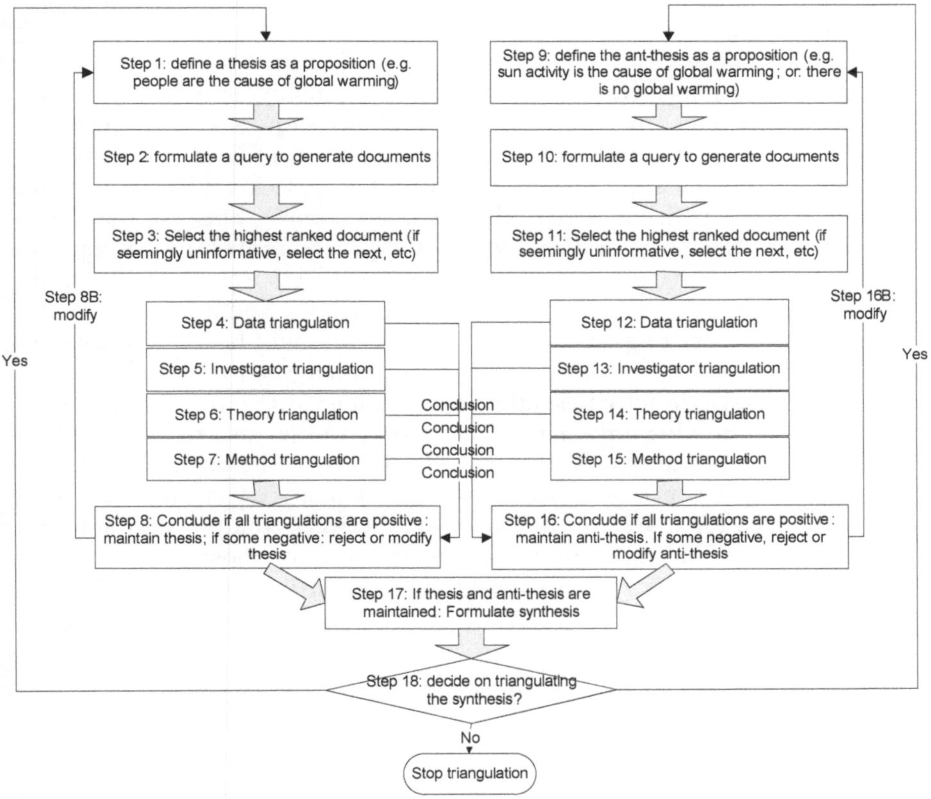


*Figure 2.3* Critical triangulation methods in Hegelian dialectics.

## 2.2.5 Singerianism and User-Oriented Revenue

Singerian pragmatism is an epistemology and ethical theory stating that the value of knowledge should be expressed in terms of how the knowledge improves the human condition and, although people have to strive for truth, they will never reach the ultimate truth and progress itself is regarded as more important than truth itself.

Singerian inquirers seek a highly idealistic purpose, the creation of *exoteric knowledge*, or knowledge for "every man", *as opposed to scientific, esoteric knowledge* that as it matures, becomes relevant to an increasingly smaller audience. The artificial division of knowledge into disciplines and the reduction of complex problems into simple components inhibit the solution of social and management problems. Solving complex problems may require knowledge from *any* source and those knowledgeable in *any* discipline or profession. Attempts to achieve such kind of pragmatic exoteric knowledge have substantial organizational and human consequences. Courtney says about this that Singerian organizations must bring in:

> multiple perspectives or worldviews and employing a holistic, systems approach in their thinking and decision-making processes. [. . .] The non-separability and irreducibility of elements in complex problems and issues is recognized. [. . .]. A critical aspect of developing multiple perspectives is open, honest, effective dialogue among all relevant stakeholders in the problem involved. Managers in such an environment must be careful to respect the rights and viewpoints of the parties involved, and be open and honest to themselves in order to gain the trust of those who will be affected by the decision. [. . .] In 'real-life' situations, managing problems consists of at least three activities: (a) analyzing alternatives, (b) making decisions about which alternative to choose, and (c) successfully implementing the chosen alternative. The Lockean, Leibnizan, Kantian and Hegelian perspectives focus most strongly on (a) and least on (c); hence the 'gap' so often deplored between analysis and action. Successful implementation depends first and foremost on the use of human resources and this means that we have to move from (a) to (c). (2001: 28)

The *Pragmatist* (Singer) is open to multiple perspectives, is innovative and adaptive, and is best in *complex situations*. Knowledge of thinking styles (Keinholz et al., 1993) can be helpful in seeking input from individuals with different ways of looking at decision problems. This will help ensure that multiple personal viewpoints are represented, rather than getting input from several who think alike. Even more, it helps in delivering substantial complementary knowledge and opinions needed to understand and manage complex challenges. Managing the diversity of the related capabilities is a key capability for effective information management. For product-oriented design theory this involves the following:

1. Integrative and free access to relevant databases, expert and model systems, enterprise systems, and opinion identification and discussion tools are requirements for analyzing problems from multiple perspectives.
2. The analysis and decision-making tools should be available for anyone who can and wants to make a substantive contribution.
3. One knows about the success of a solution only when the end-users use it successfully. Consequently, actual use has to be monitored to detect problems and improve the situation.

An information service is an integration of all these philosophical values and requirements for *pragmatic* purposes. In contrast to the Hegelian view the Singerian view states that this pragmatic purpose should serve the interests of not only the content owners, but also its potential users. This implies that content, which is the integration of data and knowledge as perceived by Kant as an integration of empirical and rationalist views, may be perceived as value by its owners, but this does not necessarily imply that it is value for its users. Much data and knowledge representation on the Internet indeed often serves only the self-representational and communication interests of its owners. To make it valuable, a consumer should be interested in it as well. If it is really of high value for users, these users may be interested in paying for it or of doing something in return, as is common in group problem-solving and learning. But, much content, though of value, does not generate any income, and people may therefore consider not submitting anymore; this is, for instance, often the case with electronic news. We therefore identify three challenges of information services from a Singerian perspective: *content is not always value*, *valuable content does not always generate income*, and much submitted and present content on the Internet is not valuable for anyone, not even for the submitter him- or herself.

### 2.2.6 Summary of Product-Oriented Design Problems

This description of inquiring systems has pointed at a list of key challenges that may be identified in the first stage of developing an information service. The identification of these challenges is of course a matter of communication, negotiation, and choice with the problem owners. The choice for one of the inquiring systems, however, determines the focus, development agenda, and limitations of the project. Table 2.1 summarizes the found problems.

*Table 2.1* Summary of Information Service Product-Oriented Design Problems

| *Inquiring system* | *Product-oriented design problems* |
|---|---|
| Lockean | Services that collect and provide reliable, complete, and retrievable data |
| Leibnizian | Decision models, correct models of reality, help to reason |
| Kantian | Integrated knowledge services |
| Hegelian | Information master services and tools to emancipate information slaves |
| Singerian | Information services to improve collaborative and multidisciplinary problem-solving |

## 2.3 PROCESS-ORIENTED DESIGN THEORIES FOR INFORMATION SERVICES

This section discusses the implications of the Lockean, Leibnizian, Kantian, Hegelian, and Singerian kernel theories for design processes of information services, which include methods and techniques for requirements definition, product design, and project management.

### 2.3.1 Empiricism and Information Service Development

Empiricism (Locke's paradigm) is a theory of knowledge emphasizing the role of experience, especially sensory perception, in the formation of knowledge. The mind as tabula rasa needs some kind of a data collection mechanism to fill it with data. These data need to be labeled and categorized such that they can be shared. It is a requirement of empirical science methods that all hypotheses and theories are based on observations of the natural world, rather than resting solely on *a priori* reasoning, intuition, or revelation. To let data become knowledge, the conclusions should be shared by the community of experts as a valid induction (e.g., sufficient number of observations in different contexts and statistically significant from at random occurrences). Much case research has this inductive theory-generating nature (Yin, 2003), and inductive empirical analysis is an important step in detecting user requirements and information needs in the information service design process. Empirical research on the motivation to submit content (Kankanhalli et al., 2005) and motivation to use and participate in networks of expertise (McLure-Wasko & Faraj, 2005) also is important for gaining realistic expectations of the impact of information services in certain information markets and contexts.

This challenge has a few problems for empirically grounding user requirements and information needs. The first problem is that in information services, the potential users are not always well known and that information about users has to be based on incomplete samples and incomplete data about these user needs. The second problem is that data collection and analysis are costly and time-consuming. The third problem is that findings from one study are difficult to generalize to other contexts, and predictions about the effectiveness of certain design decisions are therefore hard to ground on factual insights. Consequently, empirical insights are hard to collect and use during service design studies, but the systematic collection of data about an *existing* information service may be partially automatic and is very useful during the life stage or exploitation stage of a launched information service (see further Chapter 6).

### 2.3.2 Rationalism and Service Model Improvement

Leibniz states that people can strive for two kinds of truth: truth of reasoning and truth of fact. Truth of reasoning, which Leibniz names "necessary truth", can be discovered by the analysis of the notions, and "resolving it into simpler ideas and simpler truths until we reach the primitives" (Look, 2008: 24). The "principle of contradiction" is used to check if a truth of reasoning is indeed found, because contradiction is for rationalists not acceptable. Alternatively, a truth of fact, i.e., a contingent truth, exists of the detection of certain correlations between phenomena, but does not provide causes and explanations. Look states:

> According to the Leibnizian inquiring system, while the empiricist position can explain the source of contingent truths, it cannot adequately explain the origin and character of necessary truths. For the senses could never arrive at the universality of any necessary truth; they can, at best, provide us with the means of making a relatively strong induction. Rather it is the understanding itself, Leibniz claims, which is the source of such truths and which guarantees their very necessity. While we are not aware of all our ideas at any time [. . .] certain ideas or truths are in our minds as dispositions or tendencies. This is what is meant by an innate idea or an innate truth. (26)

Positivist science is the search for universal laws and causalities by deductive logic (Bernstein, 1976). Positivist non-empirical formal logic is an important technique of information systems analysis and design, especially when the requirements need to become more precise and formal (Wand & Weber, 2002).

As stated before, models aim at efficient ways of explaining or predicting phenomena and they do this by relating dependent and independent variables via causalities. Causal models can be expressed by relating independent and dependent variables by directional graphs that show the direction of the causality and also may express if the causality is positive or negative (by a "+" sign or "–" sign in the graph) or even the expression of its strength.

In design science, cause-and-effect relations are replaced by means-and-goals relations respectively, because a means should be a cause for achieving a goal. Because the collection of data in design projects is costly, many designs are predictive statements based on logical arguments alone and thus not empirical. In information systems design, design consists conceptually of a large number of mean-goal propositions (Walls et al. (1992) refer to these as "design propositions", e.g., statements like "the user-interface need not more than 7 lines on one page to avoid information clutter", and "the database needs information on individual employee performance for department members to better instruct employees"). These propositions can be logically related, or at least should not be inconsistent.

### 2.3.3 Kantianism and Service Process Development

The Kantian design theory starts with a recognition of people's freedom to take their own view of the world. Consequently, this freedom allows people to take different views even about the same phenomena. So as designers, we have to understand why people have their view, what their view entails, and how differing views can help in realizing deeper or better views of the world. This seems to be in conflict with the Lockean attempts to converge to a single consensus-based community view. It also seems to be in conflict with Leibnizian attempts to find the one single best model of the world. Although one can see one phenomenon from multiple perspectives, people will probably share sufficient *a priori* concepts so that they can understand each other and thus become suppliers of complementary information. Kant also proposes to more precisely denote Locke's labels as analytic and synthetic propositions, and describes Leibniz's logic and causality concept as synthetic propositions. Analytic a prioris are elementary words and terms people need. For example the concept of a business process may have activities, relationships, goals, beginning, end, and sequences as some of its a prioris. Synthetic a prioris combine these a prioris with a modeling language that a community can use to integrate individually owned insights into a larger coherent view of reality. The observations, statistics, and data that are enabled by the *a priori* propositions consist of *a posteriori* propositions and may be stored in a database. When using formulas for calculations, most of the formulas are *synthetic* a prioris. We need synthetic a posterioris to understand many business and organizational phenomena, but *many business and organization concepts are synthetic a prioris.* For instance, the notion that organizations have a strategy, structure, and process is a concept without experiential basis. Yet, it is a priori true, because if a unit does not have a process, strategy, and structure we may not call it an organization.

Following Kant, a prioris are given to mankind and without them people will not be able to perceive reality (Churchman, 1971: 145). Thus the objective order of nature and the causal necessity that operates within it are dependent upon the mind and its "innate" (to reuse Leibniz's term here) a prioris. Kant, however, is not a pure rationalist, who would base *all* understanding on innate human capabilities alone, but emphasizes the reciprocity of sensations and concepts. According to Churchman (1971), we should understand this as the limitations of rationality and deduction in explaining the world, and the possibility of inquiring systems to sense facts and experiences that are not fully under control of existing theories and nomological networks. This capability of confronting existing knowledge with inconsistent observation and facts is essential for human progress and scientific learning (Lakatos & Musgrave, 1970).

Kantianism also has ambitions to merge multiple theoretical perspectives into larger nomological networks (Bernstein, 1976) and multi-method-based integration of insights (Mingers, 2001). In the practice of information service development, integrating the views and knowledge of all stakeholders is possible and needed after the basic requirements have been stated in the business modeling process (to be discussed later), and before means are selected in the design stage. To realize a common way of discussing the stakeholders' requirements, languages need to be developed and applied. These languages are expected to facilitate the collection of all the views of all the stakeholders in one integrated and uniformly understandable language. Most important in this context are business process modeling languages like ARIS (Scheer, 1998) and BPMN (http://www.bpmn.org/; White & Miers, 2008). When the stakeholders agree on the business process model, more technical and implementation-oriented experts can select effective means for all the activities that have to be supported.

### 2.3.4 Hegelianism and Service Business Development

Churchman (1971) takes Hegel's view on thesis and anti-thesis as two different views about a phenomenon, based on different interests and Weltanschauungen that people may have. There are two ways of solving the resulting conflicts (i.e., realizing a synthesis). One way is the *appointment of a master* who decides like a referee, the other way is to jointly develop a resolution. *Synthesis by the master* involves a clear statement of what-side-are-we-on and working as a scientist in the service of a specific interest group or a client. *Synthesis by resolution* involves the development of criteria for the evaluation of opinions and perceptions. In information service development, synthesis by resolution is mostly the only feasible option. Understanding stakeholders' intentions and providing sufficient political sensitivity are important capabilities of successful information system project managers (Walsham, 2002).

It is essential to define the purpose of the information service as one of the first steps in the development process. A purpose statement should show what the service is supposed to accomplish and what the users will get from it. A clearly defined purpose will help the rest of the development process as the audience is identified and the content of the service is developed. Setting short- and long-term goals for the service will help make the purpose clear and plan for the future when expansion, modification, and improvement will take place. Also, goal-setting practices and measurable objectives should be identified to track the progress of the site and determine success. Although this is needed, it is more complex when stakeholders have different and even conflicting interests. For example, users may have different information preferences, computer specifications, and web experiences. Content owners may have different commercial interests and infrastructure suppliers may make a business model that satisfies the interest of all quite difficult. A good stakeholder analysis and understanding of the business motives of stakeholders are important for understanding the feasibility and business requirements of an information service. How this can be done is the subject of the next chapter. Knowing the business requirements of the different stakeholders is a first step in information service development. The next step is to check if the diverse interests can be reconciled in a set of requirements that suits all stakeholders during the life cycle of the service. This is also called business modeling. A feasible business model is a precondition for getting the stakeholders in action through a shared business *process* model.

### 2.3.5 Pragmatism and Information Service Project Management

Churchman summarizes the Singerian perspective in the following nine elements of an inquiring system:

1. The inquiring system has the purpose of creating knowledge, which means creating the capability of choosing the right means for one's desired ends.
2. The measure of performance is to be defined as the "level" of scientific and educational excellence of all society, a measure yet to be developed.
3. The client is mankind, i.e., all human teleological beings.
4. The components have been the disciplines, but the design of inquiry along esoteric, disciplinary lines is probably wrong, as we have seen, if the purpose is "exoteric" knowledge, i.e., knowledge that goes outward to be useful for all men in all societies.
5. Singer's theory of value is essentially "enabling". That is, ethical values are based on an assessment of man's capability of attaining what he wants, and not on an assessment of the goals as such. [. . .] . . . the environment which the inquiring system critically needs is a cooperative environment, where A wants that goal which will aid B in attaining his goal.
6. The decision makers are everyone—in the ideal. But at any stage there will be the leaders and the followers. For Singer the most important decision makers are the heroes, those inspired by the heroic mood to depart from the safe land of the status quo.

7 and 8. The designers are everyone—in the ideal.

9. I have purposefully stressed the theme of betterment in the foregoing account, even to the point of a kind of simplistic optimism [. . .].[5] (Churchman, 1971: 200–201).

Obviously, multi-disciplinary work and the participation of many people, academics and practitioners, under heroic leaders are needed to improve mankind. Scientists are part of the game, and not the only participants, but society expects its scientists to work in an interdisciplinary way and in close collaboration with problem owners, who have a clear stake in improving the human condition. This is a clear ethical foundation for design science, as expressed by Hevner et al. (2004), who aim at *reconciling rigor and relevance* in design research. This is an ambition shared with proponents of action research as well (Baskerville & Wood-Harper, 1998; Avison et al., 1998). Both apply similar evaluation criteria for good scientific and practical work, which integrate academic and practical needs. See Table 2.2 for an overview of design science criteria.

*Table 2.2* Design Science Guidelines (based on Hevner et al., 2004)

| *Guideline* | *Description* |
|---|---|
| Guideline 1: Design as an Artifact | Design science research must produce a viable artifact in the form of a construct, a model, a method, or an instantiation. |
| Guideline 2: Problem Relevance | The objective of design science research is to develop technology-based solutions to important and relevant business problems. |
| Guideline 3: Design Evaluation | The utility, quality, and efficacy of a design artifact must be rigorously demonstrated via well-executed evaluation methods. |
| Guideline 4: Research Contributions | Effective design science research must provide clear and verifiable contributions in the areas of the design artifact, design foundations, and/or design methodologies. |
| Guideline 5: Research Rigor | Design science research relies upon the application of rigorous methods in both the construction and evaluation of the design artifact. |
| Guideline 6: Design as a Search Process | The search for an effective artifact requires utilizing available means to reach desired ends while satisfying laws in the problem environment. |
| Guideline 7: Communication of Research | Design science research must be presented effectively both to technology-oriented as well as management-oriented audiences. |

Because we have three design aspects (content, use, and revenue) and six design layers (see Chapter 1), theoretically over 100 different scenarios may be possible when we assume that each intersection of aspects and layers needs to be taken at least once in a design scenario. Each aspect or layer also may be executed in parallel sets, increasing the possible number of scenarios even more. Because of space limitations but also because the presented scenarios are closest to current theory, we describe only five scenarios, which all quite closely relate to the inquiring systems discussed before.

A Lockean scenario , which is a typical puzzle of finding the appropriate user requirements, is described before by Albert et al. (2004) as GIST. The GIST scenario consists of gather, infer, segment, and track steps. Their approach is based on the assumption that informative websites often have very diverse and heterogeneous clients. In such situations one can best follow a marketing-like approach, which focuses on the ability to learn from client behavior. Therefore the requirements and infrastructure design layers are kept very short, and a working service is delivered as soon as possible. The key thing is to develop performance indicators, collect data (client behavior logs), and analyze these to find new business opportunities (e.g., new market segments that can be served much better with rather limited resources). GIST therefore mainly focuses on what we call "exploitation". The authors demonstrate by a case study in the financial service sector that such a strategy can be commercially rewarding. Albert et al. (2004) also plead for optimizing information services with regard to abilities to permanently learn from client behavior, and therefore exploitation design is key to information services success.

The Hegelian approach is an integration of interests among stakeholders of an information service. Such scenario focuses on owners of certain resources, like Internet and cable net infrastructures and content owners, who organize use-features (software, Internet access, security, etc.) for their clients, so that the clients can build their own websites. Hosting is mostly done using a content-blind approach (MacKie-Mason et al., 1996), although in the context of mobile Internet the Internet providers do currently organize content and define the requirements, use options, delivery processes, and business model. Software owners can specialize in solving information search and use problems on the Internet, and also enable full hosting of their clients' websites (for instance, Google and Yahoo). The competition between these providers is clearly one of who has the best use-features (and the winner will take most of the advertising incomes) and who is able to attract sufficiently high content quality and number of visitors (so-called traffic).

The Leibnizian scenario focuses on creating a logically correct design, which is typical for traditional website development approaches. This strategy focuses on delivering more value for customers from improved interactions with an existing content base. Because the business strategy is never ended and difficult to specify, this design scenario starts with what is possible to realize at the business, process, and infrastructure levels. This is typical for the exploratory way of the development of electronic newspapers and information services, which have huge and interesting collections of content and have to think about all kinds of opportunities to improve their exploitation. An interesting example here is LexisNexis (www.lexisnexis.com), which offers all kinds of customized data packages and related use-features for private or business purposes.

The Kantian scenario focuses on a fully integrated and consistent design, incorporating logical and empirical elements in an architecture. This is often called a *waterfall scenario*. Business models in fact are never complete, so such a scenario in its purest sense is difficult to find. Nevertheless, there are examples where an information service provider wants to fully consider what it wants to deliver, to whom, what the clients want, and who pays before going to any further process and infrastructure. An example is the publishing industry, which actually responded rather late on the opportunities that the Internet gave them. The reasons for these hesitations have not been the technology,

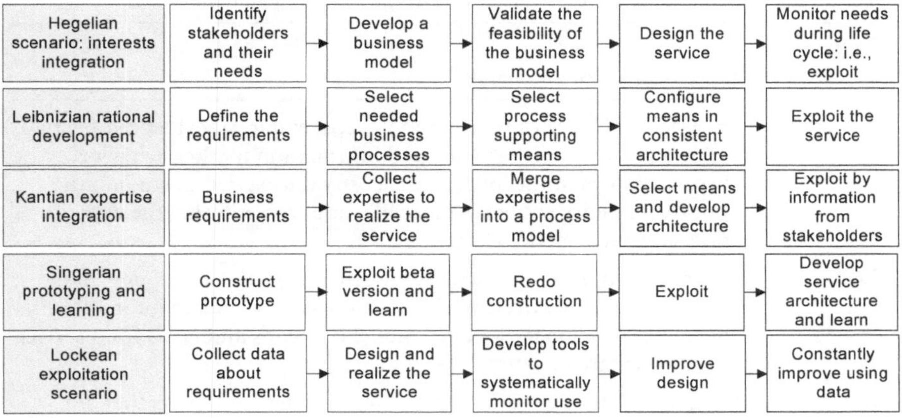


*Figure 2.4* Design project scenarios for information services.

but rather the business model. They had to answer the question of how they can earn money if the entrance barrier on the Internet is so low and how they can safe-guard proper management of the intellectual property so that quality and pay-outs can be guaranteed (Shapiro & Varian, 1999).

The Singerian scenario focuses on the actual realization of an information service by prototyping, because:

1. It assumes that not all requirements can be known in advance, which implies that at least two cycles are needed to find the real requirements.
2. It assumes that the best way of finding requirements is the construction of a prototype.
3. Prototypes have to be evaluated by use(r) data of any kind (maybe surveys, or log data). Often prototyping requires multiple cycles.
4. After several cycles, the insights gained into the systems requirements may be only marginal, and consequently the system design can be handed over to the system builders.
5. The pragmatist approach does not prescribe certain necessary sequences among aspects (content, use, and revenue) and prefers to approach project sequences from contextual opportunities and needs.

### 2.3.6 Summary of Process-oriented Challenges

The described inquiring systems (as teleological systems to produce knowledge, Churchman, 1971), provide useful kernel theories for a design science researcher. The inquiring systems point at key challenges to be aimed at, given in Table 2.3.

*Table 2.3* Summary of Process-Oriented Design Science Challenges

| *Inquiring system* | *Process-oriented challenges* |
|---|---|
| Lockean | Empirical evidence of information needs, empirical evidence of actual information service behavior and information market behavior; because information collection is costly during design studies, the Lockean inquiry system is especially applicable during the exploitation stage of a service. |
| Leibnizian | Optimization of costs (means) and benefits (goals or requirements) of information services, (rational) models that explain information behavior; a rational, designed model of means and goals for a service is called its architecture. |
| Kantian | Integrating of requirements given by the different experts that are responsible for the service's processes; this results in integrative process models. |
| Hegelian | Identifying stakeholders and what they think they need; interests of stakeholders have to be integrated in a validated business model. |
| Singerian | Information service development as a multi-actor problem-solving challenge with no clearly predefined requirements and sequences of action |

## 2.4 CONCLUSION

### 2.4.1 Summarizing the Structure of Kernel Theories for Information Service Design

Table 2.4 summarizes the product-oriented and process-oriented kernel theories, where the first states key requirements for informing services and the second mentions methods for insight generation as part of design processes. In this context, the inquiring systems provide only "instruments" for achieving real progress.

On the basis of product-oriented kernel theories we further explained theoretical notions, concepts, and methods for the three aspects for an information service, i.e., content, use-value, and revenue. This chapter explained what these product-oriented challenges imply for information services development. The section on process-oriented theory states concepts and methods for five design steps: problem analysis, business requirements, process requirements, design, and exploitation, which we identified in Chapter 1.

The next chapters will discuss each approach per design step, starting with business requirements in Chapter 3. This implies that we will focus on the process-oriented layers as the main structure for the rest of this book.

*Table 2.4* An Overview of Kernel Theories for Information Servces

| *Inquiring system* | *Product-oriented kernel theory* | *Process-oriented kernel theory* |
|---|---|---|
| Locke | Database models, user interfaces, information acquisition interface | Description and induction by empirical evidence of requirements and the impact of services in certain contexts; collecting and analyzing data for service exploitation |
| Leibniz | Expert systems, decision support systems, simulation systems, and recommender systems, which have a causal knowledge model as its core engine | Construction of causal models for explanation or prediction; testing of these models on logical consistency; application of these models as means (causes) and goals (effects) and their relations in designs and architectures of services |
| Kant | Knowledge services that integrate multiple sources of information and knowledge for different users with different questions with a common architecture using a common semantics (ontology) | Network of knowledge and requirements to accomplish the service's processes; for this a relevant, complete, and useful modeling language has to be selected up front of the modeling activities. |
| Hegel | A system for opinion articulation and sharing, discussion and conflict resolution (e.g., voting or refereeing); a valid business model for an information service is also based on interests reconciliation. | Explanatory (interpretive and critical) methods for discovering people's intentions to participate in an information service; integrate interests into a business model. The business model must be valid, i.e., sufficiently motivating for actor to participate. |
| Singer | Features for collaboration and group problem-solving | Project management theory, articulating the role of different kernel theories for realizing concrete systems and prototypes to learn about how to contribute to real human progress |

This choice is also necessary to reduce the complexity in this book and this choice will help the readers to develop projects, which are mostly organized along the process-layers and less along the product dimension.

### 2.4.2 Reflecive Exercise

Consulting firm X has 1,000 employees located in 10 towns within a radius of about 400 km. Because they want to deliver the same service for each town, a lot of expertise redundancy is needed. This was regarded as a problem, because it would disallow the experts to specialize in different fields. Therefore, the firm wants to establish an internal information exchange service.

1. Analyze what different topics will have to be covered from a product-oriented perspective.
2. Also analyze what methods and techniques will be needed to well-equip the project team.
3. To what extent do the inquiring systems successfully help in problem and challenge identification for this problem? What additional theories are needed (if any)?

## 2.5 FURTHER READING

Hevner, A., March, S., & Park, J. (2004). Design science in information systems research. *Management Information Systems Quarterly, 28*(1), 75–ind.

Walls, J., Widmeyer, G., & El Sawy, O. (1992). Building an information system design theory for vigilant EIS. *Information Systems Research, 3*(1), 36–59.

# 3 Creating Business Models for Information Services

## 3.1 FROM HEGELIAN INQUIRING SYSTEMS TO BUSINESS MODELS

The Hegelian inquiring system emphasized the existence of multiple actors (stakeholders) with different interests (stakes) that motivate them to be involved in informing actions in a certain way. Via dialectic logic these stakeholders can resolve their conflicts of interests, and so collaboration for joint purposes can be enabled. Such a synthesis may be more or less easy to establish given the context in which these actors operate.

In information services, the context can be intra-organizational, where superiors settle conflicts of interests (master models). Many information services, however, lack such superiors or have multiple masters. When these masters have complementary resources or capabilities, they may collaborate in an information service via quid pro quo arrangements, also called business models. Such business models presume an identification of the service concept and a business proposition proposed to relevant actors by a service coordinator. A business model is part of a service-business architecture, which identifies financial, technical, and organizational means to realize the business model. Before a service architecture is realized, the involved actors must be sure that the business model is valid, i.e., that all participants can expect that engaging in this business is profitable for all. Consequently, this chapter will discuss:

- Information services business contexts
- The information service business architecture
- Detecting the related stakeholders, their needs, and business models
- Validating the business models

Note that we sharply distinguish business models from process models (as mentioned in Chapter 2, where the business models are products of the Hegelian inquiring system and the process models are the product of the Kantian inquiring system, which is consistent with Gordijn and Akkermans (2001), although some authors do not prefer such a distinction (e.g., Zott and Amit 2008). Process models will be discussed in the next chapter.

## 3.2 BUSINESS CONTEXTS OF INFORMATION SERVICES

Following Boisot (1998: 14) information (goods) may be classified along their levels of *codification* and *abstraction*. Codification helps to give form to information, for instance, by representing it in a language or mass-produced artifact. High codification implies that the representation is unambiguous or less opaque (Womack, 2002) for different receivers of the tokens. Abstraction refers to the level that content of the good (information and knowledge) can be applied more generally and is less restricted in scope.

Low codification levels obstruct the market exchange opportunities of information goods, because it may be unclear for the buyer what actually will be sold. As such lowly codified goods are more effectively exchanged in networks, where credence determines much of the expected value, and higher risks of poor value deliveries are acceptable. High codification, in return, enables tagging a price to the commodity and also enables others to deliver comparable products that create market competition. Consequently, markets enable only the exchange of highly codified information goods, though if they are highly asset-specific, they will have to be exchanged via hierarchies for the sake of maximum exploitation of the property rights. Lowly codified information goods require a conversion process to make them suitable for market exchanges, if they are not asset specific. Given the different levels of abstraction and codification, several information goods may be identified (see Table 3.1).

*Table 3.1* Information Goods and Their Contexts

| *Exchange governance* | *Market* | *Hybrid/ network* | | *Hierarchy* | |
|---|---|---|---|---|---|
| *Codification* | *High* | *Low* | *High* | *Low* | *High* |
| Abstraction low | Data delivery services; news; journals; infotainment | Qualitative observations & reports | Data sets | Business intelligence reports | Databases |
| Abstraction moderate | Magazines; commercial software products | Research in progress results; ideas & notions | Shared resources for academic group | Organizational routines & norms; undocumented policies | Management reports; documented business policies |
| Abstraction high | Professional services; courseware; scientific publishing; patents; insurances | Paradigms | Scientific software; models; sponsored scientific books | Business & management consulting; skills | Business models; R&D results |

Institutional economics has identified three transaction governance models: markets, hierarchies, and networks or hybrids (Williamson, 1991). In *markets*, independent economic actors are involved in business transactions via the operation of a price mechanism. A price mechanism via markets operates via clear information about what exactly is being offered and what its payments will have to be in return. Therefore, in markets the goods traded must be comparable to a commodity. This implies that the goods must be highly codified and non-asset specific, and thus should have potential value for many buyers. The transactions are governed through classical contract law: sharp in by clear agreement; sharp out by clear performance in which the identity of the parties is irrelevant (Williamson, 1991: 271). Information goods, though, often are less codified and thus what is offered is not very sharply defined. Understanding some information goods also requires intense communications to be understood. This explains, for example, why selling training services via markets is difficult and a lot of communication and explanation is needed before a transaction will happen. Networks have a lot of benefits here. For example, for the market of books, less explanation is needed and the title and name of the author may be a sufficient reason for people to buy. Additionally, many information goods are asset-specific, implying that these goods are of use for only a limited group. For instance, an overview report of currently available production capacity of a firm may not be understandable or of any value for people other than the firm's production planners and some clients. High exchange and product uncertainties require elastic contracting mechanisms. If the contracting parties maintain autonomy but are bilaterally dependent to a nontrivial degree, the contracts will not be complete, and the actors will

1. contemplate unanticipated disturbance for which adaptation is needed,
2. provide a tolerance zone within which misalignment will be absorbed,
3. require information disclosure and substantiation if adaptation is proposed, and
4. provide for arbitration in the event voluntary agreement fails.

(Williamson, 1991: 272)

This is what Williamson calls *hybrid exchange governance*, and some other authors call clans (cf. Ciborra, 1987) or networks (cf. Liebeskind et al., 1996). It mostly does not make sense to supply high asset-specific information goods by hybrids, because (1) the firm owning it may want to apply strict ownership conditions on it when it is an important competitive asset, or (2) members in the hybrid will not be interested or they are unable to understand it. Hierarchies aim at information ownership and control and provide a context to make sense out of the information. A strong point of hybrids is that they enable informal content transfers, thus they enlarge the access to information also outside of the organizational boundaries, and hybrids are also supportive to interfirm knowledge creation and the management of tacit (low codified) knowledge (Liebeskind et al., 1996).

From the perspective of information goods buying, it may be difficult to value an information good, also because suppliers may be interested in concealing large portions of the good in the pre-transaction stage. The economic literature has introduced three attributes of goods for analyzing this problem (Nelson, 1970): search characteristics, experience characteristics, and credence characteristics.

- *Search* characteristics give a potential buyer information about the good to enable its valuation before consuming the good. In the context of information goods this may be, for instance, the occasion when you select a book on the basis of its title and list of contents.
- *Experience* characteristics enable a buyer to temporarily or partially consume the good so that the buyer can value it. This is typically the case with physical goods, like car-tests. In selling information goods, experience characteristics are problematic, because once experienced a buyer does not need to buy the good anymore. For instance, once having experienced a specific course, one does probably not need to take the course again. A seller of an information good may handle experience characteristics in three ways: (1) giving away the good for free to generate synergistic effects (e.g., academics may give away their articles to increase their reputation, which may help them to gain funds in the future), (2) excluding a buyer from further consumption by not selling an individual information good but by selling access to a constantly changing resource of information goods (this is what happens, for instance, by a subscription to a stock exchange data service), and (3) distributing demos for free (a price below cost level) to develop a client's desire for the full good.
- *Credence* characteristics enable a buyer to rely on third-party judgments or a seller's credentials. This is an important characteristic in buying information goods that require high-quality standards. For instance, certain newspapers are often bought because of their reputation. Credentials are often built by experiences of buyers and influential others.

Shapiro and Varian (1999) state that information goods as experience "goods", thus goods with experience as a *dominating* characteristic, are nearly impossible to price. If a content producer wants to earn money, he should be able to differentiate the good. Following the lines mentioned earlier, *differentiation* can be realized by delivering *use-features* as addition to content, like quality guarantees, raising the credence characteristics, or by reducing the costs of clients to find answers.

An important use-feature is the *property rights*, which states what is legally allowed to be done with the information good. Despite potentially high value of an information good, a content producer or retailer will not be able to earn a cent when he is not enabled to manage the property rights. Following Furubotn and Pejovich (1974) three types of *property rights* exist: (1) the right of use, (2) the right of changing forms and structure of the transferred good, and (3) the right to reap the profits of the good. Picot et al. (1997) add a fourth property right essential for markets: (4) the right to sell the good. Because information exchanges implicate the transfer of information (and its property rights) from a supplier to a buyer, the exchange partners may arrange some kind of payment. The actual price may result from the work of the invisible hand (the market), mutual understanding and networking (the handshaking in hybrids), and salaries in hierarchies. Because prices are hard to define in hybrids (Liebeskind et al., 1996), the payment for use mostly consists of invitations for collaboration on further development, and sharing profits when the information good can be sold or exploited. In the hierarchy, the most important ownership is the right to reap the profits exclusively. Thus despite high content value and use-features, generating revenues for information services is not trivial when the customers cannot easily identify the value or the property rights cannot be easily secured. An information service's revenue is also not always monetary; especially in networks, the opportunities to be engaged in further collaboration may be much more important than the financial benefits.

There are also *non property-rights use-features*, which include (Loebbecke, 1999):

1. *Customization*, which defines the transfer mode of the good and particularly the extent to which the good is or can be specified to the needs of a single client
2. *Timeliness*, which defines the time-slot in which the good has value; for instance, stock exchange data are very time-dependent, whereas dictionaries may be relatively time-independent.
3. *Intensity in use*, which defines if a user may use the good once (for instance, a movie) or several times (for instance, a text book)
4. *Externalities*, which may be positive when the value of the good increases when more people use it, or negative when the value declines when more people have the good

## 3.3 BUSINESS MODELS

Al-Debei and Avison (2010) identify four dimensions of a business model:

1. The web of actors and their roles (like customers, suppliers, and sponsors), relationships, channels, and networks
2. The value proposition, i.e., the product and service, and the value these are supposed to deliver to a target group
3. Financial setups and returns (revenues)

4. Value architectures, consisting of the resources, competencies, technologies, and other means to realize the value proposition

Each of the dimensions is further discussed, starting with the value architecture, which also occasionally is called the business architecture.

### 3.3.1 Value Architectures

A value architecture describes the organized means for a company or group (network) of companies to be able to create value for customers. Bouwman et al. (2008) selected the following four generic value architecture components (which they call "business model"):

- The *service concept*, which answers the question what the customer can do with the product or service offered, and includes the value proposition, which states why you should buy it. In information services the service concept can be defined at two levels: 1) the level of the individual information goods that are delivered, and 2) the level of the service platform with its features, options, and resources.
- The *technological architecture*, which specifies the technical functions needed to realize the value proposition, like data communication, privacy, and information processing
- The *organizational architecture*, which defines what organizations are necessary for offering the service or product, and how they should cooperate
- The *financial arrangements*, which consist of costs, investments, payments, revenues, and risks, and agreements on how to divide these among the actors that are participating in the business architecture

These components can be used to describe the value architecture, i.e., the main issues that have to be arranged and aligned for setting up a successful business (Prahalad & Hamel, 1994). A value architecture, of course, has to be aligned with external business developments, like new technologies, changes in the market, possible laws and regulations, and the competition. Consequently, a value architecture has to be evolving during the life cycle of the service. This evolving has to be monitored and acted upon, what we call "exploitation" in this book.

### 3.3.2 The Value Proposition: Expected Value and Revenue

A business model states the *rules that explain why some actor should supply what to another actor*. These rules explain how certain supplied *values* are expected to generate sufficient monetary or motivational *revenues* to stay in business. As such, the business model more precisely defines the arrows in the content of the actor web (see Figure 1.3), i.e., the reasons why the technology will be supplied by whom, in return of what, and for what common purpose. The main goal of a business model is to answer the question "*who* is offering *what* to *whom* and expects *what* in return" (Gordijn & Akkermans, 2001). Therefore, the central notions in any business model should be *value and revenue*, as well as the exchange of value and revenue among members of the actor web (Al-Debei & Avison, 2010).

The main questions in constructing a value model therefore are:

1. Who are the involved value-adding business actors?
2. What do their offerings consist of?
3. Between which actors are these offerings exchanged?
4. What are the value-creating activities that are present in the offerings?
5. Which value-creating activities are performed per actor?
6. How do we know that a business model will be valid?

A business model does not state *how* value-creating activities are carried out. This is an important goal of business *process* modeling (see Chapter 4).

We further illustrate the basic ideas of value and revenue models by newspaper information services.[1] This illustration further explains why values do not automatically generate revenues, and why value propositions cannot be equated with value finance.

Over 50 years ago, news distribution consisted of phoning the news into the newsroom or bringing it in by the reporter, where it was typed or transmitted over wire services to be published in the newspaper for the following day. Nowadays, the term "breaking news" has been made possible by the use of broadcast and cable news services that use live satellite technology to bring current events into consumers' homes. Events that in the past usually took hours or even days to become common knowledge are nowadays delivered instantaneously to consumers via radio, television, cell phones, and the Internet. The content on the news portal thus is delivered electronically, which has a dynamic and interactive nature, making it possible to adapt the news on the direct availability of new reports from events and the characteristics of the visitor reading it. This has large implications for the news business model (i.e., its value offerings and revenues).

The news sector has two main *values*: content and use options. Content can include news, personal ads, advertisements, and governmental messages. Together with this content, the newspaper can also provide services to its readers. These services can be, for example, brokerage services, incentives, and entertainment. These two values can be subdivided into several other values (based on Hoffman & Novak, 2005).

- *Brokerage* enables people to publish their ads and enables easy exchanges of services and/or goods.
- *Content delivery* is naturally the main value of the newspaper, which includes news about the world. Because of the availability of free news services, traditional (e-)newspapers have to differentiate themselves by background expertise articles, news archives, and additional informative services.
- *Search* enables one to browse through content or sources of information. It is naturally less easy to search through a traditional newspaper (the use of an index at the end of the newspaper will probably not be effective enough).
- *Incentive delivery* aims at creating awareness among the readers about events that have taken place in the region, country, or world.
- *Freeware* can be delivered if personal ads are published in which people offer their services for free. An example here is a software demo or trial period as part of an advertisement.
- *Communication*, such as the government using the (regional) newspaper to publish announcements that are meant for the general public (Gallaugher et al., 2001)
- *Control*, e.g. it is not possible for the reader of a traditional newspaper to filter the news he or she receives to read in the newspaper, as everything has been printed. The online newspaper, on the other hand, can be as interactive as one desires. The visitor can filter the news he or she prefers to read and use a search function that allows the visitor to search through the entire newspaper/website. The customer can deliver information so that he or she receives the proper level of codification and abstraction or the customer can receive tools to modify his or her profile.
- *Entertainment* sections usually appear in newspapers.
- *Community* is created by stimulating customers to communicate with each other using tools. This may be possible in hardcopy newspapers by send-in letters and personal ads, but e-newspapers have great opportunities of enabling discussions on topics—for example, with journalists and experts.
- *Digital rights management*, i.e., buying not only content, but also different rights if needed.

Table 3.2 summarizes the differences in value types between the traditional newspaper and the online newspaper. The traditional newspaper has most value types available but some of them in a limited form. Particular value types that are weakly present in hardcopy newspapers, like the community value, can greatly affect the success of a newspaper. A community is nowadays a must to stimulate the awareness of the service (Preece, 2001; Maloney-Krichmar & Preece, 2005).

*Table 3.2* Comparison of Value Types for Newspapers

| *Value types* | *Traditional newspaper* | *Online newspaper* |
|---|---|---|
| Brokerage | Present (limited form) | Present |
| Content | Present | Present |
| Search | Via ordering done by employees | Present, customer can do it |
| Incentive | Present | Present |
| Freeware | Maybe present | Present |
| Communication | Present | Present and more interactive |
| Control of codification and abstraction | Not present | Present and easy |
| Entertainment | Present (limited) | Present |
| Community | Present weakly with poor interaction | Present |
| DRM ordering | Possible | Easy |

As Table 3.2 suggests, the online newspaper has the potential to offer more values than the traditional newspaper. The main advantage of online news is that it can be interactive and dynamic, making it possible to achieve high levels of customization and many additional features like community building by readers. But, *values do not automatically generate revenue*. The generation of revenue is part of the business model and is essential to keep the business running. Advertising and (to a lesser extent) subscriptions are required to fund the newspaper business (Krueger et al., 2004; Swatman et al., 2006), but both are declining rapidly nowadays. When it comes to news portals, advertising is not the only source of income available; it is therefore required to analyze the different revenue streams and link these with the value supplied (Hoffman & Novak, 2005). A classification of revenue sources for news services is given here (based on Hoffman & Novak, 2005).

- *Referral fees*: Generate revenue by receiving a certain fee when attracting customers to other sites. Online newspapers can easily implement this revenue stream by logging follow-up links.
- *Subscription fees*: Regular fee that is paid to gain access to certain services; this revenue stream can naturally be present in both online and offline newspapers.
- *License fees for different digital rights management* (often shortened as DRM): Collection of fees for processes to which the company has rights, like licensing the reuse of content to other parties
- *Pay-per-view*: Charge a fee for a certain amount of views of a particular item (usually banners). This can be present only in the online

newspaper, because the offline hardcopy newspaper can unbundle its content only by producing expensive customized versions.

- *Micro-payment*: Collection of very small transaction fees, but in high volumes; this can be present in both online and offline newspapers. For example, paid services can be offered in exchange for an SMS message, which generally speaking costs less than a euro.
- *Advertising*: Allow other firms to promote their services and/or goods on the newspaper's website. This revenue stream can naturally be present in both online and offline newspapers. Advertising is also a value because it is an enriched communication method.
- *Sponsorships*: Receive fees from another, without a communication or web presence in return. This revenue stream can naturally be present in both online and offline newspapers.
- *Ransom model*: Provide a certain part of the service for free and ask for a fee for the rest of the service. This can be present in the traditional newspaper. The online newspaper can offer content that is partially free and ask for a fee to read the extended version of the content.
- *Margin on sale of goods/services*: Selling goods and services through the Internet and collecting a margin on it; this is present in nearly all newspaper business models.
- *Sale of customer data*: Collecting and then selling customer information; this is illegal in most western countries. However, customer data that does not contain personal information can be sold. This revenue stream can be used when selling anonymized primary data and derivative information regarding their readers, subscribers, and market segments.
- *Offline customer response*: Sales start through the website but are then finished using an offline solution. This is frequently done by newspapers by offering special products with discounts for their subscribers or readers (e.g., books, videos, and travel tours).
- *Value added service*: Fees are collected on new services that are provided for "free" goods and services offered on the Internet.

The many ways a newspaper publisher can generate revenue are summarized in Table 3.3.

In business models values and revenues have to be combined. A certain combination of value type and revenue stream can lead to a positive, negative, or neutral result for different actors. A negative result signifies that a given value cannot generate revenue; for example, a subscription fee can influence the amount of readers that use the brokerage service. The more people that take part in a brokerage deal, the better. A positive combination would be if the value helps a given revenue stream to improve. For example, micro-payments can enhance the brokerage service because sending an SMS message, for example, can purchase services/goods that are

*Table 3.3* Comparison of Revenue Sources for Newspapers

| *Revenue sources* | *Traditional newspaper* | *Online newspaper* |
|---|---|---|
| Referral fees | Not possible | Possible |
| Subscription fees | Possible | Possible |
| License fee | Possible | Possible (easier) |
| Pay-per-view | Not possible | Possible |
| Micropayment | Not possible | Possible |
| Advertising | Possible | Possible |
| Sponsorships | Possible | Possible |
| Ransom model | Not possible | Possible |
| Margin on sale of goods/ services | Possible | Possible |
| Sale of customer data | Possible but illegal in Europe | Possible but illegal in Europe |
| Offline customer response | Possible | Possible |
| Value-added services (i.e., free goods and incomes via related services) | Possible | Possible |

being sold at low prices. A neutral combination can be present if there is no link between value and revenue. Subscription fees have a general negative effect in combination with all the values. The more values a news agency has to offer, the more possibilities it has to generate revenue, but nowadays there is a lot of content that can be obtained for (nearly) free, so the news agency should be able to ask for a price for content that can be obtained for free elsewhere.

### 3.3.3 Value Networks and Their Assessment[2]

Markets for information goods are network-oriented constructs where several actors mutually add value. Such a network is also called an actor web (Al-Debei & Avison, 2010). Therefore, for information services development a description of the business actors, their content and value contributions, and the value objects to be exchanged between the actors is required. Validating a new business model requires the assessment of all business actors' profitability, i.e., over time all actors in the network must be able to make sufficient revenues and increase their economic utility (Gordijn, 2002). Profits of a business actor encompass the calculation of expected incoming revenue streams minus the expected outgoing revenue streams and the other operational expenses. A business model is *valid* if the expected resulting profit of *each* business actor is (1) higher than zero, and (2) for each actor higher compared to the expected profit when remaining with the current business model, i.e., not participating in the new business model. These two *business model validity norms* can be assessed by predicting the future revenue flows of all business actors. The steps for validating new information service business models therefore are:

1. Describe the current and new business structure in the industry: i.e., actors and their roles in the industry.
2. Describe the mutual content, value, and revenue exchanges between the business actors, i.e., design the value net.
3. Estimate future outgoing and incoming revenue streams, as well as the operational expenses, per actor in both the current situation and after implementing the new business model.
4. Calculate profitability for each business actor in both the current situation and after implementing the new business model.
5. Assess the profitability of the actors within the business models using the two business model validity norms.
6. Determine under which conditions the better business model is valid by changing the estimates for outgoing and incoming revenue streams and operational expenses (i.e., sensitivity analysis).

We explain each step further by the case of the digital music download industry in the Netherlands. Digital music in the Netherlands is supplied via legal digital music services by a pay-per-download revenue model. Moreover, many consumers obtain digital music from "illegal" channels, including file-sharing networks, e-mail, and FTP servers. Musicians and music producers lose substantial profit opportunities by the existing illegal channels. As a solution to this loss, the levy model is often proposed. Key characteristics of this business model are as follows (Fisher, 2004; Netanel, 2002; Oksanen & Välimäki, 2005):

- Every broadband consumer is obliged to pay a fixed monthly levy upon his or her broadband subscription.
- The total amount of money thus collected is distributed among the property rights owners of music goods based on the relative usage of their digital music in a certain period.
- Every Internet user is allowed to download from every download service (including peer-to-peer networks) and to non-commercially distribute and share digital music.
- Commercial distributors of digital music (e.g., advertisement-based music services) are obliged to obtain a distribution license and provide download statistics in return.

This levy business model has many drawbacks, including:

- Not all broadband subscribers are digital music consumers.
- Determining the relative legal usage of a digital music good in a specific period is difficult, because download statistics do not include only the downloads from legal services.
- Determining the total amount of levies to be collected requires a currently non-existent trusted collection agent for the industry.
- It is difficult to cope with the use of digital music from other countries and it is also difficult to control how the use by people in other countries is compensated to the music actors.

The case study was conducted in a time frame of three months (April 2007 until June 2007), and analyzes the profitability of music actors for the year 2006. We have limited ourselves to the Dutch download market of music singles and albums, allowing better estimations of exchanged monetary revenues. This excludes other types of digital music content (e.g., ringtones), mobile music downloads, and streaming of digital music content (e.g., online radio), digital music incorporated in other content or bundled with other products.

As data sources, we used both interviews and documents. The interviewees we had access to are:

- Manager public relations and communication of the Dutch association of music producers and importers
- Vice president global royalties of a major Dutch record label
- A manager of new media from the same record label
- Business developer of a former Dutch download service that recently stopped its activities, because it saw no future in the sales of music downloads anymore

The documents consist of quantitative and qualitative sources, including market statistics, market forecasts, websites, and literature sources on the music industry. The documents are used to describe business models and to estimate the exchanged value objects and expenses of actors. In addition, we analyzed the websites of Dutch download services in order to determine their revenue structure (pay-per-download, subscription, advertisements) and if they used their portal to sell advertisement space. The obtained information was used to describe and construct a first version of the value models. The interviews are used to validate estimates of exchanged value objects and expenses of actors. After each interview, we updated the value models and used it as an input for the upcoming interview.

### *Step 1 The Business Architecture Model*

Figure 1.3 identified the following actors of an information service: suppliers, consumers, the information service manager, subcontractors, and sponsors. The information service manager coordinates the value net and maintains it. The subcontractor increases the value offered by the information service by offering additional use-values to both the information service and the consumer. Two types of subcontractors for information services exist: commerce service providers, like a payment service offered by a bank, and infrastructure service providers, like the provision of a communication platform for consumers and the information service. The sponsors monetarily support the information service. Figure 3.1 outlines the actors of the pay-per-download business model.

The suppliers of digital music goods consist of music performers, composers, and text writers, as well as the companies that produce and publish music. The value contributions of composers and text writers consist of the design of the music good. They are represented by publishers who ease that their designs are recognized by producers. Moreover, they collect copyright remuneration from commercial users of digital music goods. Producers ensure that the designs are produced into actual music goods using performing artists and music studios to record the music good. Moreover they promote the music goods into the marketplace by advertisement campaigns.

The information service manager in the pay-per-download business model is the digital music service. Their value contribution is the online distribution of music goods fulfilling consumer demand. This role is performed by two actors: content aggregators and download portals. Content aggregators are the information service interface to suppliers of digital music goods and are responsible for receiving authorization to distribute digital music goods from producers, digitization of music into digital music goods, and the hosting of digital music libraries. Moreover they digitize and compress digital music

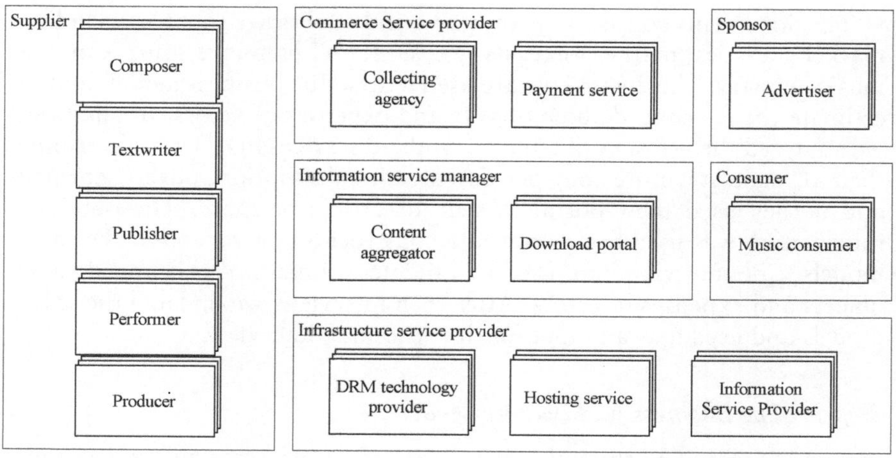


*Figure 3.1* Business actors in the digital music industry.

into music catalogues. These catalogues are mostly stored at hosting services, which provide storage and delivery of downloads to the consumer. During the digitization, music is compressed with Digital Rights Management (DRM) technology. Producers require content aggregators to compress music downloads with DRM technology as part of their license agreement. DRM technology embeds the use-values of digital music goods into the good itself, ensuring that the music good is used according to the requirements and conditions licensed. Content aggregators have to obtain a license from a DRM technology provider in order to use their technology. The hosting service and the DRM technology provider are hereby infrastructure service providers that facilitate both the (secure) distribution of digital music. Consumers search and download digital music goods from download portals. Hereby they are supported by ISPs, which offer them an Internet connection to actually access the portal. Download portals are the service's client interface and are a platform where supply meets demand. Moreover they reduce consumer search costs by filtering out inferior goods and informing consumers about music goods. The use-values they deliver are embedded by means of DRM technology. Payment services are used to securely transfer the money from the consumer to the download portal. Portals obtain music downloads from the music catalogue of their content aggregator. Furthermore, they have to obtain a distribution license from a collecting agency, which ensures remuneration to composers and text writers. The payment service and the collecting agency are the commerce service providers supporting the transaction of digital music. In addition to the download revenues, download portals offer advertisement space to third-party advertisers and promotional places to producers.

The collecting agency collects remuneration together with download statistics from the download portal for all music downloads that are sold and pays royalties to the publishers of the composers and text writers, which transfer part of it to the composers and text writers. In return download portals are authorized to commercially distribute music.

Producers require part of the advertisement income to be transferred to them. Part of the download portal's advertisement space is filled with advertisements from producers in order to promote their artists. In return, download portals are allowed to use the content to attract traffic. The revenues are transferred to performing artists in the form of royalty payments. Table 3.4 gives a summary of the business actors within the download industry, including their value contributions, the offered and received value objects, and the exchange partner.

Applying the levy business model would change the structure of the described pay-per-download business model. The main adjustment would include the change in transaction flows from consumers to suppliers. The download portal still remains the platform where supply meets demand for digital music goods, but at the download portal *no direct financial transaction takes place anymore.* The revenues are gathered by the Internet service provider, where broadband consumers have to pay an obligatory levy. The

*Table 3.4* Actors, Value Contributions, and Value Objects Summarized

| *Role* | *Actor* | *Value contributions* | *Offered value objects* | *Received value objects* | *Exchange partner* |
|---|---|---|---|---|---|
| Supplier | Composer & text writer | Design and write musical compositions and lyrics | Exploitation rights | Royalties | Publisher |
| | Performing artist | Music performance | Exploitation rights | Royalties | Producer |
| | Producer | Produce music goods; selection of superior musical compositions; contract superior performing artists; promotion of music goods | Music good; distribution license | Fee | Content aggregator |
| | | | Advertisements | Fee | Download portal |
| | Publisher | Promote musical compositions; Collect royalties on musical compositions and lyrics | Collective administration | Royalty | Collecting agency |
| | | | Royalty | Exploitation right | Composer & text writer |
| | Content aggregator | Receiving authorization for distribution of digital music goods; creating digital music goods; hosting digital music good's libraries | Fee | Music good; distribution license | Producer |
| | | | Fee | Hosting | Hosting service |
| | | | Fee | DRM license | DRM technology provider |
| | | | Music good | Fee | Download portal |

*(continued)*

*Table 3.4* (continued)

| *Role* | *Actor* | *Value contributions* | *Offered value objects* | *Received value objects* | *Exchange partner* |
|---|---|---|---|---|---|
| Information service coordinator | Download portal | Fulfill consumer demand; filtering out inferior goods; inform consumers about music goods | Music good | Fee | Consumer |
| Infra-structure Provider | Collecting agency | Cashing money from ISPs and redistributing it to rights owners | Fee | Music good | Content aggregator |
| | | | Audience | Advertise-ments; fee | Advertiser |
| | Payment service | Efficient payment processing | Promotion | Advertise-ments; content attractiveness | Producer |
| | Hosting service | Hosting of Inter-net service access | Fee | Content attractiveness | Producer |
| | DRM technology provider | Digital rights preservation | Fee; download statistics | Distribution license | Collecting agency |
| | Internet service provider | Consumer access to Internet services and download portals | Fee | Payment support | Payment service |
| Sponsor | Advertisers | Source of income | Advertisements; fee | Audience | Download portal |
| Consumer | Consumer | Source of income | Fee | Music good | Download portal |

ISP transfers the money to the collecting agency, which repartitions among producers and publishers based on relative download popularity in a given period. The producers and publishers use the levy income to pay the composers, text writers, and the performing artists. Compared to the pay-per-download business model, the changes are:

- The download portal is no longer the financial interface with the consumer and it therefore financially fully depends on sponsors.
- The ISP is becoming a commerce service provider because it is responsible for the financial transaction from consumer to a central collecting agency.

- The central agency collects the levy income from all ISPs and repartitions it among the producers and publishers.
- Content aggregators and download portals still require a distribution license to offer their digital music commercially (ad-supported) in return for delivering their download statistics.
- The collecting agent requires estimation of the download popularity of its total catalogue. A media measurement service could fulfill this role by monitoring households and peer-to-peer file sharing networks.
- The commerce service providers (i.e., collecting agent and payment support) are not necessary anymore to support the commercial transaction.
- The DRM technology provider becomes obsolete for enforcing requirements and conditions.

### *Step 2 The Value Net*

The e3value technique is useful to represent actors and their value activities. Value objects are exchanged between these actors via value interfaces. These value interfaces are part of actors or their value activities. Value interfaces have value ports that offer or request value objects. These value objects are obtained from other value ports via value exchanges. Minimally two value exchanges, one incoming and one outgoing, make up a value offering (Gordijn & Akkermans, 2001).

Value offerings fulfill a certain consumer or organizational need. Within e3value, scenario paths are used to model which value offerings fulfill these needs. A scenario path consists of a start stimulus representing a need, a stop stimulus indicating the end of the scenario path, and several connection elements that connect the start stimulus, stop stimulus, and the intermediate value offerings. A scenario path can consist of a pure linear process, but can also have several AND or OR elements representing alternative paths that can be used to fulfill a particular need. Figure 3.2 shows the visual representation of the e3value modeling elements. For a detailed description of these modeling elements, see Gordijn and Akkermans (2001). The software for e3value modeling can be downloaded for free via www.e3value.com.

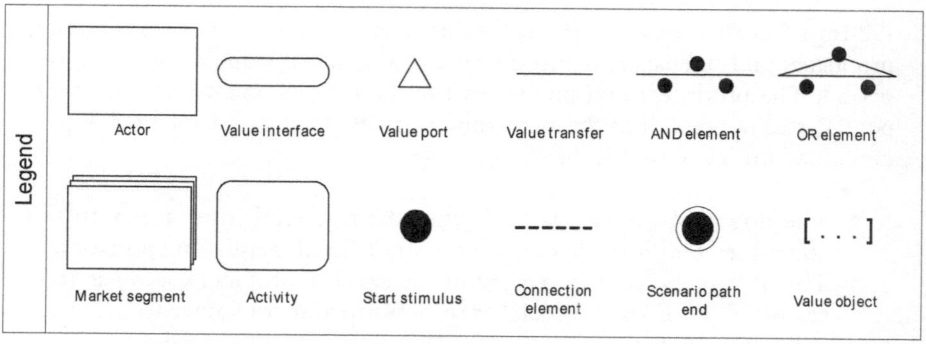


*Figure 3.2* Elements of the e3value modeling technique.

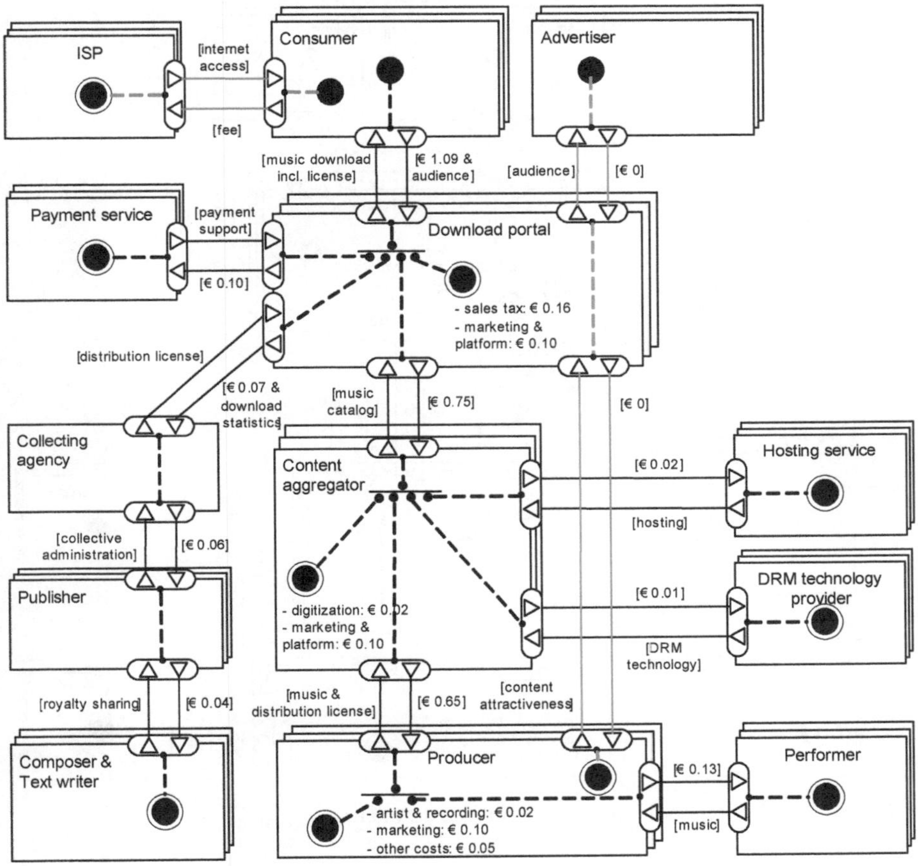


*Figure 3.3* Value net of the pay-per-download business model.

*Note* that for a business model, we do not need the "activity" object mentioned in Figure 3.2.

Figure 3.3 shows the value model of the *current Dutch download market*. Although we did not explain the estimation of the figures yet, the value of the exchanged value objects are also shown within the figure. In reality the value model is much more complex because each market segment consists of several organizations. Moreover, organizations could operate in different market segments. For example, Apple's iTunes Music Store is a download portal and content aggregator. For practical reasons, market segments are used to represent all organizations, assuming that the economic profitability of a market segment represents the economic profitability of all organizations within the market segment. In addition, we assume that all download portals obtain their music from a content aggregator.

The value model for the pay-per-download model consists of many scenario paths. These scenario paths can be merged into two main paths:

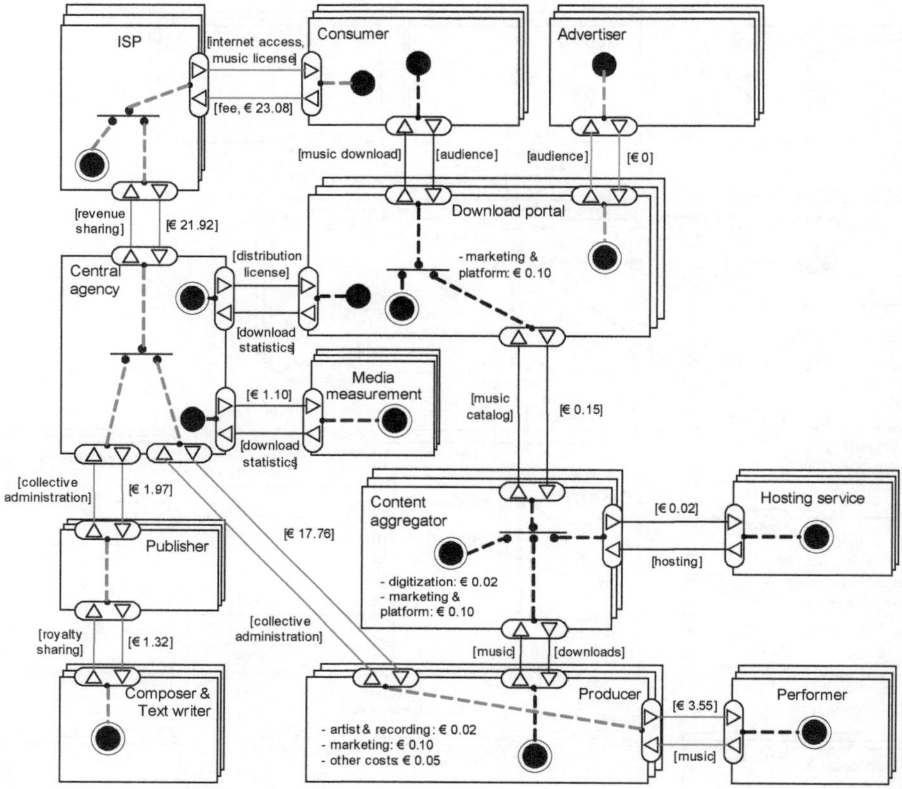


*Figure 3.4* Value model of the levy business model.

1) consumers buying a digital music download and 2) third-party advertisers advertising on the download portal.

Figure 3.4 visualizes the value model of the *levy business model*. In addition to the two main scenario paths of the pay-per-download business model, a third path is the payment of the levy fee via the ISP.

### *Step 3 Value Exchanges*

Table 3.5 outlines the estimates of the value exchanges and costs of the download portal, content aggregator, and producer market segments. These estimates are from five different sources: Piet (2005) (A) and OECD (2005) (B) and interviews with a major record label [Producer] (C), the Dutch association of producers and importers (NVPI) (D), and an organization that formerly owned a download portal (E). The estimates are divided into a low and a high value for the respective value exchange or cost and should be read as value per download. In the average column these

*Table 3.5* Estimates of Value Exchanges and Expenses of Download Portals, Content Aggregators, and Content Producers

| *Actor* | *Value exchanges (v) or operating costs (o)* | *Low* | | | | | | *High* | | | | | | *Average* | *Adjusted* |
|---|---|---|---|---|---|---|---|---|---|---|---|---|---|---|---|
| | | *A* | *B* | *C* | *D* | *E* | *Min* | *A* | *B* | *C* | *D* | *E* | *Max* | | |
| Download portal | Download price (v) | 0.99 | 0.99 | 0.99 | 1.10 | 0.99 | 0.99 | 0.99 | 1.39 | 0.99 | 1.10 | 1.19 | 1.39 | 1.19 | 1.09 |
| | Producer advertising (v) | | | 0.00 | 0.01 | 0.00 | 0.00 | | | 0.00 | 0.01 | 0,. 0 | 0.01 | 0.01 | |
| | Copyright license (v) | 0.10 | 0.10 | 0.07 | 0.06 | 0.08 | 0.06 | 0.12 | 0.12 | 0.07 | 0.06 | 0.08 | 0.08 | 0.07 | 0.07 |
| | Payment support (v) | 0.10 | 0.10 | | 0.11 | 0.05 | 0.05 | 0.15 | 0.30 | | 0.11 | 0.15 | 0.15 | 0.10 | 0.10 |
| | Music catalog (v) | 0.62 | 0.50 | | | 0.70 | 0.50 | 0.81 | 0.92 | | | 0.75 | 0.75 | 0.63 | 0.75 |
| | Sales tax (o) | | | 0.16 | 0.16 | 0.19 | 0.16 | | | 0.16 | 0.16 | 0.19 | 0.19 | 0.18 | 0.16 |
| | Platform & Marketing (o) | | | | 0.39 | | 0.04 | | | | 0.39 | | 0.18 | 0.11 | 0.10 |
| Content Aggregator | Platform & Marketing (o) | 0.10 | 0.10 | | | | 0.04 | 0.18 | 0.25 | | | | 0.18 | 0.11 | 0.10 |
| | Digitization (o) | | | | | 0.02 | 0.02 | | | | | 0.02 | 0.02 | 0.02 | 0.02 |
| | DRM license (v) | | | | 0.03 | 0.01 | 0.01 | | | | 0.03 | 0.01 | 0.02 | 0.02 | 0.01 |
| | Hosting (v) | 0.02 | | | | 0.01 | 0.01 | 0.05 | | | | 0.01 | 0.03 | 0.02 | 0.02 |
| | Music license (v) | 0.50 | 0.40 | 0.60 | 0.34 | 0.65 | 0.34 | 0.58 | 0.67 | 0.70 | 0.34 | 0.70 | 0.70 | 0.52 | 0.65 |
| Producer | Marketing (o) | | | 0.12 | 0.08 | | 0.08 | | | 0.14 | 0.09 | | 0.14 | 0.11 | 0.12 |
| | Artist & Repertoire (o) | | | | | | | | | | | | | | |
| | Digitization (o) | | | 0.19 | 0.17 | | 0.10 | | | 0.23 | 0.17 | | 0.23 | 0.17 | 0.22 |
| | Recording (o) | | | | | | | | | | | | | | |
| | Royalties (v) | | | 0.12 | | | 0.07 | | | 0.14 | | | 0.14 | 0.11 | 0.13 |
| | Other (o) | | | 0.05 | 0.05 | | 0.05 | | | 0.05 | 0.05 | | 0.05 | 0.05 | 0.05 |
| | Profit | | | 0.12 | 0.04 | | 0.04 | | | 0.14 | 0.04 | | 0.14 | 0.09 | 0.13 |

*Note*: A=Peit (2005); B=OECD (2005); C=Producer interview; D=NVPI; E=Portal manager interview.

low and high values are used to calculate the average per value exchange or cost. The final column interprets the averages and displays the estimates that are used within the case study.

The figures are adjusted by expert opinions. A music license is more likely to be €0.99 per download, because both insiders C and E validated this figure. This resulted in a correction of the music catalogue price paid by the download portal and a correction in costs of producers in terms of artist and repertoire, digitization, and recording. The download price is also more likely to be around €0.99. This is mainly because the major seller of music downloads, iTunes, asks a price of €0.99 per download including transaction costs. The other services ask a bit more (ranging from €0.99 to €1.39) and also surcharge transaction costs. Because numbers about segmentation within the download portal market segment are unknown, we assume the price to be €0.99 excluding, and €1.09 including transaction costs. In addition to the estimates of the music delivery channel from producer to consumer, also margins of the collecting agency and the royalty sharing percentages of the publishers have to be estimated. In this case study these estimates are [Producer]: 10% for the Buma/Stemra and 33% royalty sharing for the publisher.

The value model of the pay-per-download business model consists of two scenario paths. The triggers for these scenario paths are: 1) the number of music downloads that consumers trigger and 2) advertisement payments by sponsors. The number of legal downloads are yearly reported by the NVPI in their estimated value of the Dutch music industry. In 2006 the total Dutch music market is estimated at €317 million. Downloads account for approximately 3% of this market, resulting in a total of €10.1 million or 10.1 million downloads [NIVP, 2007a]. Only 4 of the 34 Dutch download portals have advertisements from third-party advertisers. These four portals also are small players within the download portal market segment and the income from third-party advertisers is therefore assumed to be zero. The main reason for this is that producers demand a percentage (50–70%) of the income generated from advertisements [Producer]. Most download portals therefore do not choose to advertise within the download shops, but on earlier pages.

In the case of the levy model, no price per download is paid, but instead there is a fixed subscription fee per year. It is suggested to determine the height of this fee based on the loss in revenues of the music industry due to (illegal) file sharing. NVPI reports on its website a list of academic and non-academic sources that have calculated this loss in revenues. It concluded the total loss in the period 1998 to 2004 was 22% [NIVP, 2007b]. BREIN, the Dutch anti-piracy organization, reports approximately the same figure: 15–20% (Brei, 2007). The drop of 20% is also visible in record sales in that period from 1998 to 2004. In the period from 2004 to 2006, record sales dropped even further. The loss in sales of recordings now grows to 40% or €200 million. Making this figure the total levies that should be collected by Internet service providers is not completely correct. It is based on the sales price of CDs and includes retailer margins, distribution costs, and sales tax in total approximately 40% of the revenues. These costs do not have to be covered by the levy, resulting in a total of 60% of €200 million or €120 million that does have to be collected per year.

The levies will be collected on broadband subscriptions. The Netherlands is one of the countries with the highest broadband penetration in the world. In December 2006, the number of broadband subscribers was approximately 5.2 million (OECD, 2007) of the total of 7 million households (CBS, 2007). The resulting subscription fee for broadband subscribers would therefore be around €20 per year. The number of broadband subscribers (5.2 million) forms the trigger of the third scenario path in the value model of the levy business model.

Finally, the collected levies have to be distributed among the right owners. Moreover, the margins for the ISP, central collecting agent, and the media measurement actor have to be determined. In our model we estimated the margins to be 5% per actor, leaving 85% of the total levy revenues for the digital music suppliers. The division of the remuneration between digital music suppliers is done based on the same division of the download money (10% for the publisher, composers, and text writers and 90% for the producer and performing artist).

### *Step 4 Calculate Revenues*

The value model represents all incoming and outgoing value objects in a structured way. These value offerings constitute the major incoming and outgoing revenues and costs of the actors. The incoming value objects represent revenues and, together with other expenses of actors, the outgoing value objects are costs. Subtracting the total costs from the total revenues results in the profit of an actor or market segment in the value model (Gordijn, 2002).

The economic profitability can be generated from the value model when all value objects and fixed expenses and investments per actor are estimated. In order to estimate the profitability, the scenario paths are triggered using 10 million downloads, zero advertisement income, and 5.2 million broadband subscribers. The estimation of fixed costs for commerce and infrastructure service providers are not included, because these are costs of actors within the primary distribution of digital music goods. Moreover the fixed costs of composers, text writers, and performing artists are not estimated because the goal of this evaluation is to see if they are able to receive a higher compensation and not to be able to make profit. Finally, no estimate of the the fixed costs of a music publisher, concerning the online distribution of music is given. These can merely be seen as commerce service providers enabling the transaction between composers and text writers as well as collecting agencies.

### *Step 5 Assess Revenue Distributions*

The first business model norm (each actor has a profit larger than zero) is not reached, because the download portal will lose money in the levy model (see Table 3.6). The main reason for the loss is its inability to recover the distribution, platform, and marketing costs. Moreover, we assumed the advertisement income to be zero to compare the two models correctly. In the levy model, advertisement income is the only possible source of revenue for download portals resulting in zero revenues. The second business model norm (for each actor the expected revenue is higher than what can be gained by the existing business model) is not reached because the download portal is less profitable than in the current pay-per-download business model. In conclusion, the levy model is not an economically feasible alternative compared to the pay-per-download model, because the download portal is not profitable.

### *Step 6 Sensitivity Analysis*

Sensitivity analysis encompasses the effect of changing the estimated variables in the value model. This is necessary because the profitability of the music actors is calculated based on estimates. These estimates could vary from reality and could affect the reliability and validity of the conclusions. These variables include the exchanged value objects, the expenses of actors, and the triggers (in our case, number of downloads, advertisement payments, and number of Internet subscribers). The following variance of estimates is analyzed:

- Effect of minimum estimates for the exchanged value objects and expenses of actors
- Effect of maximum estimates for the exchanged value objects and expenses of actors
- Effect of changes in size of the triggers

The results of using minimum and maximum estimates are given in Table 3.6. As is clear from the figures this analysis does not change the results found in step 4: the download portal is not profitable and even less profitable in the levy model.

The only way the download portal could get higher profits compared to the pay-per-download model is by higher advertisement income. The reason is that within the levy model, the download portal does not have to share their advertisement income with the producer. In other words, whenever the advertisement income is high enough, this will result in a profitable download portal and a feasible levy model. Changes in the number of broadband subscribers would not have an effect on the

*Table 3.6* Profitability of Actors Using Minimum and Maximum Estimates

| *Role* | *Actor* | *Minimum estimates* | | *Maximum estimates* | | |
|---|---|---|---|---|---|---|
| | | *Download* | *Levy* | *Download* | *Levy* | |
| Supplier | Composer & text writer | 360000 | 6,840,000 | 480,000 | 6,840,000 | V |
| | Publisher | 180.000 | 3.420.000 | 240.000 | 3.420.000 | |
| | Performing artist | 700,000 | 18,468,000 | 1,400,000 | 18,468,000 | V |
| | Producer | 400,000 | 71,572,000 | 1,400,000 | 69,672,000 | V |
| Information service | Content aggregator | 800,000 | 100,000 | -2,000,000 | 100,000 | X |
| | Download portal | 1,800,000 | -1,200,000 | 500,000 | -4,100,000 | X |
| Commerce service provider | Collecting agency | 70,000 | 5,700,000 | 80,000 | 5,700,000 | V |
| | Publisher | 303,750 | 4,104,000 | 405,000 | 4,104,000 | V |
| | Payment service | 500,000 | - | 1,500,000 | - | V |
| | Internet service provider | - | 5,700,000 | - | 5,700,000 | V |
| Infrastructure Service Provider | Hosting service | 100,000 | 100,000 | 300,000 | 100,000 | V |
| | DRM technology provider | 100,000 | - | 200,000 | - | V |
| | Media measurement | - | 5,700,000 | - | 5,700,000 | V |

*Note*: All estimates are in euros.

feasibility of the levy model. It simply means that the total amount of levies that have to be raised should be paid by fewer or more subscribers. Finally, the number of downloads does have an effect on the feasibility of the levy model. The levy model has a maximum total market value based on the loss in revenues from CD sales. Theoretically, the pay-per-download model could grow above this figure whenever enough downloads are sold. The effect is that especially the producers earn more money when the number of sales increases, because of their high margin on download sales, which implies that the second norm is not reached (the producer earns less money within the levy model compared to the pay-per-download model in cases of sales growth).

The comparison of the levy model and the pay-per-download model showed that the levy model is not a very profitable and viable alternative. It is not evident that it would result in a profitable situation for the download portal.

## 3.4 CONCLUSIONS

### 3.4.1 Summarizing Conclusions

Based on Al-Debei and Avison (2010), this chapter has discussed business modeling for information services in the following successive steps:

- A business model includes a business or value architecture, which defines what means are needed to realize a certain value proposition. The value architecture requires specific content and services, financial, organizational, and technological means.
- A business model development should consider correctly how content can realize value, and how value can be transformed to revenues. Content is not always value for clients and value does not automatically generate revenues.
- The business model of an information service should be valid, i.e., should result in an outcome that is at least as good as the existing business model for each participant in the value architecture.

To realize a business model, a complex dialectic process is needed that never will be completed because actors and business environments constantly change. This makes sensitivity analysis an unsure activity.

### 3.4.2 Discussion

Table 2.5 summarized the following challenges for information services from the Hegelian process-oriented theory:

1. Creating explanatory (interpretive and critical) insights: Several insights have been created by which we can explain why actors want to be engaged or not in a certain business proposal.
2. Methods for discovering people's intentions to participate in an information service: We detected different actors with different interests for information services.
3. Integrate interests into a business model: We used value architecture and valuenet concepts to integrate interests, although they basically will be the result of (dialectic) negotiations in changing contexts.
4. The business model must have a valid valuenet for the actor-web.

This chapter has the following lessons related to these challenges.

Lesson 1: People in information markets do not automatically (via an invisible hand) generate joint interests. The role of an *information entrepreneur* (the information service manager or coordinator) is vital, and thus we define different roles: coordinator, suppliers, clients, sponsors, and infrastructure suppliers. It is up to the coordinator to get these roles established, i.e., to find actors who can take these roles such that it is in their interest to perform these roles. At the end the coordinator also has to be able to cover its costs.

Lesson 2: We noticed differences in *context* and *content* of information services. With respect to context, some information services are not in a market governance context but may be in a hierarchy (like corporate websites and portals) or in a network (like virtual community of practice sites). In both cases, monetary transactions may be counter-effective in realizing effective exchanges of content. For instance, in hierarchies, an information goods pricing scheme may turn into dysfunctional behavior—for example, under-utilization of content or over-delivery of irrelevant content (Roll, 1984). Some pricing, however, may result in efficient use of shared resources, i.e., the avoidance of over-use of free services. With respect to networks, the high cost of knowledge and information sharing via face-to-face meetings may result in less than optimal knowledge sharing. A solution in both cases may be the creation of information services that can substantially reduce the costs of sharing (Kankanhalli et al., 2005). These information services should not become a dump place of content but can better be moderators of communities (Bourhis et al., 2005; also see Chapter 5 for more details). Motivational balances and game theoretical dilemmas in a context of uncertain returns have to be understood well. Especially in contexts where pricing is a difficult-to-use coordination mechanism (networks and hierarchies), game theoretical dilemmas may obstruct potential useful sharing of information (see Wijnhoven et al., 2010).

Lesson 3: Although it is important to be able to predict the success of an information service, its actual success is not only based on its initial design, but also on continuous negotiations with it actors to improve the total value of the service in changing environments. These negotiations may follow a Hegelian dialect process, in which all statements of negotiators need to be critically evaluated using triangulation methods, and in which the debate between thesis and anti-thesis should result in a synthesis that is surprisingly better than what individual participants could accomplish in their own. These dialectics, however, never end.

Lesson 4: The nature of the content is also an important element in information service design. From the prior analysis, we can recognize that music is a clearly defined information good, with a clear volume definition (track) and almost standard pricing per unit. The more the content is uncertain (thus less codified), difficult to define, and highly subjective in its understanding (thus more abstract), the more difficult business modeling becomes. This is much the case with news, and even worse with substantive academic and intellectual products. Nevertheless, to let such services flourish in the information age, we will need new concepts and principles to define valid business models. The traditional hardcopy versions are becoming out of date, as exploitation problems of newspapers and the development of open source products demonstrate.

### 3.4.3 Reflective Exercise

Exercise 1: Use the insights on business model validation to design and validate a business model for e-newspapers while checking the opportunities that (1) e-readers can give, and (2) differentiate between national, international, and local news.

Apply the Hegelian triangulator to find and assess evidence on this topic from the Internet.

Exercise 2: Do a similar analysis for management reporting within your organization. How could management reporting change and improve while applying the insights of this chapter?

## 3.5 FURTHER READING

Al-Debei, M., & Avison, D. (2010). Developing a unified framework of the business model concept. *European Journal of Information Systems, 19*, 359–376.

Clemons, E., & Lang, K. (2003). The decoupling of value creation from revenue: A strategic analysis of the markets for pure information goods. *Information Technology and Management, 4*, 259–287.

Gordijn, J., & Akkermans, H. (2001). Designing and evaluating E-business models. *IEEE Intelligent Systems, 16*(4), 11–17.

# 4 Creating Process Models for Information Services

## 4.1 THE KANTIAN INQUIRING SYSTEM AND INFORMATION SERVICES

Chapters 1 and 2 have introduced the Kantian inquiring system. We described there Kant's interests in understanding the elementary categories for human thinking and how these enable people to perceive reality. These pre-given categories are called analytic a prioris. Typical analytic categories mentioned by Kant are space and time (Hartnack, 1967), which are important for both natural sciences and management sciences. For information science some other additional key categories are task, resource, actor, sequence, and information. Without these categories it will not be possible to organize any kind of service. Many of these categories can be combined with a language for discussing and documenting services. Some of these languages are process analysis and design languages like ARIS (Scheer, 1998) and BPMN (White & Miers, 2008). Such languages are synthetic a prioris, i.e., combined a prioris. These a prioris or languages also have to be shared among the stakeholders involved. This implies that the business process modeling, as a process of integrating the different stakes, goals, objectives, and needs of involved actors, has to be well done before it is feasible to talk about what tasks and processes are needed for the realization of value propositions aimed at via the process models. The information systems and business process analysis disciplines have developed several languages for process modeling, and we follow Stabell and Fjeldsted (1998), who identified three languages for the modeling of business processes: value chains, value shops, and value *process* nets. After having introduced this classification of business process modeling languages, we describe each of them by examples in the following sections. Finally, we follow Kant's interest in empirical observations via the construction of what he calls a posteriori propositions. This is realized in two ways:

1. By testing the quality of existing business processes and possibly identifying best practices

2. By integrating the expertise and insights of multiple actors in a business process to realize an integrated business process in reality, which thus extends over the insights of individuals

Consequently, this chapter discusses:

- Context and content implications for informing process models
- Modeling information service value chains
- Modeling information service value shops
- Modeling information service network processes
- Kant's a posterioris and ways of business process model validation

## 4.2 INFORMATION SERVICE CONTEXTS, CONTENT TYPES, AND INFORMING PROCESS MODELS

Chapter 3 mentioned three information service contexts (markets, hierarchies, and networks) and three *levels of abstraction* of information goods. For simplicity, only two levels of abstraction are discussed here, i.e., information goods that are simple because anyone will straightforwardly understand what they mean, and more *abstract* goods that require professional understanding and multiple interactions to be well understood. This dichotomy also explains the utility of Stabell and Fjeldsted's (1998) distinction between value shops (as abstract-content suppliers) and value chains (as simple-content suppliers). The distinction between networks, hierarchies, and markets identifies different relationships between suppliers and clients. In hierarchies and markets, internal or market prices and contract relations will regulate the relations between suppliers and clients, whereas in network the regulation may be more diffuse and patterns of interaction may be based on shared norms and potential mutual benefits of collaborations (Liebeskind et al., 1996; Williamson, 1992). In network contexts pricing may be nearly impossible and contracting for exchanges is too expensive or time-consuming.

We thus identify three analytically distinct classes of information process models, each with different a prioris:

1. *Value chain* analytic a prioris are the time-related concepts of start and finish, and sequences of increased value, i.e., for information service: product design and creation, production and reproduction, and sales, delivery, and after-sales service. Each of these processes can be decomposed into activities depending on the nature of the information good to be supplied, and will have a dedicated management and possible infrastructure support. These analytics can be combined by a value chain modeling language as developed before by Porter (1985). An example of a value chain is shown in Figure 4.1.

Section 4.3 further applies value chains to information service processes.

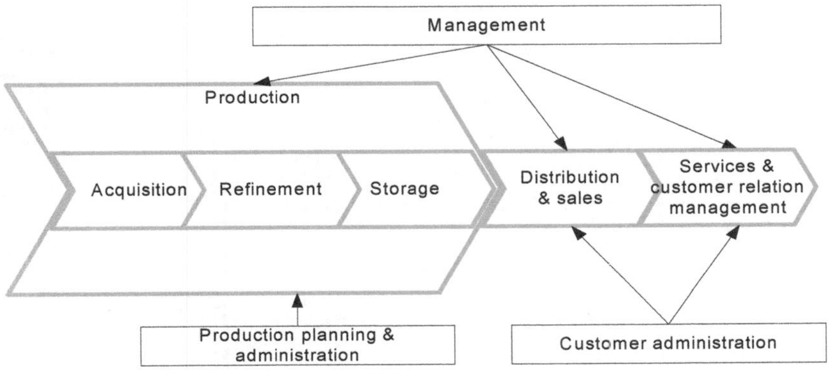


*Figure 4.1* A value chain model.

*Note*: This figure demonstrates "management" on top; "support" below; "processes" as open arrows, and "decomposition" within one arrow.

2. *Value shop* analytic a prioris consist of interactions between a client (problem owner) and service provider. The last can be an expert or an intermediary between the problem owner and one or more experts. The interactions consist of information search by a problem owner, followed by a possible question or problem articulation by a solution provider. These searches are responded to by information deliveries or offerings to submit questions and problems. The solution provider matches the problems with available solutions, or redirects the problem to an expert. Available solutions may be submitted by experts and stored to an expertise database (after a possible review by the provider). The dialogues between problem owners and service providers finish when a solution is reached or when the problem owner or expert terminates the dialogue (e.g., because of lack of time or interest, or low expectations of improvements). We thus identify the following analytic a prioris for value shop modeling, which connect to Kant's time (T)-space (S) a prioris:
    - Start and stop for dialogues (T)
    - Actions, consisting of registrations, submissions of content, and submission questions (T)
    - Databases that store registration information, content, questions, and analysis routines (S)
    - Evaluations of results (T)
    - Flows of data (S)
    - Sequences of actions (T)
    - Three types of actors: problem owners, content suppliers, and the service intermediary (S)
    - Shops nearly always have a public part (the public website) and a private part (accessible only after login) (S)

Figure 4.2 shows the related elements to model a value shop.

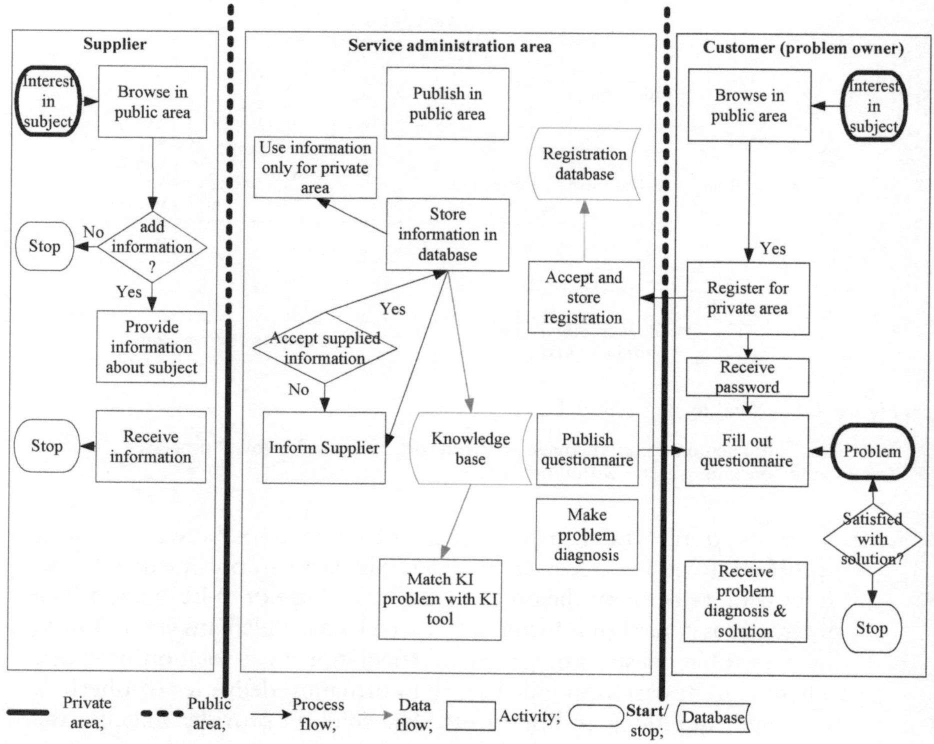


*Figure 4.2* Modeling constructs for value shops.

Section 4.4 further explains the modeling language and an example will be given as well.

*Value net process* analytic a prioris consist of multiple actors who can all play the role of supplier or client of content in a network. All interactions start with the creation of a membership account, and people can actively deliver content and search content from others. To handle the complexity of such networks, a network facilitator exists, called the information service, and the service combines and groups all interactions using possible technical means and possible resources from a sponsor. Figure 1.3 already described actors and their interactions in a network, which can be extended by adding process components to the network models. For modeling this value net process, the e3value method of Figure 3.2 is used again, but additionally the "activity" object of the legend becomes important. Section 4.5 introduces the e3value tool as a technique for networked business *processes*. After the discussion of the information service process modeling techniques, section 4.6 discusses opportunities of assessing their quality. The chapter finishes in section 4.7 with conclusions, discussions items, and reflective exercises.

## 4.3 VALUE CHAIN MODELS FOR LOW ABSTRACT INFORMATION GOODS[1]

In value chains, information goods creation processes make information goods to a commodity that can be easily sold and (automatically) delivered to generate the highest revenues. Some of the most important sub-processes of this activity are to help clients find the product (search), to realize the authenticity of the product (e.g., by copyrights), and to make attractive product representations that help clients to make buying decisions. Information goods theoretically have nearly unlimited opportunities of mass customization. Also after-sales services may be developed to increase the client's expected future product value. This results in the following classification of activities and processes for information goods trade (Clemons and Lang, 2003).

1. Information goods *creation* process, by e.g., artist, writer, reporter, researcher, photographer; publishers and other goods managers may facilitate the creators by delivering content-creation (e.g., templates), and access to resources that may be used as base materials.
2. Information goods *management* includes the selection of content, promotion, contract writing, editing, generating sponsorship, certifying correctness, accuracy control, timeliness and suitability management, and managing the intellectual property rights. Many information goods creators want to save costs by avoiding using a specialist publisher, though promotion, contract management, and delivery of a production platform are specialist expertises needed for high-quality professional product management.
3. Information goods *production* includes bundling data to packs, combining it for cross-selling (e.g., advertisements), printing, and distributing to subscribers and retailers. Because the basic good has already been created in the initial stage of the value chain (and may already be in a state of access to consumers), information goods producers are basically information *re*producers.
4. Information goods *retail and distribution* includes the realization of subscription services, news agencies, newsstands, convenience stores, and other outlets. *Transaction-focused approaches* of e-commerce have been developed to support these processes. Kambil and Van Heck (1998) distinguish several trade support processes:
    - *Search*: Search engines, portals, and electronic agents reduce the search costs for information goods. The number of potential offers may be over-abundant, requiring evaluation by credence and search information.
    - *Valuation*: A variety of electronic price discovery means (e.g., electronic auctions, bidding processes, and negotiation via electronic agents) exists that differentially attributes costs to information goods buyers, sellers, and intermediaries.

- *Logistics*: Information goods offer opportunities for transaction costs reductions via Internet delivery. The high levels of divisibility of most information goods enable customization.
- *Payment & settlements*: Third parties may provide the infrastructures to reduce for exchange risks, consisting of banking and legal services. The divisibility of information goods enables stopping delivery when payment is not done.
- *Authentication*: The authenticity of the trading parties in electronic commerce is required. Third parties may monitor conformance to the contract or agreement among parties, so that dispute resolution can be based on agreed data.
- *Communications & computing:* Improved processing, storage, input-output, and software technologies transform the coordination capabilities of stakeholders in each process.
- *Product representation*: Product representation determines how the product attributes are specified to the buyer or third parties. Too much representation, though, removes the trade value of information goods.
- *Legitimization of transaction*: Trade and exchange agreements can be validated online by connections with credit card firms (which guarantee payment) or checking the authority for transactions by PIN codes and membership numbers.
- *Influence structures and processes*: Explicit mentioning of the terms and conditions of the trade may reduce dispute problems.
- *Dispute resolution:* Probably legal institutes must be adjusted to settle legal problems in information goods commerce; however, information goods property rights are hard to describe and secure.

At least three different value chain models can be identified for low abstract information good services: *data refineries*, which create information from pools of data, *infotainment*, which deliver fixed packs of information, and *magazines*, which deliver data with added informative content. These will be further described later.

Information suppliers deliver elementary data to data refineries' acquisition processes (Meyer & Zack, 1996). Next these data may be analyzed, integrated, synthesized, added, and standardized, and consequently stored and made available to clients to facilitate customized client needs. These acquisition, refinement, and storage and retrieval facilitations are the information goods creation process. The distribution process is similar to the retail process and thus also includes the contracting and product presentation. The buyer receives information packages, and submits information needs specifications to the access tools and information product family resource. These data delivery services thus deliver customized information packs and access to large data resources. See Figure 4.3a for a model of the data delivery service.

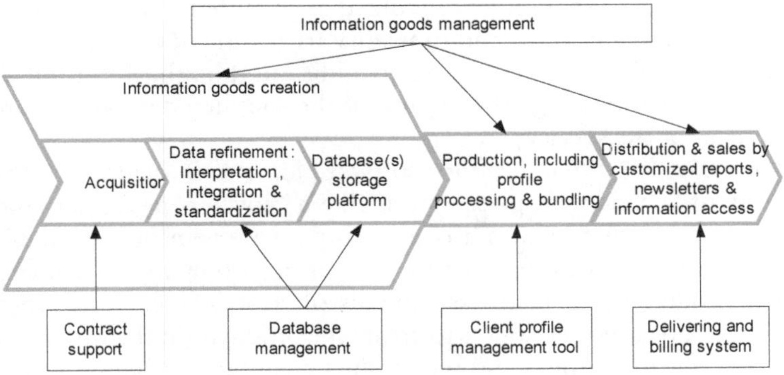


a. Data refinery.

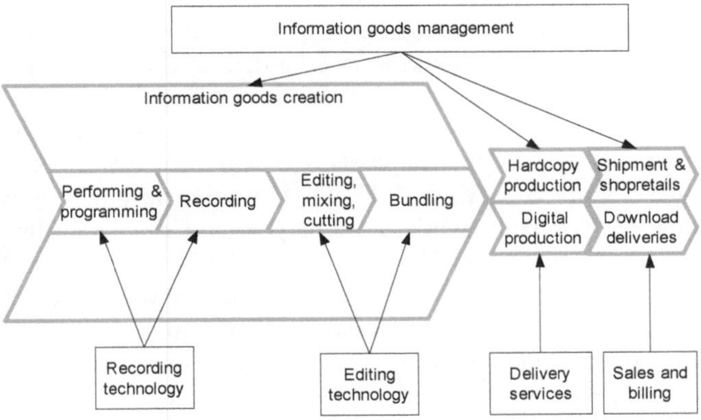


b. Infotainment.

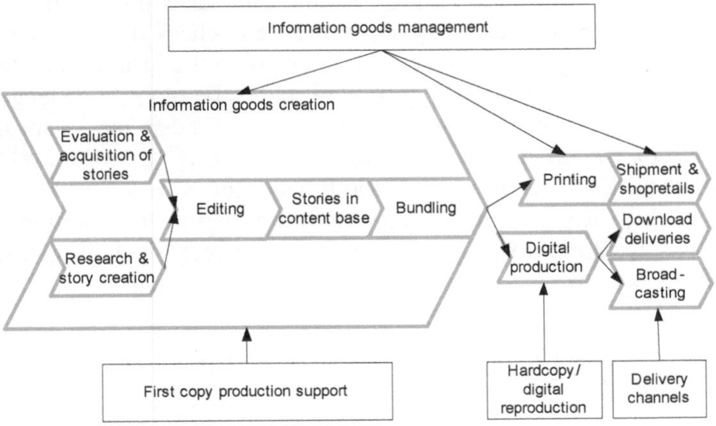


c. Magazine.

*Figure 4.3* Value chains for low abstract information goods.

Modern news services can be organized as data delivery services, while improving the customization and topicality (real-time news), and reducing the production and delivery costs. As an addition, though, they need a *certification* process to manage the quality of the supplied data and maintain the reputation of the service.

*Infotainment* is a broad term for software for fun. Basically an artist or group of artists produces a piece of art, like a movie, a piece of music, or a game. The artist first creates a composition, arrangement, script, or initial game design and tries to convince a recording company to arrange the facilities to produce the idea, and sell and distribute it. There is a tendency for music groups and game developers to create the products on their own, which means that the artist (group) and the product creation management firm are the same people, but often their investments and the commercial expertises needed are insufficient (cf. Clemons & Lang, 2003). The information goods creation manager also facilitates the bundling of pieces of the art product to optimally suit specific market groups and so to make the product more attractive. Information goods of this kind can be delivered in hardcopy and digital form. The digital form, though more sensitive for violations of copyrights, enables more flexibility in the delivery and customization of the good. Also the distribution and reproduction costs are near zero (so-called "first copy cost principle", Shapiro & Varian, 1999). Many infotainment services require continuous development, while users/players and designers discover new opportunities or generate new ideas related to the basic product. After some time, the many new ideas may be combined in a new release, which may be supplied via a download site. Consequently, the management of the exchanges of users and designers is a most important part of product management in infotainment services.

*Magazines* publish articles with a higher level of abstraction than news services. This implies that more expertise is added. Consequently, the information goods creation process is more intense and takes more time. Additionally, magazines have to hire external expertise to check the quality of the product or to add to it when the editors have insufficient depth of knowledge. Some information goods buyers may be expected to be more knowledgeable and can add to it by delivering their comments. The readers may want more resources and may be interested in reusing articles, though they do not know which and when. The most important additions to the news services thus are (1) the research process, (2) acquiring external expertise for additions and review, and (3) resources like links to portals for readers. See Figure 4.3c for a model of a magazine.

## 4.4 VALUE SHOPS: PROCESSES FOR ABSTRACT INFORMATION GOODS

Many examples of highly abstract information goods exist, like professional services, scientific publications, patents, and insurances. We identify complete and incomplete online interactions via value shops.

### 4.4.1 Value Shops with Incomplete Online Interactions

Professional services have a high level of abstraction and consequently it may be difficult to codify them fully. As far as they are not fully codifiable, other trade mechanisms than markets are more useful (Liebeskind et al., 1996; Williamson, 1991). Most hospitals, organization consultants, and educational institutes have websites, which help clients to make an initial diagnosis or an initial analysis, or give information concerning research results and courses. Many of these sites are free of charge, because they help to develop a need among prospects for more profitable services, which are difficult to codify. To understand the typicalities of such professional services marketing, we analyze the case of e-consultancy services. E-consultancy clients can fill out a form consisting of benchmark items. The data submitted are compared to data from other firms, and a diagnosis and advice are given. Via the system, clients receive well-grounded advice, combining theoretic insights, expertise, and data. They may pay a small fee for the service. On the basis of this advice, a client may sometimes be able to solve the detected problems, but he or she may also hire the professionals from e-consulting firms or another professional. At least two different types of products may be delivered: (1) electronic advice via the website, and (2) professional skills. The information goods production thus has two production lanes, and these lanes build on data, expertise (case experiences), and theoretical insights that are modified to the consultancy systems and the consultancy method.

Typical for this information trade process is that some of the information goods are hard to codify, and thus are difficult to trade via markets and are certainly not to be traded by electronic commerce. These low-codification goods, though, are important complements to the codified goods.

Another example is *patents trade*. Patents are representations of highly abstract knowledge, and are suitable for codification. This means that they are described such that other people can use them in a profitable way when they pay for their use. This makes patents as information goods particularly suitable for market trade. Because using a patent is possible only through coming to an agreement with a patent owner, the actual production requires the publication of the patent, a valuation of the patent, and negotiation and contracting. These production processes are combined by the *Yet2.com* site. Yet2.com wants to be a global patent marketplace, by giving clients (searchers and potential buyers of patent licenses) access to owners of advanced technologies. Several leading technological firms sponsor Yet2.com, and they share their patents via Yet2.com with the market. The Yet2.com site gives information for valuation and pricing of patents via its "done deals database", assists in structuring a deal by providing past deals as a frame of reference, and helps the user learn about royalty rates in similar transactions. Yet2.com also gives assistance by legal services. The site is also a portal to other firms that can help by providing their professional services, and as such is a professional services marketing site as well. The information good is created via the review of a patent submitted for publication and the actual delivery of it as an information good via publication (hardcopy or online). This review (the job of patent and trademark offices and authorities) focuses on removing ambiguity in the patent description, and checking the novelty of the invention. The results of these reviews are processed by specialized publishers like Derwent via hardcopy prints and online databases.

### 4.4.2 Value Shop with Complete Online Interaction: The KINX Portal[2]

This section describes the development of value shop processes with online highly codified knowledge using the example of the KINX portal. The KINX portal aims at the constant submission of new problems and solutions, and the development of the matching of both in the area of knowledge management for small and medium-sized enterprises (SMEs). The ambitions of the portal are described in the following six points:

- Informing small and medium-sized enterprises (SMEs), consultants, researchers, and others about knowledge integration (KI, i.e., the reuse of knowledge from other firms in own products and processes) problems and solutions for new product development (NPD) in high-tech SMEs
- Helping SMEs in their process of identifying and defining the problems they encounter with knowledge integration in the NPD context
- Matching available solutions and problems; by matching their problems with solutions, the KI portal limits the efforts the SMEs have to make searching for an appropriate solution to their problem. The portal will, therefore, (partly) fill in the gap between solution developers and users (SMEs).
- Providing additional information about solutions so that problem owners can make informed decisions on adopting and using the solutions offered
- Providing a platform to exchange experiences, feelings, ideas, and views on KI
- Improving problem identification and problem classification, developing new solutions and improving existing ones, as well as improving the matching mechanism between problems and solutions

Like most information services, the portal links people with problems and questions on the one hand with resources having solutions and answers on the other hand in a direct or indirect way. The *direct* way consists of a forum in which people can discuss problems, solutions, and experiences with regard to knowledge integration. This gives many opportunities of exchanging implicit knowledge. The *indirect* way consists of the exchange of information, like problem and solution descriptions, and mechanisms that match both, thereby enabling the exchange of *explicit* and *represented* knowledge on KI. The matching mechanism selects and shows the most appropriate solution(s) for a given problem. Additionally, the portal gives derivative information about these solutions, e.g., information on documented experiences and information on suitability and use of the solution(s).

Due to the multiplicity of its functions the portal in its present state has a highly elaborated process model. The elements of this process model are described later and finally we describe some of the major challenges regarding the matching mechanism.

### *Knowledge Integration Portal Description*

Figure 4.4 gives an overview of the activities that the KINX portal performs to realize matches between KI tools and techniques suppliers and KI problem owners.

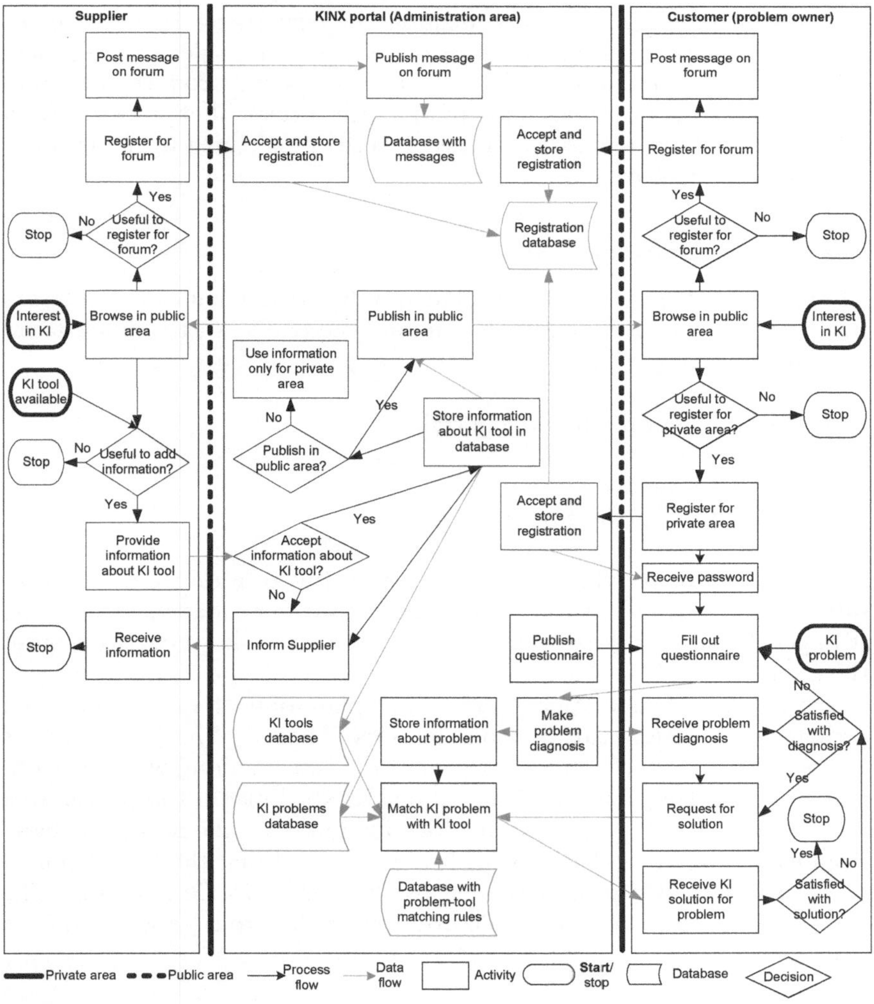


*Figure 4.4* A value shop model of the KINX information service.

The KINX portal has three domains:

- A public area through which external KI problem owners and KI solution providers can browse to find out what the KINX portal is all about; the solution owners also can submit content (meta- and derivative information on their solutions) via the public area to the portal.
- A private area in which problem owners can interact with the portal to generate a problem diagnosis and potential solution
- An administrator area that performs activities to increase the value of the portal; these activities consist of the admission of the problem owner to the private area, maintenance and development of the diagnostic questionnaire, maintenance and development of the classification of problems, evaluations of information from solution owners, classification of these solutions in relation to problems areas, development and maintenance of the matching rules, management of the forum, and possibly creating new insights from the forum to improve the matching rules and publish successful experiences from the matching activities and forum to the public area (if the problem owners involved agree).

### *The KINX Portal Public Area*

The *public area* of the KINX portal holds information that can be accessed by any portal visitor without registration. The public area is divided into the following subsections:

- General description of the portal
- Common KI problems
- List of KI solutions
- Successful experiences

The main goal of the public area is to show at a glance the kind of information that the visitor can find on the site. The idea of this section is to get the visitors' attention, and invite them to ask for registration to the private area.

On the home page appears a basic explanation of the services and contents that a user can find on the KINX portal. The Home link is always visible on the right upper part of the screen, along with the Contact link, the Help link, and the About KINX link (in the public area only). The Contact page contains localization data about the company responsible for the KINX portal. It is also stated that the KINX portal is the outcome of a project funded by the European Commission. The About KINX page contains a description of the project's goals and its main contributions.

The "common KI problems" section presents some aggregated tabular and graphical data obtained by the analysis of the daily data gathered by the portal. This aggregation includes data about the type of problems found in each sector. The goal of this section is to show general information that can be extracted from the database in order to demonstrate the capabilities and the benefits of the KINX portal beyond the provision of customized solutions for KI problems.

The KINX portal holds detailed information about different tools and/or techniques related to knowledge integration. An information template supplies information on more than 40 KI solutions, which are used as suggestions to solve the problems recognized as user problems. This template is structured in two levels, one of which contains basic information and the other one has detailed information about the given solution.

The information fields defined for each solution on the first level are:

- *Name*: A short name assigned to the solution
- *Type*: Used to distinguish between tools or techniques or both
- *Concise Description*: A two-line description of the solution, which is returned as a result of a text search over all available solutions
- *Basic Description*: A detailed description (several paragraphs) of the solution that is shown when the user asks for information about a solution
- *Related Solutions*: A set of links to related solutions in the database

The information fields defined for each solution on the second level are:

- *More Details*: This contains more concise information by several paragraphs about the solution found in the first level.
- *Implementation*: This section provides information about the application of the given solution.
- *Case Study*: A situation where the given solution has been applied is described.
- *Suitability*: Data about the implementation time, the price, and the maturity of the solution.
- *References*: A list with available web links or other information references.

The List of Solutions section also allows for text search through the text fields defined for the available solutions. To see the details of each of the solutions, the user clicks the corresponding title. By clicking the links shown in the result list, the pop-up windows with the previously described information for each solution are shown. Furthermore, an Advanced Search section is available, by which more detailed search conditions can be stated. The criteria that can be used to filter the available solutions are the same as the ones defined for the Suitability subsection of the solutions information window.

The Successful Histories section contains examples of problems detected with the help of the portal, including success stories about proposed solutions and characteristics (description and suitability features) of these solutions. Of course, the user must explicitly permit the use of the problem definitions stated when using the KINX portal. None of the examples presented will show the company name or person that stated the problem, unless the corresponding user has given explicit permission. The main goal of this section is to show casual visitors the capabilities of the KINX portal by presenting some of the real interactions performed by registered users.

### *The Private Area*

A registered visitor of the KINX portal is called a basic user (i.e. not an administrator). This registered visitor can interact with the portal to define a specific problem and obtain the most appropriate solution(s). The main sections for this kind of user are the "In progress problem definitions" and the Diagnosis sections. In the first step, the provided questionnaire must be answered to allow the identification of the most relevant problems in the user's organization. The next step is to get a diagnostic about potential problems. In a final step, several solutions (techniques and/or tools) will be provided along with their relevance according to the problem at hand. A basic user can also see a report with information about his previously stated problems, solutions offered by the portal, or aggregate non-confidential data about the rest of the users that interact with the system (but only aggregate data). A basic user can configure the portal not to share information about some or every previously executed problem identification process(es) and result(s). Part of this data would then be used to build the "Successful experiences" public subsection.

The Diagnosis section is designed to assist the user in defining a KI problem. This process is divided into the following steps:

- State your problem
- Diagnosis
- Solutions
- Suitability

A menu appearing on the left side of the browser window when the user visits the Diagnosis section serves to ease navigation across these different sections. Every step can be accessed at any moment.

*State your problem:* This is the initial step of the problem definition process. Here, a name is given to provide a unique identifier for the data that is going to be supplied. This name will be used later to return to the process. As mentioned before, each problem definition is called a run or execution.

*Diagnosis:* The user has to answer several questions (a variable number depending on the answers given). For each question, the user can state how important the question is for his or her specific situation. For this purpose, a relevance box is provided on the upper right-hand side of the screen. Given answers can be modified at any moment.

The submission of information can be interrupted at any point in order to get a problem analysis on the basis of the information supplied so far. The portal analyzes the answers given hitherto and provides a description of the problems detected with possible causes. To get a diagnosis, it is not necessary to complete the entire questionnaire; the portal will do its best with the answers provided.

*Solutions:* The answers to the questionnaire are also used by the KINX portal to search for the best available solution (tool and/or technique) in order to solve the recognized problem. Solutions are provided also on the basis of partial information.

The KINX portal contains detailed information for more than 40 solutions (tools and/or techniques). Detailed information for each solution can be accessed from the Solutions list by clicking the name of the desired element.

*Suitability:* The last step in the process is the suitability section, where all suggested solutions are compared according to the different parameters. In the first view, solutions are compared according to implementation costs and ease of use. This information is shown in a tabular format (see Figure 4.5).

A registered user can see here a complete list of previous problem definitions s/he has stated on the KINX site. The Personal Reports section includes different reports about previous interactions of the user with the KINX Site. These reports include data of the problems detected and the solutions proposed, as well as tables comparing different solutions and problems. The main goal of these reports is to serve as interaction summaries for the user of the KINX portal. The user will be asked whether a personal report may be used as input to build the content of public sections such as "Successful experiences" and "Common problems".

### *The Administration Area*

In the administration area functions for the daily maintenance and operation of the portal are provided. The various functions include:

- *Portal content snapshot*: This option facilitates storage of (parts of) the data contained on the database portal. This file contains the

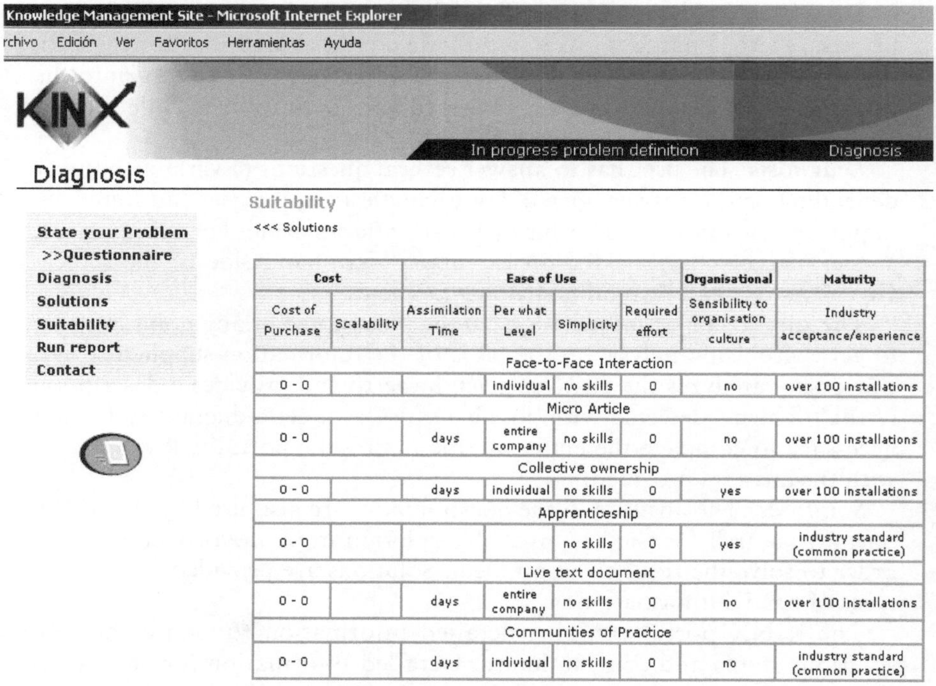


| Cost | | Ease of Use | | | | Organisational | Maturity |
|---|---|---|---|---|---|---|---|
| Cost of Purchase | Scalability | Assimilation Time | Per what Level | Simplicity | Required effort | Sensibility to organisation culture | Industry acceptance/experience |
| Face-to-Face Interaction | | | | | | | |
| 0 - 0 | | | individual | no skills | 0 | no | over 100 installations |
| Micro Article | | | | | | | |
| 0 - 0 | | days | entire company | no skills | 0 | no | over 100 installations |
| Collective ownership | | | | | | | |
| 0 - 0 | | days | individual | no skills | 0 | yes | over 100 installations |
| Apprenticeship | | | | | | | |
| 0 - 0 | | | | no skills | 0 | yes | industry standard (common practice) |
| Live text document | | | | | | | |
| 0 - 0 | | days | entire company | no skills | 0 | no | over 100 installations |
| Communities of Practice | | | | | | | |
| 0 - 0 | | days | individual | no skills | 0 | no | industry standard (common practice) |

*Figure 4.5* Solution suitability information on the KINX portal private area.

questions and answers for the questionnaire, and the data for all the runs performed by the users.

- *Load a new questionnaire for the portal*: Using a predefined format in a MS Excel file, it is possible to change the set of questions (the order in which they are presented and the associated weights to state their importance) presented by the portal. Questions and problems are characterized by a set of features or variables (for example, the way in which information is codified) previously defined and identified.
- *Load new problem definitions*: New problem descriptions and the way they are characterized by a set of predefined features can be loaded into the portal to be used in the problem identification stage. For this purpose, a preformatted MS Excel file must be used.
- *Load new solution descriptions*: New solution descriptions can be loaded using an MS Access file. If the content of this database is stored as text files, this subsection allows loading these text files onto the portal database. In this way, the process of updating the content related to the information regarding solutions is automatic, without needing specialized staff intervention.

The matching of problems and solutions proceeds as follows. First, using the questionnaire, the internal logic of the portal will score the problem for each of the KI activities. Once the problem vector has been constructed, the portal will use a set of rules to transform it into two different spaces:

- The diagnosis space, used to communicate the interpretation of the problem to the user
- The solution space, used to construct the list of suitable solutions

This means that—starting from the set of problems identified—a matrix is constructed to obtain a universe of vectors. The coordinates of these vectors in a multi-dimensional space indicate how well each solution and each diagnosis option fit to a specific problem. Using a mathematical standard function for measuring the distances between the needs and the possible solutions, the best set(s) of solutions and the most suitable diagnoses are identified.

## 4.5 VALUE NET PROCESS MODELS

Different actors may take the roles of suppliers of content, sponsors, customers, and subcontractors. Together these realize the flows of content, content use-features, and revenues intermediated by an information service. Consequently, information service business models may be conceptualized as value nets (Stabell & Fjeldsted, 1998), where actors take roles as suppliers or collectors of content, suppliers of use-features, and revenues; some of these supplies are required and others are optional for a successful information service.

Value net processes define actors in a network and their interlinking processes. In these network processes, information services manage these interlinking processes. This implies that information service network processes must have at least four core processes:

- Network membership management processes, consisting of, e.g., subscription processes and customer relationship management. This also involves guarantees and arrangements for user privacy, security, and property rights.
- Delivery or submission, which can be content logistics (i.e., information services that acquire, store, and distribute content), or content transformations that improve value over what the supplier already delivered, which thereby increases value by delivering the proper kind of representation (reducing overload) and the proper kind of conceptualization (reducing cognitive distance and misunderstanding)

- Use facilitation, via delivering content-interaction means or meta-information (e.g., accuracy indicators) about the content delivered (Vishik & Whinston, 1999)
- Transaction processing, which compensates suppliers and external use facilitators by collecting funds from customers and sponsors, and to cover the service's own costs (Strens et al., 1998)

The processes are related to the stakeholders in a value net process model. Figure 4.6 gives the value net process model.

These four interlinking processes each have their own sub-processes, which can be an iterative value shop (e.g., for content-interaction), a value chain (e.g., for payment processing), or a value net process (e.g., the co-creation of a website by multiple suppliers with customer involvement and the involvement of a publisher).

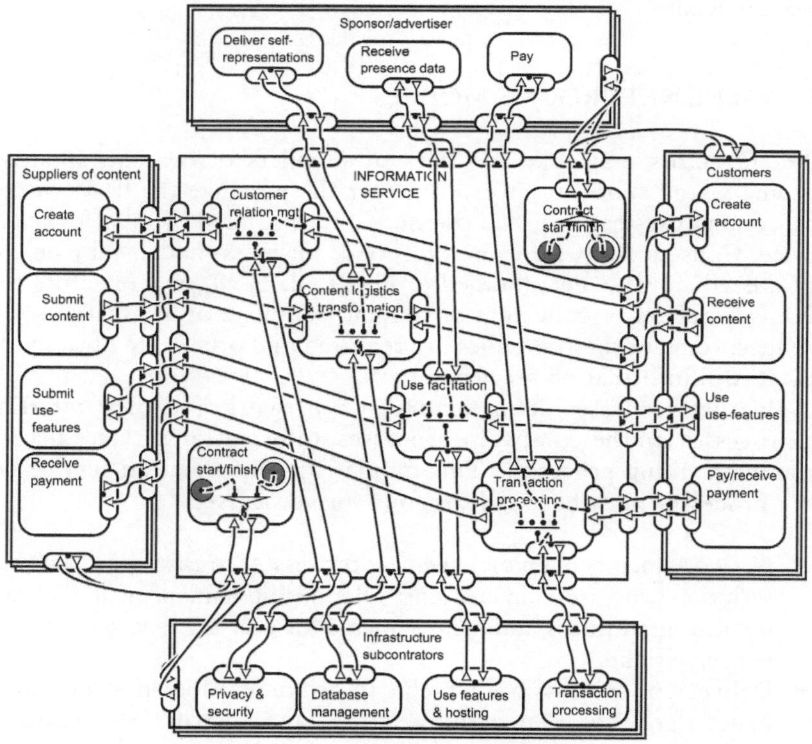


*Figure 4.6* A value net process reference model for an information service.

*Note*: Depending on a specific instance several activities will have to be decomposed or may be irrelevant.

## 4.6 A POSTERIORIS: VALIDATION OF PROCESS MODELS

One can validate the a prioris of a process model in at least five levels:

1. The quality of the *modeling language* if related to an ontology. This would imply that a generic and correct basic statement of "what is" a process model exists. We have followed Stabell and Fjeldsted's classification and conceptualizations, but other approaches and ontologies (e.g., Green & Rosemann, 2000) may exist, resulting in different basic a prioris. One can check existing modeling languages, like the one presented in this chapter, regarding their completeness in covering the main constructs of a process-ontology. For example, one can criticize value chain modeling for not including constructs for information objects. To solve this, the flow arrows in value chain models can be extended with information denoting labels that identify the type of information that flows between the processes. One also can criticize value shop and value process nets for a poor treatment of time and sequences of activities (so-called control flows). In some contexts, like in more formal and legal contexts, the explication of control flows is very essential and thus has to be added (see, for example, Van der Aalst & Van Hee, 2004).
2. The quality of the *chosen techniques as representation mechanisms*. A technique should express the chosen ontology. As far as discussed here, techniques were presented that are able to express the required ontologies. A technique, though, also has to be evaluated from the perspectives of its efficiency (no conceptual overload; Green & Rosemann, 2000), usability (e.g., user interface and graphics), practical usefulness, and costs (Recker et al., 2010).
3. The *empirical validity of the created model*. "As-is" models should correspond to the actual practice of a process. This is often difficult, because people need work-arounds to solve problems quickly and efficiently and therefore deviations from the formally agreed processes are common in many organizations and business. To be able to cover processes fully, a substantial level of detail is needed, which is nearly never feasible given the limited time-space of business modeling in most (information service development) projects. So deviations from models will be common, but we should be able to create and test models on their usability of detecting the key issues of relevance for a specific problem or project. Sometimes modeling less (abstraction) can be better.
4. The *normative validity of the created model*. "Should-be" models have to correspond with certain (legal or ethical) norms and objectives that are aimed at. Many engineering models have this nature and thus require the operationalization of norms into process characteristics (like what decision has to be made in what sequences, with what data, and who will be involved).

5. The *correspondence of the created model with best practices*. This is also often called "reference" models, and requires the ability to prove that certain process models are the best given optimum possibility (Becker et al., 2009). Such a proof can be reached via empirical evaluations of the performance of different models given the same context, or can be found via simulations and mathematical proof (e.g., Petri-Nets; Van der Aalst et al., 2004). If a best practice model is known for a situation, a designed model can be tested on best practice criteria.

## 4.7 CONCLUSIONS

### 4.7.1 Summarizing Conclusions

This chapter has discussed the Kantian foundations for information services design processes. This contribution consists of the identification of:

1. The analytic a prioris for information service process models
2. The synthetic a prioris of languages and ontologies for modeling information service processes
3. Best practices based on empirical analysis of existing reference cases (a posterioris)
4. Given different contexts and content, different modeling methods are needed. Therefore, service value chains, service value shops, and service network processes as distinguished as most suitable in different contexts and abstraction levels.

### 4.7.2 Discussion

Chapter 2 (Table 2.5) identified the following Kantian guidelines for process-oriented kernel theories: a network of knowledge and requirements is needed to accomplish the service's processes. For this a relevant, complete, and useful modeling language has to be selected ahead of the modeling activities. This chapter identified the following lessons related to these insights.

Lesson 1: There are currently no synthetic a priori modeling languages specifically developed for information services. Probably the existing modeling languages can do all that is needed, but it is unclear if existing modeling languages, like EPC (Scheer, 1998) and BPMN (White & Miers, 2008), have any biases that make information service modeling not sufficiently rich and effective. To answer this question, we need an ontology for information service processes (Green & Rosemann, 2000). Such an ontology does not exist yet and is an issue for research.

Lesson 2: Value chains and value shops are more likely process models for markets and hierarchies, and networks require value net process models. This is also related to the content type, because low abstract content can be efficiently handled via value chains or value net processes, but highly abstract content requires value shops. Lower levels of content codification require a value shop.

### 4.7.3 Reflective Exercise

Several questions can be raised about these insights:

- Hierarchies and markets are definitely different, but this distinction has not been discussed in this chapter. What will be the main consequences of these differences for information service processes?
- Low and high abstraction levels of content are distinguished, but how would an analysis improve if we add a third level—moderate abstract?
- For network processes, interlinking processes are modeled. The e3value process model is only a reference (that is, generic) model. The reader is invited to create a value net process model for his or her department's website service or the information service of your company's PR home page. Use the e3value technique (which is available for free at www.e3value.com).

## 4.8 FURTHER READING

Green, P., & Rosemann, M. (2000). Integrated process modeling: An ontological evaluation. *Information Systems, 25*(2), 73–87.

Robertson, S., & Reese, K. (1999). A virtual library for building community and sharing knowledge. *International Journal of Human-Computer Studies, 51*, 663–685.

Scheer, A. (1998). *Aris: Business process frameworks*. Heidelberg, Germany: Springer.

Stabell, C., & Fjeldsted, O. (1998). Configuring value for competitive advantage: On chains, shops, and networks. *Strategic Management Journal, 19*(5), 413–437.

Van Der Aalst, W., & Van Hee, K. (2004). *Workflow management: Models, methods and systems*. Cambridge, MA: MIT Press.

White, S., & Miers, D. (2008). *BPMN modeling and reference guide: Understanding and using BPMN*. Lighthouse Point, FL: Future Strategies Inc.

# 5 Designing the Information Service Infrastructure

## 5.1 LEIBNIZIAN RATIONALISM AND SERVICE INFRASTRUCTURE DESIGN

An information service can enable its *goal* (informing) by 1) acquiring, aggregating, displaying, processing, creating, and delivering *content* relevant for its clients, 2) delivering additional *use-features* to increase the value experience for information users, and 3) realizing a stream of *revenues* and possible financial transactions for the information good supplier and the information service owners (Bhargava & Choudhury, 2004; Strens et al., 1998). These business processes need *human and information technological means* to become efficient. Together, these means are called the *infrastructure* of an information service (Maglio & Barret, 2000; Meyer & Zack, 1996). The design of an infrastructure is called its architecture here.

According to the Leibnizian inquiring system, knowledge consists of causal understandings (i.e., explanations and predictions). A well-described and consistent causal model enables reasoning about the relations between the phenomena it refers to. Also designs are based on causal theories, which reason about the effectiveness of certain means for certain goals. In Chapters 1 and 2, we distinguished (following Walls et al., 1992) product-oriented and process-oriented design theories. Product-oriented design theories focus on features of the end product; that is, these provide *meta-requirements* and *meta-designs* that help to solve classes of problems and create classes of artifacts as possible solutions. Requirements consist of specified goals for a problem. A design includes the selected means and relations between these means to meet the requirements. These means or components for information services consist of databases, organizational structures, people with certain skills and tasks, work processes, and information technologies. Product-oriented design theories require *kernel theories* to select meta-requirements and meta-designs that may solve the informing problems in reality (Markus et al., 2002). Given an understanding of the requirements, designers may select specific design options that they think will be effective. Product-oriented *design hypotheses* link meta-requirements to meta-designs in context. When these design propositions are incorrect, the design will be based on incorrect views of reality and the resulting design may probably (although not necessarily) fail (Gregor, 2006). We have summarized the main causal statements for information

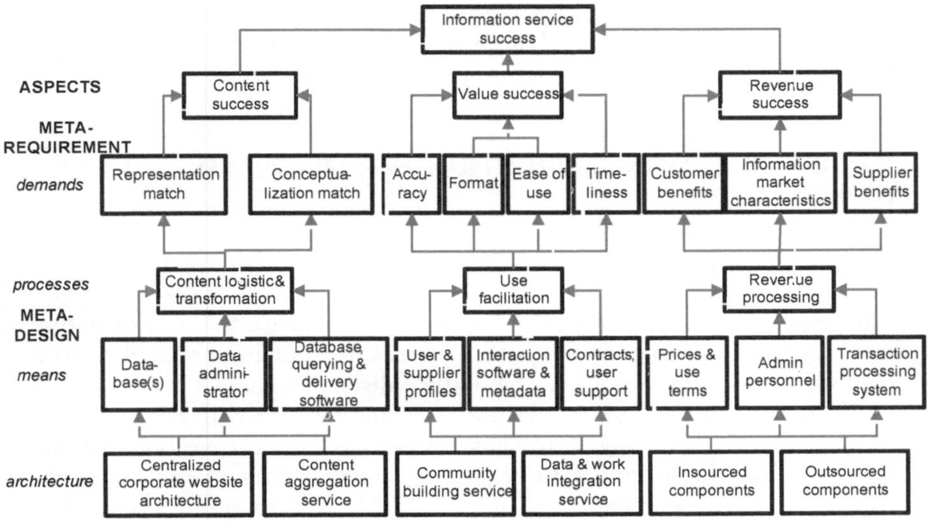


*Figure 5.1* A causal model of information service design propositions (each proposition is presented by one arrow in this diagram). Note that the aspects have been described in Chapter 2, and that demands and processes have been described in Chapters 3 and 4.

services in Figure 5.1. Each arrow in the diagram presents a causal proposition. Details about this model will be explained in the rest of this chapter.

Process-oriented design theories focus on the methods, techniques, and procedures by which people are able to design successfully. Following Sowa and Zachman (1992), an information systems design process has design steps corresponding with different design layers; i.e., layers of decomposition from abstract notions of a system (the business model) to its realization in concrete databases, organizational and technical means (the infrastructure).

This chapter further discusses the concept of design theory and applies this for the requirements analysis, meta-design, and infrastructure development of an information service in the following sections:

- 5.2: A summary of product-oriented design theories for specifying information service requirements and solutions
- 5.3: A summary of process-oriented information service design theories for analyzing needs and solutions
- 5.4: The means and infrastructure for an information service
- 5.5: Architecture design of an information service
- 5.6: A summary and reflection

Before continuing, note the difference between information services and information systems. Whereas information services aim at intermediating between content owners and potential users, information systems process data. An information service thus needs one or several information systems for realizing efficient operational processes.

## 5.2 INFORMATION SERVICE PRODUCT-ORIENTED DESIGN THEORY

### 5.2.1 Meta-Requirements

The kernel theories presented in Chapter 2 have described that information service design has to cope with three classes of challenges related to content, use-value, and revenue, which will be discussed here.

At the end of the 1960s, the use of computers for delivering *content* resulted in questions concerning how to express an information need and how to transform this into a query (Taylor, 1968). This is a persisting problem in information retrieval (Cole, 1998). An information service may reduce information overload by deciding on what is a relevant information product or service for the customer. The core meta-requirement related to the content aspect therefore is relevance of the information good. Relevance is more difficult to specify for digital goods than for physical goods. A physical good can be presented to a buyer by pictures, animations and simulations, or temporal use. This is possible for information goods as well, but the unlimited opportunities and variations of information goods make it difficult to precisely state the user's needs, and interpreting the relevance of retrieved documents from a query is difficult (Spink, 1997).

The problems of information overload and relevance can be described by the dimensions: representation and conceptualization. *Representation* describes the relation between the set of content that is actually wanted and what is actually supplied after a query. Three values may be given to this variable: under-representation (insufficient content is delivered), match (exactly enough content is delivered), and over-representation (too much content is delivered). In the database literature also the terms recall and precision are used to describe representation match. Recall refers to the number of *relevant* documents retrieved by a search divided by the total number of existing relevant documents (which by the way may be hard to assess if you do not have them and thus do not know them). Precision is the number of relevant documents retrieved by a search divided by the total number of documents retrieved by that search (thus including the overload, which you do not want) (Baeza-Yates & Ribeiro-Neto, 1999). Conceptualization defines what level of abstraction a user wants or is able to process cognitively. Seven levels can be distinguished here ranging from the presentation of primary data to the presentation of tested scientific formulas (Bohn, 1994). It also involves the match between the languages and meanings of the potential information consumer and information provider, i.e., the sharing of terminology and jargon via a shared ontology. In the beginning of the 20th century, semantic web technologies have been developed as part of search engines to increase the relevance of query results and reduce information overload by the processing of search history and user characteristics data (Berners-Lee et al., 2001). This requires information services like Google to process massive amounts of data, which as a by-product realizes very profitable marketing information (see further Chapter 6).

*Use-value* can be approached by the user satisfaction construct, which is a multi-dimensional concept involving accuracy, format, ease of use, and timeliness in addition to content (Doll & Torkzadeh, 1988). Vishik and Whinston (1999) give a role to information services in guaranteeing certain *accuracy* levels by checking the correctness, validity, and reliability of the information they intermediate, and as such reduce uncertainty in information markets. Poston and Speier (2005) propose the following concrete meta-information that can be used and supplied to content consumers to judge the accuracy of retrieved content: indicators of the number of raters of content, indicators of raters' expertise, and collaborative filtering. Choi et al. (1997) and Loebbecke (1999) mention the following *ease-of-use* characteristics of information goods that information brokers can facilitate: interactiveness, temporality, locality, use duration and use intensity, opportunities of using information in products and services of the information consumer, reducing information asymmetry (and thus increasing information externalities), or explicitly not doing so by creating asset-specific information goods. Benbunan-Fich (2001) emphasizes the role that information services can play in *ease-of-use* aspects, like formats (e.g., natural language options and visualizations) and Chen and Yen (2004) emphasize the realization of interactivity (playfulness, connectedness, reciprocal communication, information collection, and choice). Also the handling of intellectual *property rights* (e.g., by delivering information regarding the conditions in which certain information can be used, Picot et al., 1997) and annotations of the *context* of the information's origin and relevance (Sowa, 2004) can be regarded as useful services that may increase the perceived usefulness (Karahanna & Straub, 1999) and value of intermediate information. The development of mobile broadband Internet and smartphones has resulted in a substantial reduction of information access efforts and 24 hours' availability of data nearly everywhere. The so-called app markets (like the OVI store for Nokia phones and Android Market) supply easily usable apps as interfaces to these Internet information resources. In contrast to the content aspect, here the core issue is not relevance but the core meta-requirement is optimized perceived usefulness for the content consumer as well as for its content owner.

With respect to *revenue* requirements, we must understand that each of the actors involved in the service's actor web must be able to realize sufficient revenues. These actors consist of the information good suppliers, content consumers who take or buy the content, and some ancillary services (like payment and information service provision) and sponsors. Suppliers of content may have high development costs, but reproduction and distribution costs in the digital era are near zero. This eases property rights theft and a tendency of information goods to have a price of zero (Shapiro & Varian, 1999). The value of an intermediary for a buyer relates to the number of goods and sellers that can be reached by it, and the value of the intermediary for a seller depends on the size of the demand it can reach. Such a service thus involves asymmetric network effects: one type of users is interested in the number of users of another type. Moreover, different types of users buy different services and they face different types of prices. It thus combines asymmetric network externality and third-degree price discrimination (Caillaud & Jullien, 2001: 798–799).

Suppliers and customers thus may be charged or paid out differently. Sponsors are often important for realizing information services (Womack, 2002) but attempts of services to raise advertising incomes may result in high use costs, so-called clutter costs, which are fictive prices for the consumers (Dewan et al., 2002). Consequently, it is important to know when it is appropriate to ask prices or to define motivational structures in non-monetary terms. Different actors may also deliver different contributions and thus cross-subsidizations may happen.

On the basis of this review, the requirements for information services are summarized in Table 5.1 as a set of demands and required processes for information services.

*Table 5.1* Requirements for Information Services

| | *Problems* | *Requirements (demands)* | *Requirements (processes)* |
|---|---|---|---|
| Content | Difficulty of selecting the right level of conceptualization and representation for potential consumers | Achieving high information recall and precision by linking relevant information goods to specific clients or target groups<br>Client group–targeted information and match with the user's ontology and semantics (conceptualization match) | Delivery of content |
| Use-value | Supplying proper levels of accuracy, format, usability, and timeliness | Perceived usefulness indicators; accuracy checking; ease-of-use (including format); property rights handling; context metadata; accessibility anytime and any place | User facilitation |
| Revenue | Pricing is difficult and not equivalent to value; costs coverage uncertainties; importance of ratings and credibility; first copy costs; high development costs; prices are pushed to zero on the Internet. | Charging of suppliers, customers, and sponsorsPayments of suppliers, customers, and subcontractorsA business model that results in an equitable balance of charging and payments, resulting in a sufficient surplus to cover the service's costs; price discrimination and cross-subsidization | Transaction processing |

## 5.2.2 Meta-Design of an Information Service

Based on the meta-requirements, this section identifies the design *components* and service *architectures*.[1] These components consist of service processes supporting *databases* (containing primary data, meta-data, information for service management like contract data and user log data), *organizational structures and people* (with expertise and tasks for, e.g., web development, transaction processing and administration), and *information technologies* (e.g., data communication, web services, security and payment systems). These components should be clearly *aligned* to business process activities. Table 5.2 groups the related components per process.

With respect to *content*-related process requirements, an information service needs different components:

*Table 5.2* Groups of Possible Components for Information Services

| | | *Information service infrastructure components* | | |
|---|---|---|---|---|
| | | *Information and databases* | *Organization and people* | *Information technology* |
| *Service processes* | *Content logistics and transformation* | Information products and product families with different conceptualization and representation levels; database(s); customer and supplier information | Data administrator; web developers | Querying system; database management system; HTML and style sheets; content aggregation tool (e.g., RSS); web server |
| | *Use facilitation* | Personal user profiles; user needs; metadata (e.g., reviews); user log data | Contract with users; user support personnel (e.g., developers); use-feature suppliers; intellectual property right handling | Visualization, analysis, interaction software; data and text mining tools; annotation tools; community building tools (e.g., del.ic.ious) |
| | *Revenue: Transaction processing* | Prices, sales volumes, invoice information, contracts with external stakeholders; user log data | Administrative personnel | Transaction processing system; billing and payment systems |

1. For acting as a *content logistic* portal, the service does not change anything with respect to the supplied good, and just transfers the good as it was supplied to the service. In performing this function, an information service is an aggregator and distributor of information goods like www.comtex.com.

   Comtex (www.comtex.com) provides real-time, economically relevant information. Comtex customers receive select content from key sources which is further enhanced with stock tickers and an extended lexicon of relevant terms. With a specialization in the financial news and content marketplace, Comtex receives, enhances, combines and filters news and content received from national and international news bureaus, agencies and publications, and distributes more than one million total stories per day. Comtex also provides a line of SmarTrend products to consumers, including a daily stock market letter (Morning Call), selected stock news and market analysis (SmarTrend Spotlights), and its banner product, SmarTrend Alerts (via subscription at www.mysmartrend.com).

   Such a service may have an important role in reducing search costs for customers. Personal profiles of clients (Orwant, 1996), databases, and product families are vital elements in such a design. A difficult problem in this context is coping with diverse ontologies, classifications, and languages held by different information sources and information consumers (Wu et al., 2001). For this human brokers can have an important role, although a number of technical developments also exist that support brokers or replace them, such as collaborative filtering technologies that use opinions and evaluations of many users for improving the relevance of query outcomes for each user (Belkin & Croft, 1992; Grote et al., 2002), retrieval feedback, which improves query results by using evaluations of past query outcomes (Spink, 1997), and RSS feeds, which enable Internet users to receive customized information on the basis of pre-given user profiles.

2. For *transforming* the levels of representation and conceptualization of the supplied information, an information service needs different means. The level of representation and conceptualization can be changed by offering different versions of information goods that serve different user profiles and needs. For instance, a university can offer a website about its newest research findings that serves academic and general audiences by more conceptualization for the first group and less for the second group. It can also deliver summary reports (low representation) and access to the full original data resources (high representation).

3. The content bases, sponsors, and subcontractors also have to be acquired, and thus contracts have to be managed.

*Content transformations* are often realized by delegating the transformation efforts to the information service consumer by giving them the tools to compose their own information goods. This results in two types of information service architectures:

1. With the *centralized website architecture*, the information service provider takes all the responsibilities for providing its target clients with the right kind of information through definitions and production of target group–related product families. This especially happens when the information supplier has a clear and targeted set of communications to its target groups, like with most company websites or product support sites. An example here is the Derwent World Patent Index, which tries to cover all the patents in the world in its database, and sells access to its database to engineers and technology strategy managers in companies (see http://scientific.thomson.com/derwent/). The Derwent Database has a set of tools for searching, comparing, and gaining additional information (e.g., concerning specific property right issues) for its users, but is also incorporated in a broader set of tools for (content) analysis and intellectual property rights management (named Aureka), and search (Delphion), and is also accessible from, for instance, the intellectual property rights marketplace www.yet2.com.
2. With the *aggregator architecture*, the information service provider enables the information service consumer to find and compose information goods, and it helps the customer to find what he needs. This is often the case when the information service wants to help specific groups with similar interests, which are often difficult to specify in advance. An example is the website of the British Horn Society (http://www.british-horn.org/links.html), which contains little information about itself, but has a huge collection of links for French horn enthusiasts (amateurs, professionals, and general audience) to find more information about topics like French horn producers, composers, and orchestras. A content aggregator can also explicitly push acquired content to clients according to client profiles by providing webfeed tools like RSS and ATOM. An advanced version of so-called syndication channels is Yahoo Pipes (see http://pipes.yahoo.com/pipes/docs and Vossen & Hagemann, 2007: 167–171).

These two service architectures are modeled in Figure 5.2.

a. The centralized (website) information service architecture.

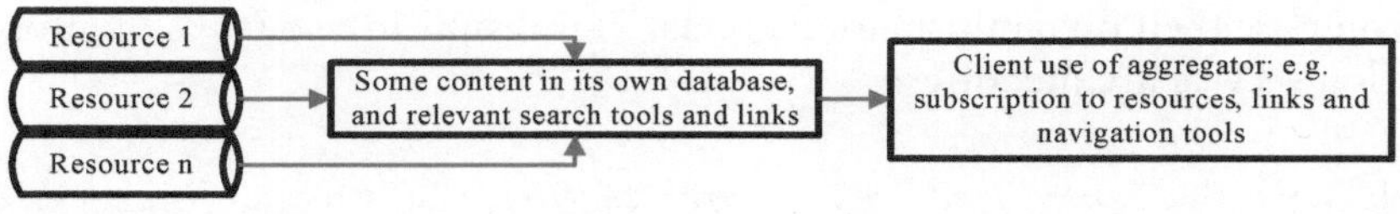


b. The aggregator information service architecture.

*Figure 5.2* Two architectures for *content-based* information servies.

With respect to the *use-value* requirements, we identified different opportunities of users to interact with the content and the delivery of meta-information, which all require specific IT facilities. For *content-interactions*, we identify:

1. Translation, which comprises giving information about the language in which the information is coded, technical language translations (code and format), and natural language translations
2. Format variation by delivering only standard formatted reports, delivering standard reports with customized formats, giving opportunities of analyzing data by a set of given models, and analyzing data by models that the users can create easily themselves or by data and text mining tools
3. Temporality and locality of the good can be varied by intentionally delaying information delivery or by alerting on the basis of location indicators via mobile devices.
4. Use duration can be varied by giving a time-slot with a certain duration for accessing.
5. Operational use can be varied by delivering only descriptions of the content, delivering a design of the content, delivering executable software, and delivering source code (which enables the receiver to act as co-producer of the software).

For meta-information we identify:

1. Enabling externalities by supplying information with respect to the level of *acceptance* of the good by the general audience. Information may also be kept secret when needed.
2. Delivery of quality certificates, by providing reputation information about the good and the source, and by providing opportunities to verify the information by other sources (Poston & Speier, 2005).

3. Intellectual property rights information can be delivered consisting of the right to use, the right to change form and structure of the good, the right to reap the profits, and the right to (re)sell (Picot et al., 1997).
4. Ontologies for standardizing and integrating data from different sources in one (virtual) database. This may be extremely valuable in environments where data consolidation is feasible (e.g., in standard management reporting) or where standardized data exchanges in a value chain are needed (e.g., electronic data interchange enables inter-firm business processes), but it is extremely challenging in the world of distributed Internet-based resources (Berners-Lee et al., 2001; Guha et al., 2004; Lei et al., 2004). Several initiatives for developing common ontologies for an industry exist, like the edifact standard for the chemical industry (http://www.unece.org/trade/untdid/d00a/tred/tred3055.htm; accessed September 28, 2010). For ontologies of other industries (like music and food), although with a less formal status, see the ontology directory http://ontologyonline.org. Human information broker expertise is essential for developing and maintaining these ontologies and for generating high quality retrievals in the many contexts where ontologies are not existing (Vishik & Whinston, 1999).

This discussion of use-value indicates at least two other information service architectures:

1. The *community architecture*, which does not aim at full information integration but aims at providing ways of interacting with content such that it enables community building by metadata processing. An example here is www.YouTube.com, which allows members of the community to share metadata by tagging of video material. These comments can be used to develop communities of people with common interests or expertise and help others to develop their interests. The tagging of content by information service customers can result in folksonomies (i.e., taxonomies for search and data management by the community of interested users). Sharing tags can also result in socialization, because it enables the service to combine users with possibly shared interests. Flickr.com has interesting features here worth trying. Social bookmarking tools like Del.icio.us are interesting tools for improving search while reusing bookmarks of people in the same social network (probably people with whom you socialize have similar interests and thus reusing their bookmarks may increase the relevance of search results) (Vossen & Hagemann, 2007: 183–198).
2. The *integrated data architecture* aims at the consolidation of data from different sources by a common data standard or ontology.

A well-known variant of this is the data warehouse (Kimball & Merz, 2000), which integrates data from different resources. Such data integration is much more difficult when more text-based or multimedia data have to be integrated via the Internet (McIlraith et al., 2004). Some interesting options exist by applying text and data mining tools. Vossen and Hagemann (2007: 163–167) mention also so-called page-scaping with wrappers, which search other sources according to search criteria and transform (not solely transfer) the acquired data to the specific formats of the service before delivering the content to the customer. This, though, requires substantial engineering of search filters and format transformation and therefore is useful only in repetitive search and delivery processes (e.g., daily management reports).

Following these two descriptions, these are two architectures in Figure 5.3.

For the *revenue*-related design, suppliers and buyers may pay an access rate, a registration price, or a transaction tax. The gross income of the service consists of the contributions of customers, sponsors, and affiliates

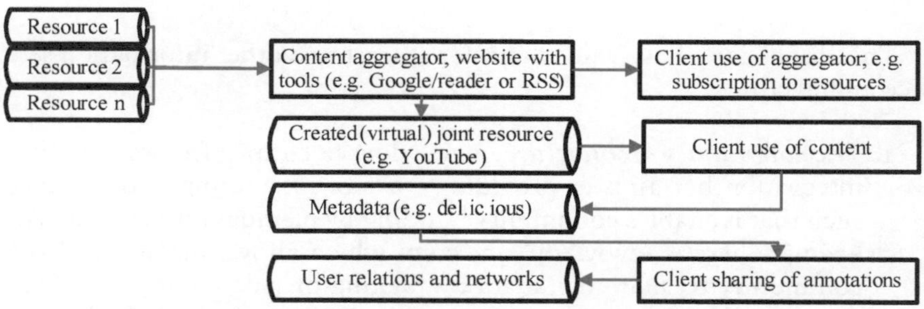


a. The community building information service architecture.

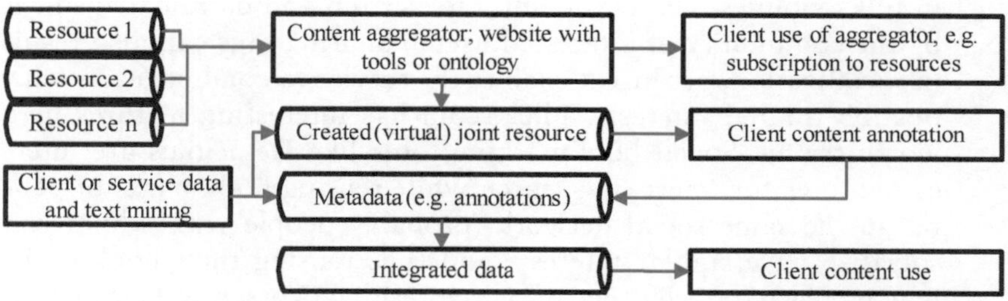


b. The data and work integration information service architecture.

*Figure 5.3* Two information service architectures for *use-value*.

minus the pay-outs to suppliers and (sub)contractors. The collection of *payments* and processing of *pay-outs* for the service may need the following administrative procedures (Gallaugher et al., 2001):

1. *Advertising*: In this process, the buyer does not pay directly for the content received, though the buyer may pay indirectly by clutter costs or increased costs of the products and services of the sponsor. The sponsor also does not directly pay for content, but the sponsor pays for presence.
2. *Subscribing*: Here the buyer does not pay for a single item but for a collection or bundle of information goods that may be supplied periodically or through access periods of the source. This revenue collection method is rather simple, because there is no need for separate pricing of individual items and the total transaction costs for the buyer are very low. A disadvantage of this system is that the buyer also pays for unwanted items.
3. *Online ordering/off-line payment of printed documents*: This process involves documents delivered in hardcopy versions, and the delivery is accompanied by a bill. This is a revenue collection method for online newspapers and magazines. For instance, *National Geographi* allows people to access its items via its website. The website is funded by customers of hardcopy versions and sponsors for which the website generates interests.
4. *Syndicating*: This process is an intermediation between content owners and potential content buyers. Here the syndicator can consist of a portal that sells content of others, collects the money from the buyers, and transfers the funds to the owners.
5. *Paying per unit*: This process requires that the units are well defined, that they are correctly priced, and that the transaction costs per individual transaction are low enough to make the transaction economical. With small units, like a weather report or telephone number request, this requires small prices and revenue collection mechanisms that are able to process micro-payments.
6. *Selling additional merchandise*: Many commercial content suppliers deliver content for free to attract other (but related) business that can be priced. For instance, www.euronorm.net gives away all kinds of useful reports and advice to entrepreneurs to enable them to conform to industrial norms. To be able to perform according to these norms, firms need measurement equipment and training, which they may buy from the owner of the website.
7. *Affiliate program processing*: This process enables incomes for portals and websites when they redirect clients. In some models a click-through is directly paid to the portal; in other instances the websites have agreed to show to each other what business has been generated by them and some sharing of the profit then is executed.

Additionally, we identify:

8. *Paying per data packages*: This process is important when prices are hard to define from the semantic value of the unit delivered, or when the supplier wants to be content-blind (e.g., like in the telephone industry; MacKie-Mason et al., 1996). In this case, the supplier calculated the number of data (bits) or access time, and thus prices and bills per data and time units.
9. Paying-out of subcontractors who delivered supportive services, like software licenses and fees for the hosting firm.

Because these revenue processing mechanisms are a common part of the electronic commerce literature, they are not treated in detail here; however, at least some of its components should be kept in-house by the service, whereas other components can be better left to a supporting firm (e.g., a bank). Consequently, the architecture for such revenue processing systems is not discussed here.

## 5.3 PROCESS-ORIENTED DESIGN THEORY FOR INFORMATION SERVICES[2]

### 5.3.1. Elements of Process-Oriented Design Theories

This section gives an overview of existing information systems techniques that are useful to all stages of the design of an information service. These techniques are integrated into a design framework called the information service design approach (ISDA). Hereby it is not the purpose of this section to give an exhaustive set of techniques or a single approach, but to offer some techniques that serve information service *design tasks*.

Figure 5.4 visualizes the purpose and contents of the ISDA. A development project is a process to design and realize a product. The product of ISDA—artifact—is an information service consisting of a design, including the required organizational embedding. The purpose of the ISDA is to support the process of creating the information service design by providing a set of techniques.

We use the case of the vtsPN (voorziening tot samenwerking Politie Nederland—Dutch Police organization for cooperation on information technology (IT)) to illustrate the main ideas. The vtsPN was founded in 2006 to support the Dutch Police with high-tech IT assets to improve efficiency, offer new initiatives, and increase the cooperation of the largely autonomic Dutch Police regions. Since its founding the vtsPN has focused on the development of IT and, relating to this, advising about governmental and organizational issues. In 2007, around 55,000 people

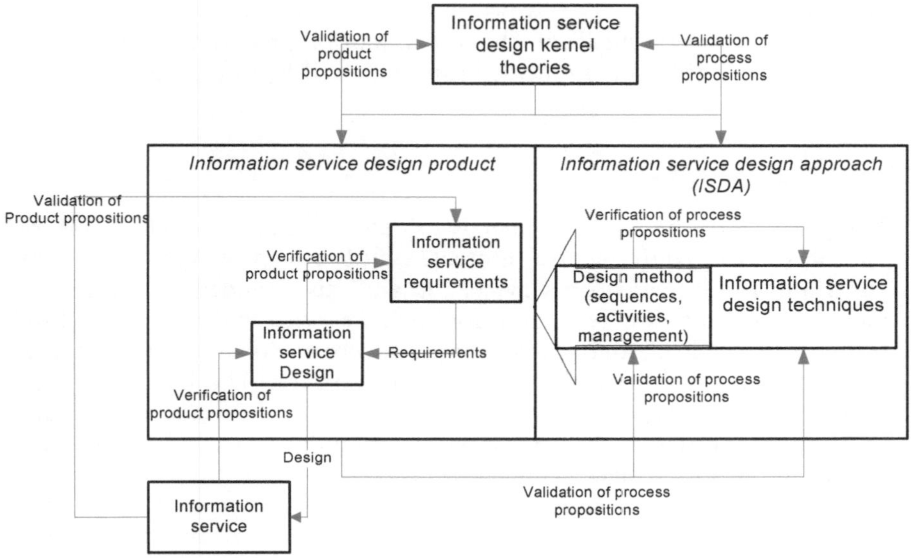


*Figure 5.4* The ISDA design science framework.

were working for the Dutch Police, and vtsPN had approximately 2,000 employees. As the central IT organization for the police it is important for the vtsPN to inform their clients—the users of the police departments—about their organization, products, services, and common IT developments. A newly developed information service should support realizing this goal.

Following Wieringa (2003), a *method* is defined as a problem-solving procedure and a *technique* is a tool for representing the knowledge that resulted from of applying the method. The techniques of the ISDA are partitioned in two layers.

1. *Analysis*: Techniques to represent the (organizational) context in which the information service will operate; this results in information service requirements.
2. *Design*: Techniques to describe and model the information service design; design is about the selection of solution components per aspect, such as the application and infrastructure components and organizational structure.

These two design layers are common phases of systems development processes. Even though many design projects start with an analysis phase, the order of application of the techniques in the different phases does not suggest that this is always the best prescribed order. It gives only a logical treatment of the tools, not a procedural treatment, because depending on project contingencies, different sequences may be chosen.

### 5.3.2 Analysis Layer

The purpose of the analysis layer is to determine and model the information service requirements. To create a fit between the organizational goals and the information service, the analysis includes techniques to model the context wherein the information service will operate and its business goals. Each analysis technique covers one or more of the three design aspects: content, use-features, and revenue. The business goals cover all three design aspects and the business model covers primarily the revenue design aspect. A system boundary method is included to determine the project scope, including the connections with other information systems and actors, and thus covers the content and use-feature aspects. The requirements description is divided into techniques to describe the data (i.e., content aspect); domain-level—functional level (i.e., the use-features aspect); and critical quality requirements (i.e., covering content, use-features, and revenue design aspects) (Lauesen, 2002). Figure 5.5 gives a summary of the analysis layer methods.

After application of the analysis layer techniques, context, development opportunities and limitations, and information service requirements must be clear.

At the beginning of a design process the relevance and business goals of the product to develop must be formulated. The same holds for the design process of an information service. The "mission-vision template" (Johnson et al., 2008) is a method to describe the business goals of the information service on a high level and to describe how these information service goals are related to the organization's overall business goals. The *mission-vision template* consists of eight fields—mission, vision, goal, objective, strategic capability, strategies, business model, and control—of which the first four

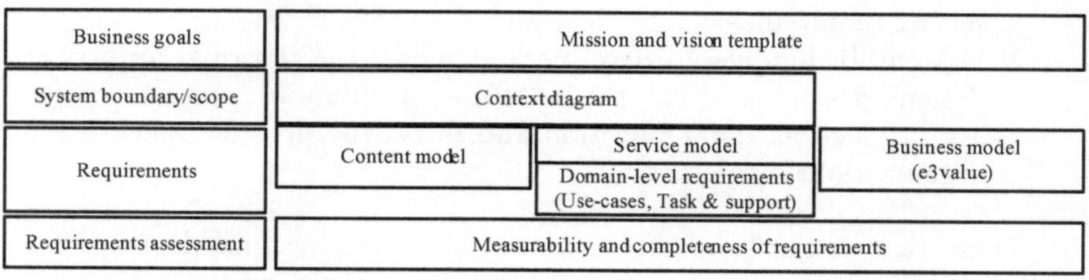


*Figure 5.5* Analysis layer techniques.

are useful to describe the business goals of an information service. The mission-vision of vtsPN is given here:

- *Mission*: vtsPN wants to contribute to public safety in the Netherlands by improving the existing products and services by standardization and simplification, broadening the product supply to all public safety organizations, and renewing the product and service supply by founding shared services, and focusing the service provision of products and services on the primary police processes.
- *Vision*: Within the next four years the vtsPN wants to become the professional partner of the police regions and the public safety organizations for advice, services, and facilities. vtsPN wants to develop itself as the number one service provider and knowledge institute for the Dutch public safety sector. One of the initiatives to realize these goals is the development of an information service for the clients of the vtsPN.
- *Goal*: The vtsPN business goals include the realization of an information service with the goal to market itself as the knowledge institute for the public safety sector. The target groups of the information service are the police officers of the police regions (primarily the IT policy makers) and the employees of the vtsPN. The primary supplier of content is the vtsPN.
- *Objective*: The information service satisfies the vtsPN if the information service satisfies the content and functionality requirements of its users. The content to deliver will include (1) product and services supplied, (2) product support, (3) news, (4) developments and innovations related to it and public safety, and (5) information about product development.

For the development of an information service the business goals description should include a first description of the target groups and the global contents. The arguments for the information service development often include a description of the gap between the current situation without information service, and the desired situation, with information service. When necessary a *problem tree* (e.g., represented by a fishbone diagram) can be created as a supporting tool to analyze the business problems that cause this gap.

When the business goals and problems are known, the scope of the project must be determined. A technique to do this is *context diagramming*. A context diagram gives an overview of the actors who will use the information service, which roles these actors can fulfill, and which connections there are between the information service and eventual other information resources. The context diagram represents which external information resources and actors are part of the information service development project. The actors of the information service and their roles are determined using the business goals. The system boundary for vtsPN with its two main components of the information service information system—the CMS and information service front-end—is shown in Figure 5.6.

The business goals and organization problems are the reasons to develop the information service. The business model elaborates how the information service is supposed to support the creation and sharing of values in a network of actors (Gordijn & Akkermans, 2001). Eventual legal and technical issues will have to be described in addition to the business model. These legal and technical issues can limit the solution space or offer possibilities for the information service design. These issues can be further elaborated in the data requirements and critical quality requirements.

The content model describes in abstract terms the subjects of knowledge and a description of potential users and suppliers of the content. By grouping the abstract knowledge, according to their contents, type, users, and suppliers, a model is made of the knowledge groups: what subjects they represent, how they are related to each other, and what kinds of abstract knowledge subjects are assigned to which groups. During the design phase this *content model*—with its knowledge

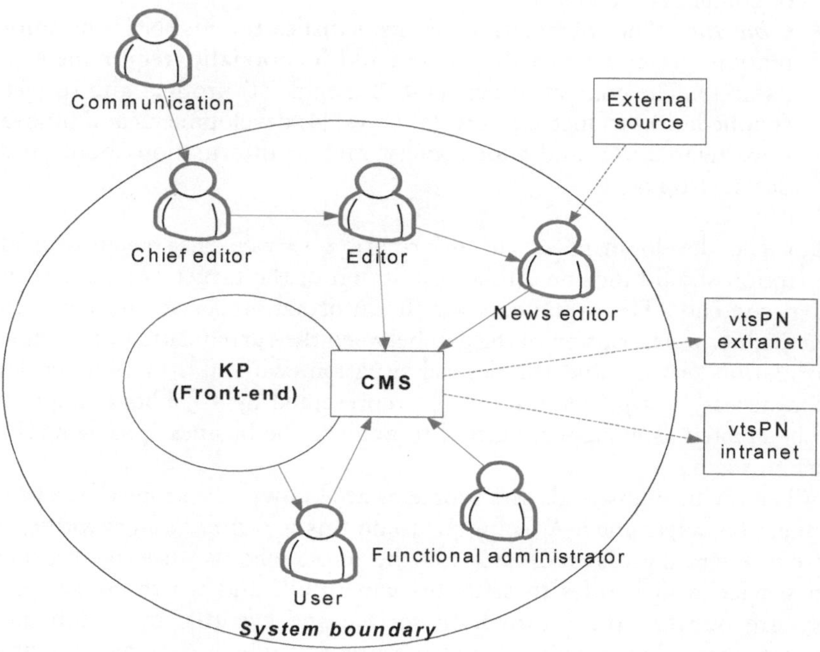


*Figure 5.6* vtsPN information service system boundary.

groups—can be used to create a navigational map of the information service application.

The *service model* describes what kinds of services and features are required to deal with the specified contents. Also the service model describes under which circumstances and conditions the knowledge can be handled by different actors. Which features and conditions are relevant for designing the information service varies from one situation to another. Some examples are:

- Content type, for example, plain text, documents, or multimedia
- Delivery mode, i.e., knowledge accessibility via push or pull mechanisms
- Actor relations, which describe how the users interact (suppliers and acquirers of information) with each other
- Legal, which describes the owner of the content and how to deal with the intellectual property
- Security, which describes what requirements must be fulfilled to supply the knowledge in a secure way
- Source, which describes the source of the content and how the information service will be fed with new knowledge and information

A simplified version of the service model of the vtsPN information service is given in Table 5.3.

The domain-level requirements are descriptions of the functionality of the information service on the business environment level. The requirements describe in which way the users have to be supported by the information service. The domain-level requirements can be described by UML use-case techniques. To make the use-cases more accessible for non-technical users and managers, the "task and support" roles can be described to make a clear description of every use-case. Task and support tables can contain the necessary steps and alternative scenarios to perform the use-case (a part of functionality) and how this is supported by the information service information system (Lauesen, 2002). Figure 5.7 gives the Unified Modeling Language (UML) use case diagram. A UML activity diagram can also be used to model the interaction between use cases (Laganiere and Lethbridge, 2001).

Besides the domain-level requirements that describe what information the information service will supply and process, requirements have to be specified to enable their assessment. These requirements are called *critical quality requirements* (Lauesen, 2002). Critical quality requirements are about usability, performance, reliability, accuracy, and security of the information system. In the ISDA the critical quality requirements can be partially subtracted from the technical and legal aspects of the business model.

*Table 5.3* The vtsPN Information Service Model

| Information object | Content type | | Delivery mode | | Actor relations | | | Legal | | | Source |
|---|---|---|---|---|---|---|---|---|---|---|---|
| | Plaintext | Document | Pull | Push | KP - S/U | S - U | U - U | vtsPN | Police | External | |
| Organization chart vtsPN | X | | X | | | X | | X | | | Manual edit |
| Enterprise architecture | X | X | X | | | X | X | X | | | Manual edit |
| vtsPN goals | X | | X | | | X | | X | | | Manual edit |
| Explanation IT-decision model | X | X | X | | | X | | X | | | Manual edit |
| Explanation IT-planning | X | X | X | | | X | X | X | | | Manual edit |
| Siminar calendar | X | | X | X | | X | | X | | | Manual edit |
| Publications related to police and/or IT | | X | X | X | | X | | X | X | X | Manual edit |
| Wikipedia for police departments | X | | X | | | X | X | X | X | | Manual edit |
| News about research projects | X | | X | X | | X | | X | | | Manual edit |
| Department description | X | | X | | | X | | X | | | Manual edit |
| Procedures central service desk (CSD) | X | | X | | | X | | X | | | Manual edit |
| Functional application manuals | | X | X | | | X | X | X | | | Manual edit |
| Domain description | X | | X | | | X | | X | | | Manual edit |
| Domain architecture | X | X | X | | | X | X | X | | | Manual edit |
| Police process architecture | X | X | X | | | X | | | X | | Manual edit |

*Note*: Actors can be the knowledge portal (information service), its suppliers (S), and its users (U). The legal column identifies the owner of the content, which can be vtsPN, police departments, or externals (e.g., a research institute, a government ministry, or a municipality).

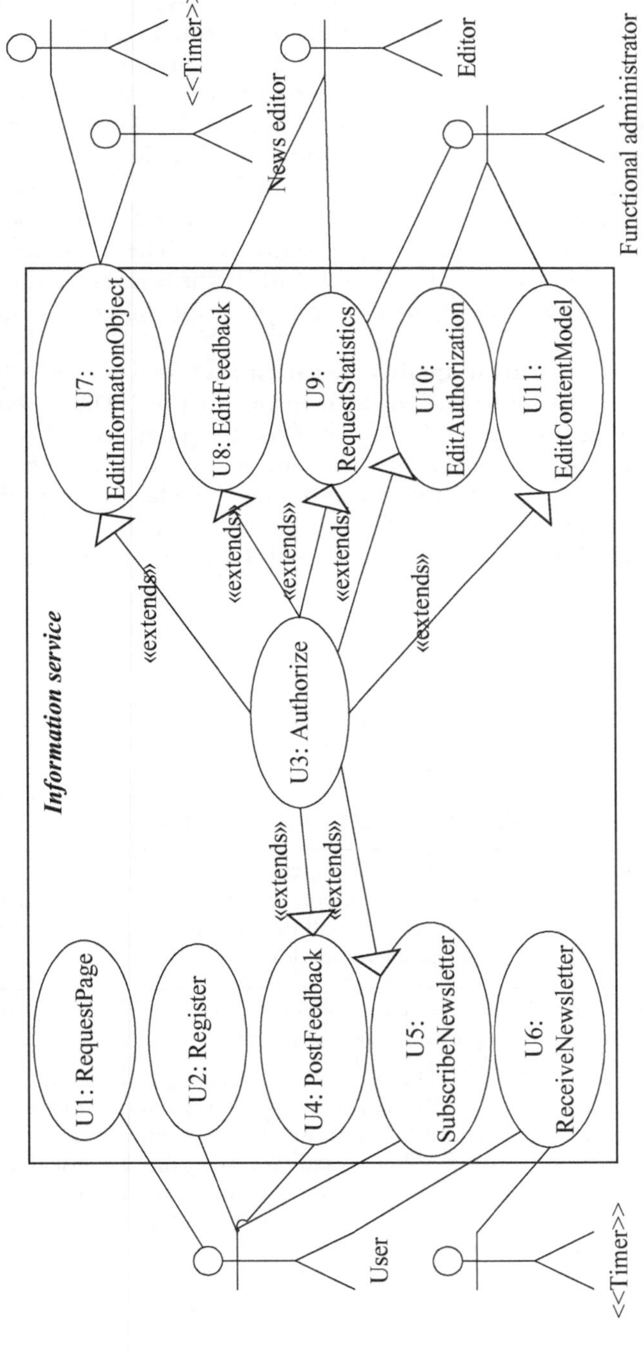


*Figure 5.7* vtsPN information service UML use case diagram.

One approach to create measurable critical quality requirements is applying the Gilb-template. The Gilb-template describes a number of fields that have to be fulfilled for every requirement. These fields are: tag (or name), gist (or description), scale (measurement unit), meter (measurement method), and the measurement values to obtain (must, plan, wish, past—the value of the old system) (Lauesen, 2002). For every critical quality requirement of the information service, the threshold value of the measurement values to obtain must be known. The "must" value has to be obtained to accept the design. The "planned" value has to be obtained to fulfill the critical quality requirement. The "desired" value has to be obtained to ensure the design fulfills the wishes of the users. Table 5.4 gives an example of the *Gilb-template* for the vtsPN information service.

The number of critical quality requirements varies per information service, so it is not possible to mention in the ISDA when your critical quality requirements list is (sufficiently) complete. The information service requirements at least have to consider the three information service design aspects and may be checked on product operation, product revision, and product transition or functionality, reliability, usability, efficiency, maintainability, and portability (ISO norm 9126).

*Table 5.4* Gilb-Template Example of the vtsPN Information Service

| | | | | | | |
|---|---|---|---|---|---|---|
| Quality factor: | **Efficiency and accuracy** | | | | | |
| Tag (name): | **R9. information service responsiveness** | | | | | |
| GIST (description): | One of the success factors of an information service is related to the responsiveness of the application. The user experience will decrease when the loading times of the pages are too long. | | | | | |
| Scale (measurement unit): | The time span in seconds between the moment of requesting a page and the moment the page is fully displayed | | | | | |
| Meter (measurement method): | Randomly browsing through the information service on different hours (for ten hours in total), especially during office hours, and measuring the response time using a stopwatch; the information service responsiveness is sufficient when the requested page is fully displayed within two seconds. | | | | | |
| Measurement values to obtain | Must | 75% | Plan | 95% | Wish | 99% |

### 5.3.3 Design Layer

Designing the information service is describing how the information service goals and revenues can be achieved, how the actors work with the information service, how the content, use-features, and functionality are implemented in the information service, and how to ensure that the information service satisfies the desired quality level. An overview of the techniques is given in Figure 5.8. Some techniques for the design layer are:

- A data model diagram (DMD) to create a database model—covering primarily the content aspect
- UML WAE to model objects of the information service application
- A navigation structure diagram for modeling the navigation paths of the information service application—covering both the content and use-features aspects
- A description of the organizational structure, supported by an organization chart and a role actor diagram (RAD)—covering the revenue and use-features aspects
- An architecture description technique to represent the relationship between the processes, services, applications, and infrastructure—covering all three design aspects

The knowledge that the information service delivers is described in the content model. This model is translated to a database layout, which provides a view of how the information (i.e., documents, text, links, media, etc.) is stored in the information service application. The relational structure in which all data are stored depends on the results acquired from the information model. The DMD method consists of tables with attributes and relations between tables consisting of attributes that point to other attributes and give a structure to a relational database (Hoffer et al., 2002). The DMD also includes the required data for use-features and revenue processing. A DMD can directly and one-on-one be implemented in an information service application. When it is difficult to translate the information service application objects and navigational structure

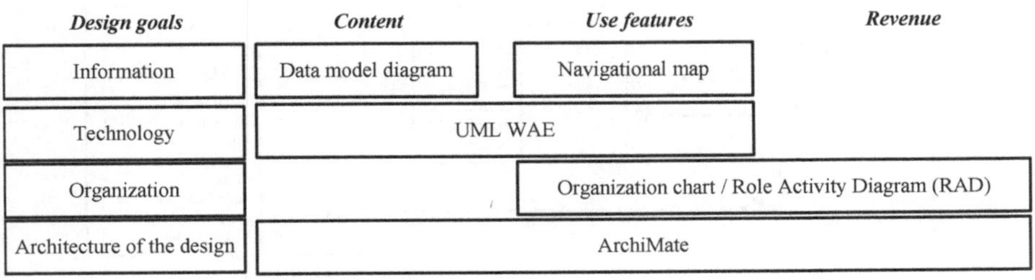


*Figure 5.8* Design layer techniques.

directly to a DMD, it is possible to construct an entity relationship diagram (ERD) first (Hoffer et al., 2002). Figure 5.9 is an example of a DMD for the vtsPN information service.

To design a highly usable information service, the information must be organized and navigation inside the portal should be easy (Palmer, 2002). Content presentation, website structure, and navigation are important factors with regard to information service usability (Yang et al., 2004). A navigational map is an abstract diagram to show where—on which screen—and how the users can access this information service functionality. In the navigational map every web page is modeled as a rounded rectangle. Arrows indicate which pages are connected to each other and show how a user can navigate from one page to another. For more details see Larsen and Conallen (2002).

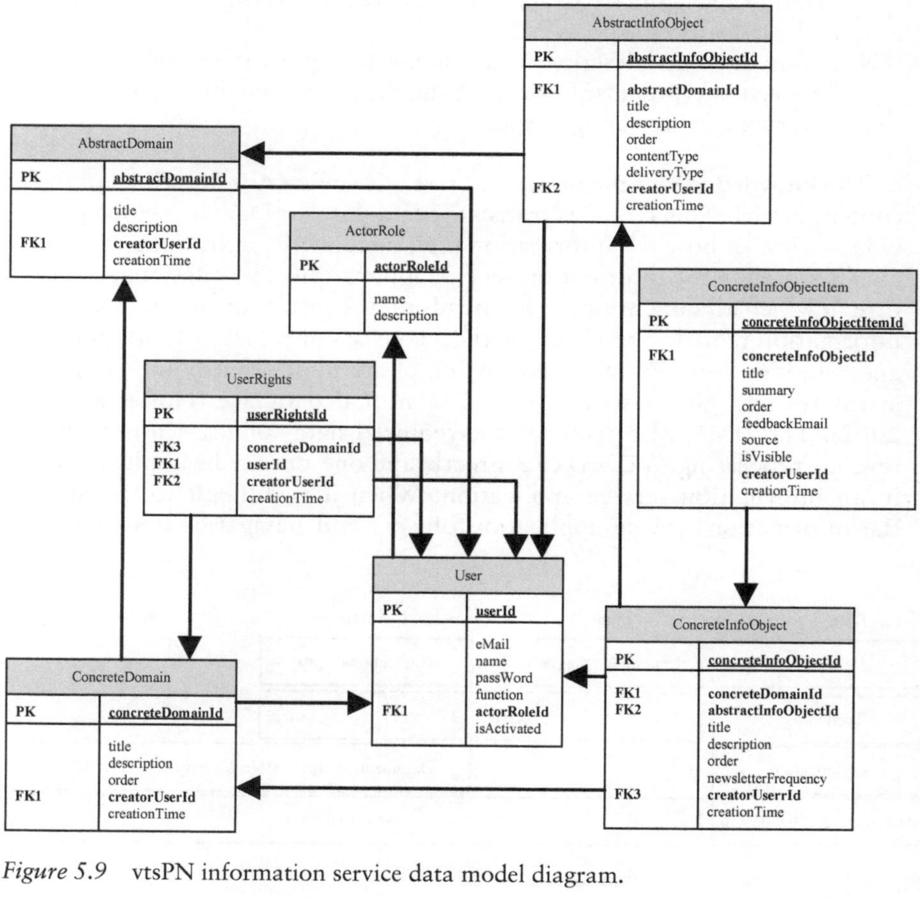


*Figure 5.9* vtsPN information service data model diagram.

Based on the business goals, stakeholders, and actors of the information service, an organization chart can be made to model the organization structure on an operational level. An organizational chart provides information about authority and responsibilities of the stakeholders and actors of the information service.

## 5.4 SELECTING ELEMENTS FOR THE INFRASTRUCTURE

Although most of the previous has been written with the interest of a pragmatic multi-disciplinary problem solver in mind, to achieve real progress the selection and implementation of means identified in the *architectural design* are necessary. These means can be several and have a multi-disciplinary (i.e., technical, human, and organizational) nature. Given the three aspects of an information service (content, use, and revenue), we will need the means as listed in Table 5.5. This section will not go into details regarding revenue means yet. Revenue is a major issue for the life-long continuation of an information service, which deserves a chapter on its own (Chapter 6).

### 5.4.1 Acquiring Data

There are two fundamentally different ways of data acquisition for information services:

- By creating data as a service by the information service, called internal content creation here

*Table 5.5* Information Service Infrastructure

| *Aspect* | *Processes* | *Means* | *Section* |
|---|---|---|---|
| Content | Data collection | External resource acquisition tools; internal content creation tools | *5.4.1* |
| | Data management | Content management systems | *5.4.2* |
| Use | Content search, interaction, and manipulation | Mashups, calculation tools, personalization tools | *5.4.3* |
| Revenue | Payments, monetary and non-monetary | Payment systems and evaluation and monitoring | *Chapter 6* |
| All | All | Human-organizational means | *5.4.4 & 5.4.5* |
| All | All | Integrating means into one architecture | *5.5* |

- By accessing other sources, and thus syndicating the other's content

### *Internal Content Creation*

*Web templates* can be used to set up any type of website. Once a template is purchased or downloaded, the user can replace all generic information included in the web template with his or her own personal, organizational, or product information. A common goal among experienced web developers is to develop and deploy applications that are flexible and easily maintainable. An important consideration in reaching this goal is the separation of *business logi* from *presentation logic*. Developers use web template systems (with varying degrees of success) to maintain this separation. The distinction between "presentation" (front-end) and "business logi" (infrastructure) is an important one, because:

- The presentation source code language may differ from other code assets.
- The production process for the application may require the work to be done at separate times and locations.
- Different workers have different skill sets, and presentation skills do not always coincide with skills for coding business logic.
- Code assets are easier to maintain and more readable when disparate components are kept separate and loosely coupled.
- Not all potential users of web templates have the willingness and ability to hire developers to design a system.
- Although web template reusability is useful for even highly skilled and technically experienced developers, it is *especially* critical to those who rely on simplicity and "ready-made" web solutions.

Such "ready-made" web templates are sometimes free and easily made by an individual domestically. However, specialized web templates are sometimes sold online. For an overview see, e.g., Wikipedia.com pages on *web templates* and *template systems* and the web template at the Open Directory Project.

Some web developers have a graphic arts background and may pay more attention to how a page looks than considering other issues such as how visitors are going to find the page via a search engine. On the other side, search engine optimization consultants (SEOs ) are concerned with how much traffic it generates via search engines, and how many sales it makes, assuming looks do not contribute to the sales. As a result, the designers and SEOs often end up in disputes where the designer wants more "pretty" graphics, and the SEO wants lots of "ugly" keyword-rich text, bullet lists, and text links. But, how well a site works may depend on the graphic designer's visual communication ideas as well as the SEO considerations. A problem when using lots of graphics on a page is that download times can be greatly lengthened, often irritating the user. This has become less of a problem awith the current high-speed Internet and the use of vector graphics, although it is urgent again in the growing market of cell phone applications.

On the Web, the designer has no control over several factors, including the size of the browser window, the web browser used, the input devices used (e.g., mouse, touch screen, voice command, text, and cell phone number pad), and the available fonts. Some designers choose to control the appearance of the elements on the screen by using specific width designations through the use of HTML tables or cascading style sheets (CSS). Whenever the text, images, and layout of a design do not change as the browser changes, this is referred to as a *fixed width design*. Other designers choose a liquid design, which allows the flow of content into the whole screen, or a portion of the screen, no matter what the size of the browser window. Proponents of *liquid design* prefer greater compatibility and using the screen space available. Liquid design can be achieved through the use of CSS, by avoiding styling the page altogether, or by using HTML tables set to a percentage of the page. Both liquid and fixed design developers must make decisions about how the design should degrade on higher and lower screen resolutions. Sometimes the pragmatic choice is made to flow the design between a minimum and a maximum width.

Similar to liquid layout is the optional *fit to window* feature for Adobe Flash content. This is a fixed layout that optimally scales the content of the page without changing the arrangement or text wrapping when the browser is resized. Adobe Flash (formerly Macromedia Flash) is a proprietary, robust graphics animation or application development program used to create and deliver dynamic content, media (such as sound and video), and interactive applications over the Web via the browser. Many graphic artists use Flash because it gives them exact control over every part of the design, and anything can be animated and generally "jazzed up". Some application designers enjoy Flash because it lets them create applications that do not have to be refreshed or go to a new web page every time an action occurs. Flash can use embedded fonts instead of the standard fonts installed on most computers. Other sites may use Flash content combined with HTML but with smaller vector file sizes to generate faster loading animations.

### *External Content Acquisition*

The Internet is full of providers of content, named *resources* here. Many of these content providers allow the free reuse of their data, others require special licenses. For example, Google Maps allows the free reuse of its resources and the integration of these resources into another's information services. Integration of these external resources can be achieved by 1) the reuse of technical means for automatic access and integration and 2) the explicit services of information intermediaries.

Technical-automatic access and integration can be achieved by webfeeds and mashups. Webfeeds, e.g., RSS and ATOM, enable one to integrate original data or store links to data of others in a site. A more advanced use of RSS is Yahoo Pipes, which enables one to define more advanced rules for data acquisition. Mashups (e.g., via Google Maps APIs, see http://code.google.com/apis/maps/) enable one to add information on incorporated external data sources. Besides the automatic content aggregation and integration tools, information service companies nowadays are actively engaged in the business of context-aware external content acquisition for providing highly relevant information to their clients. In the past publishers did this as best they could, but the Internet realities resulted in a huge supply of content with problems of getting control over the information overload. This requires a new kind of intermediation or publishing, of which two types can be identified:

1. The aggregation of content and content-syndication services, like EBSCO and Google Scholar, by which a huge number of consumers can be given access to content of a huge number of information goods suppliers and property owners
2. Publishing platforms, which request a payment from content suppliers to enable access to their content by clients for free, and by which the intermediary thus exploits the value of communication and externalities of the goods as part of larger information resources with a certain quality stamp attached to it (e.g., Springer's open access model; see http://www.springeropen.com/)

### 5.4.2 Web Content Management Systems for Efficient Maintenance and Delivery Processes[3]

#### *Necessity of Web Content Management Systems*

As amounts of content increase, editing web pages becomes more complex and the use of a content management system (CMS) becomes unavoidable. If websites have complex divisions of work or large amounts of content, manual editing will be inefficient, and CMSs are developed to give support.

Content management systems support the following tasks in the back-end.

1. Web page presentation tasks like designing templates for content; layouts and appearances

2. Content life cycle tasks like authoring, reviewing and publishing content, updating and removing expired content
3. Systems management tasks like managing use, managing user roles and permissions, and system configuration.

### *Web Page Presentation Tasks*

According to the AIIM (Association for Information and Image Management), content implies both structured and unstructured information. Content is any type or "unit" of digital information. It can be text, images, graphics, video, sound, documents, records, etc.—or in other words, anything that is likely to be managed in an electronic format. On the back-end, CMS cuts content into the following components: 1) primary data that are created by users, 2) metadata, 3) templates for composing and arranging components. It combines these components into displayable web pages on the front-end. The final content format is usually in HTML and can be accessed through web browsers, whether the content is saved in a database, XML, or other types of files.

An important presentation success factor is the type of navigation that the CMS supports. Well-designed *navigations* avoid end-users getting lost in websites and provide contexts for retrieving content in websites. Embedded navigations are located on each web page. Global navigation is the same on every page. It is usually located on headers or footers, like a privacy policy and copyright. Local navigation tools, like menus, also appear on each content page, but they may change according to which sub-areas they are located in, if websites are divided into subsites. Both global navigation and local navigation structurally categorize content. Bread crumb navigation is another way to indicate where end-users are on websites. Contextual navigation, though, provides flexible ways to connect pages by subjects—for example, a hyperlink connected to a specific piece of content. This is helpful when pages of the same subjects are located in different places of website. Supplemental navigation is an extra way to help end-users find content, like site maps and site indexes. A site map is a "table of contents" of a website. It enumerates content according to tree structures of web pages. Additionally, a site index may be provided, which is especially suitable for large websites. Each content page is given a title, and site index pages list these titles by alphabetical order. Additionally, end-users usually expect a search function somewhere on websites. But search is a supplementary way to look for content, not a main way. Main ways are embedded navigations. If embedded navigations are not good enough so that end-users have to use "search" frequently, then improving embedded navigations should be considered.

### *Content Life Cycle Management*

The *content life cycle* is the development of content from the beginning until the end. The content life cycle can be divided into the following phases: authoring, approval, management on the back-end, and publishing on the front-end. Detail activities and features in each phase are explained here.

Some *features* exist in all phases, like layout, metadata and audit trail. Some activities are the responsibility of web designers and are independent of substantive content, but facilitate the actual appearance of the content. Layout involves the positioning of elements like menus, navigations, headers, footers, and content on a web page. Appearance involves formats for styles of websites, like background color, font size, and font name. CSS is the most direct way to control both. A ready-made way to control layout and appearance is called "theme", which is also called a "skin" or "template".

*Metadata* is used for managing content and describes properties of it. Owing to content formats, some content is difficult to index and search, e.g., images, graphics, media, and not text-based files. Metadata are used frequently for making such content retrievable. The Dublin Core Metadata Initiative (DCMI) defines a set of basic metadata elements for describing electronic resources. There are 15 elements in Dublin Core: contributor, coverage, creator, data, description, format, identifier, language, publisher, relation, rights, source, subject, title, and type. Users can define their own metadata by extending these elements. Many metadata schemes extend Dublin Core for different purposes.

*Audit trail* logs events happening in the content life cycle—for instance, who authored what content and when—and compiles statistics. (This is named operational data by Floridi, 2005.) Common events include creation, update, revision, and deletion of content. Hits of content or reading content are also recorded in some CMS products.

In general, the basic unit of content is one content item displayed on one web page. But content items can be divided into different components, like body and form. Users *author* the body part by editors. This is the most common way to edit content in CMS systems. As to form, one content item has only one form at most. Customized forms are usually built by line-by-line programming, especially when forms contain inputs and business rules.

*Approving* is examining content in order to prevent publishing of improper content. Reviewers may approve or give authors comments for revisions. Until content is approved, it is not qualified for publication. In Drupal and Joomla!, if content is created by someone who does not have permission to publish content, then the content must be forwarded and reviewed by administrators.

Content management on the back-end consists of version control, content scheduling, and permissions management. *Version control* may be helpful when users find problems within new versions and may need rollback options. Users could also compare modifications among versions of content to trace changes of content. A related option is "check-in and check-out" for collaborative authoring. When more than one person has permission to edit the same content, it is possible that users author at the same time. In order to prevent overwriting others' revisions, check-in and check-out are necessary.

*Content scheduling* means content is automatically displayed on websites at a planned moment. Users set starting dates and expiry dates to control for content obsolescence. This function is useful when content must be published and removed at appropriate moments.

*Permissions* set who has privileges to act on existing content. Common permissions include view, edit, and delete. Granularities of permissions are decided by units of content and roles. The most detailed level is that privileges are assigned per content item and per user basis. This function prevents improperly acting on content. For example, if content is for inner use, then the permission of viewing this content is granted to inner users only.

Finally, each CMS has at least five *publishing* options:

- *Static*: Content authors provide content in XML, and then pages are transformed into HTML and delivered to websites. This benefits the performance of websites, because websites provide web pages without parsing script languages.
- *Multiple renditions*: After content is created, it may be rendered to different formats, like PDF and e-mail. This gives end-users more choices to access content.
- *Dynamic at publish-time*: When content is created or updated in a repository, it is not published right away. Publishing engines regularly check content and publish to websites at pre-given moments.
- *Dynamic at run-time*: Contrary to dynamic at publish-time, as soon as new or updated content is stored in a repository, it is instantly available. This kind of delivery needs server-side scripting, like ASP, JSP, PHP, and ColdFusion. When end-users request content, web servers receive requests and send queries to get content. After getting content back, web servers combine content with page templates, and then deliver to end-users
- *Live from repository*: When end-users request content, web servers pass requests to the repository. Content is delivered from repositories to end-users. This delivery mode requires the least effort of websites, because websites just pass requests.

Table 5.6 summarizes requirements of CMS software for life cycle management.

*Table 5.6* Summary of Life Cycle Requirements

| *Content life cycle* | *Requirements classes* |
|---|---|
| All phases | Layout and appearance |
| | Metadata |
| | Audit trail |
| Authoring content | Components of content |
| | Editor |
| | WYSIWYG editor for HTML |
| | Customize client-side code |
| | Customize server-side code |
| Approving content | Approval |
| Enhancing & managing content | Version control |
| | Content scheduling |
| | Permission per content |
| Publishing | Sandbox |
| | Renditions |
| Archiving | Archive |

### *Systems Management*

A good overview of CMS products is given at CMS Matrix.[4] Here, CMS products are described by operating systems, application servers, web servers, databases, and programming languages. After that, user interface aspects are described and the different ways CMsystems can handle the content life cycle. The end describes generic functions of a CMS and technical issues for systems management.

Drupal and Joomla! both have high rankings on CMS Matrix,[5] and catch the attention of users on the Internet. Besides, the two products received the 2006 Open Source CMS Award. Drupal is also voted as one of the best web applications in 2007 on the website WebWare, which is supported by CNET.[6]

Drupal, Joomla!, and CMPro are all open source software, but not all of them are free—CMPro is commercial, so the owner (ZMPX) provides support and upgrades. Drupal and Joomla! are supported and maintained by open source communities. CMPro is developed on ColdFusion, and supports several databases, even commercial ones. The common way CMsystems integrate with existing systems is by offering application protocol interfaces (APIs). Through APIs, CMS systems are more easily extended with functions and can be accessed by other systems. Drupal and Joomla! supply complete API documentation on the Internet for developers.

Besides the system requirements, the main differences among CMsystems are how users get support. For organizations that have no technical staff or IT departments, it may be hard to use freeware products like Drupal and Joomla!, since each step in deploying and maintaining such a CMS system requires substantial IT professional knowledge. But, because Drupal and Joomla! are supported by communities, more modules and themes are contributed than for a proprietary tool. If users can handle technical tasks, they may consider Drupal and Joomla!.

General modules for CMS systems management are:

- Authentication system
- Site statistics report
- Workflow
- Multi-language support
- Multi-site deployment, i.e., that one system is able to host multiple sites.

*Peripheral modules* provide more functions to use on product websites, like enabling different types of interaction. Interaction can be simple, like end-users giving comments to content. It could be complex, like online shopping, personal information, shipping address, bill address, and paying bills. Other common functions are shopping carts, forums, polls, and comments for content. Because Drupal and Joomla!, are supported by communities, there are many modules. More modules are available on their website product.[7] As for CMPro, it has polls, a shopping cart, and an e-learning tool. Many others items exist (more than 100), listed on the website of CMS Matrix. Boiko (2005) wrote a 57-page guide for selecting a CMS system.

### *5.4.3 Use-Features*

The Internet-related industry has developed many use-features. The most frequently mentioned and easiest to use are listed here:

1. Mashup tools, which we already discussed via Google Maps API
2. Tagging, by which information users can annotate information retrieved and also possibly share these tags for building folksonomies of Internet topics and as such increase relevant retrievals; people can also annotate sites as useful, trustful, and relevant for specific topics, and use Rollyo (http://rollyo.com/bookmarklet.html) for inserting this information to increase the quality of retrievals.
3. Social bookmarking and filtering also allow the building of social networks around shared opinions, interests, and views. Del.icio.us (a Firefox add-on) is a well-known tool for this purpose.

4. User-generated content tools, like Flickr.com and YouTube and co-editing tools like Wikis; this collection of tools is also named social media or Web 2.0. Social media is a group of Internet-based applications that build on the ideological and technological foundations of Web 2.0, and that allow the creation and exchange of user-generated content (Kaplan & Haenlein, 2010). Social media utilization is believed to be a driving force in defining the current time as the Attention Age, exploiting attention economics (Shapiro & Varian, 1999). The term Web 2.0 is commonly associated with web applications that facilitate interactive information sharing, interoperability, user-centered design, and collaboration on the World Wide Web. A Web 2.0 site gives its users the free choice to interact or collaborate with each other in a social media dialogue as creators (prosumer) of user-generated content in a virtual community, in contrast to websites where users (consumer) are limited to the passive viewing of content that was created for them. Examples of Web 2.0 include social-networking sites, blogs, wikis, video-sharing sites, hosted services, web applications, mashups, and folksonomies.
5. Software-as-a-Service (SAAS) may consist of many easy-to-use for one moment and often free tools, for example, statistic calculations and video manipulation. Two sites that are offering SAAS are www.sourceforge.net (all kinds of open source software) and www.wolframalpha.com. Service-as-a-Service is also a part of the so-called cloud computing offerings (http://www.europeancloudcomputing.nl/en/).
6. Infrastructure services, like storage space (e.g., Amazon S3) and computing capacity (Amazon EC2); in the context of computing this is called infrastructure-as-a-service (http://www.europeancloudcomputing.nl/en/; accessed September 28, 2010).
7. Finally noticeable here are the many interesting tools and gadgets that are provided by Google via its labs (www.Googlelabs.com).

## 5.4.4 The Organizational Infrastructure

To have an information service working, besides its software, it requires an organizational infrastructure, i.e., managers, developers, support people, and organizational procedures to run the service. These will be discussed here.

### *Webmasters and Related Actors*

The webmaster, also called the web architect, the web developer, the site author, or the website administrator, is the person responsible for designing, developing, marketing, or maintaining a website. On community websites, webmasters are able to change and manipulate any comment that the users make. Webmasters are practitioners of web communication. Typically, they are generalists with HTML expertise who manage all aspects of web operations.

On larger sites, the webmaster will act as a coordinator and overseer for the activities of other people working on the site and is usually an employee or the owner of the website; hence webmaster can also be listed as an occupation. If the webmaster is hired by a larger website, or promoted to the position, he or she could do anything from web design to project management or employee supervision.

In the early days of the term "webmaster" (a takeoff on the term "postmaster", the administrator of an e-mail system), this role encompassed all aspects of planning, coding, production, and user interface. The webmaster may have many of the duties of an information architect, including ensuring site usability, user experience, and menu taxonomy. However, since the late 90s, this type of webmaster role was typically found only on small websites that could be managed by one person, or in environments where there was not a great deal of role definition. The current model tends to be more team-oriented, with a website manager or online producer leading a team consisting of web developers, designers, programmers, quality leaders, Adobe Flash developers, and often at least one usability expert on user interfaces. In established web development companies, especially those existing since the 90s, the term webmaster may be used by senior officers of the company, and may include usage such as "webmaster-in-chief." A broader definition of webmaster is a business person who uses online media to sell products and/or services. This broader definition of webmaster covers not just the technical aspects of overseeing website construction and maintenance but also management of content, advertising, marketing, and order fulfillment for the website. Core responsibilities of this webmaster include the regulation and management of access rights of different users of a website, and the appearance and setting up of website navigation. Content placement can be part of a webmaster's responsibilities, while content creation is typically not. Typically, the webmaster is the agent who reads user feedback and complaints about site functionality. The webmaster is actually in charge of the server more so than the actual web pages. The web pages are handled by the senior designer.

### *Community Roles of Information Service Managers*

Information services often have a role in facilitating effective networks of people, resulting in social network roles besides technical, commercial, or content roles. A *network* here is defined as: ". . . a collectivity of individuals among whom exchanges take place that are supported by shared norms and trustworthy behaviour" (Liebeskind et al., 1996: 430). In terms of "who pays what" two *network contexts* can be distinguished:

1. Community networks, where seekers and suppliers jointly pay for the expertise exchange—no one earns from this relation at the expense of the other.
2. Sponsored networks, where the expertise exchanges are free

In either case, the ideal norms of networks of expertise are reached (Liebeskind et al., 1996). When only the seekers or suppliers pay, market-like relations exist, and thus the exchanges are not according to network norms (Liebeskind et al., 1996). Additionally, Bourhis et al. (2005) emphasize demographics (e.g., age, size, dispersion, member selection rules, and member stability) of the expertise network's membership as context characteristics, which may affect performance demands and how various services are valued.

Market-like and hierarchical relationships are considered ineffective for expertise sharing, while network structures offer several advantages—such as greater interaction flexibility and the absence of complex contracting—as reported by sociologists (e.g., Liebeskind et al., 1996) and economists (e.g., Williamson et al., 1991). Expertise intermediaries, like joint databases, newsletters, and network organization activities help reduce search costs and cognitive distance (Van Baalen et al., 2005), overcome the disadvantages of weak ties, and reduce the costs of creating and maintaining strong ties (Brown & Duguid, 2000; McLure-Wasko & Faraj, 2005). Expertise intermediaries also may facilitate communication and collaboration through virtual means (Herbsleb & Mockus, 2003). Consequently, expertise intermediaries (i.e., services that mediate between owners and seekers of expertise; cf. Wijnhoven, 2002a & 2002b; Womack, 2002) may improve the *performance of networks of expertise*, as assessed by the ability of the network to deliver actionable knowledge (Cross & Spoull, 2004), such as solutions, referrals to people, databases, or other sources, problem reformulation, validations of delivered answers, and "legitimations" (e.g., indicators of reputation and recognition of the sources). Expertise intermediaries also may improve network performance by increasing the value of the network for members and non-members (McLure-Wasko & Faraj, 2005) and by increasing the members' mutual utilization of each other (i.e., network density; Carrington et al., 2005).

The intermediary problems can be partially overcome during design, but also require better *management* during the usage stage. Bourhis et al. (2005) identify four groups of management roles to enhance the value an expertise intermediary has for a network of expertise:

1. *Knowledge domain roles*: Including making decisions for service alignment within the network context
2. *Leadership roles*: Being the initiator of intermediary services
3. *Knowledge intermediary roles*: Taking responsibility for usefulness of intermediation between members
4. *Community support roles*: Administrator, event coordinator, and technologist

In addition, taking these roles and making appropriate decisions require the managers to have information about the network and its performance.

Figure 5.10 integrates the mentioned variables that influence expertise network performance in a research framework for this study.

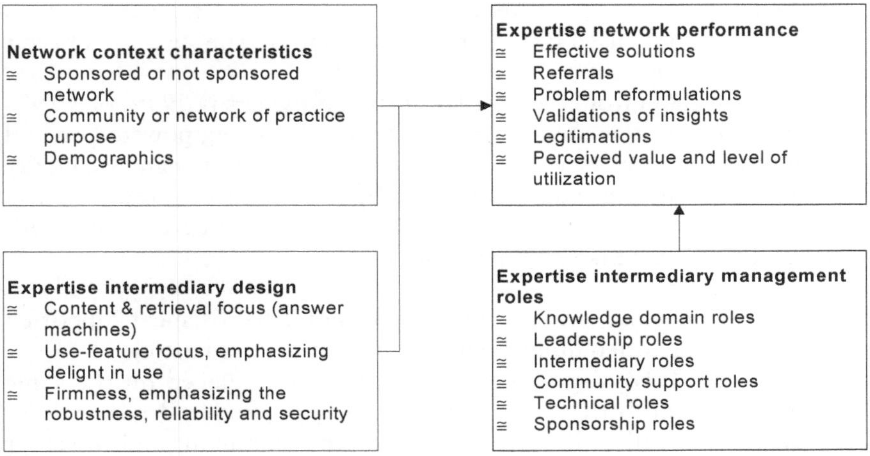


*Figure 5.10* Framework of possible relations between variables in a network of expertise.

### *Web Hosting Service*

A *web hosting service* is an Internet hosting service that allows individuals and organizations to provide their own website accessible via the World Wide Web. Web hosts are companies that provide space on a server they own for use by their clients as well as provide Internet connectivity, typically in a data center. Web hosts can also provide data center space and connectivity to the Internet for servers they do not own to be located in their data center, called collocation.

The scope of hosting services varies widely. The most basic is web page and small-scale file hosting, where files can be uploaded via File Transfer Protocol (FTP) or a web interface. The files are usually delivered to the Web "as is" or with little processing. Many Internet service providers (ISPs) offer this service free to their subscribers. People can also obtain web page hosting from other, alternative service providers. Personal website hosting is typically free, advertisement-sponsored, or cheap. Business website hosting often has a higher expense.

Single-page hosting is generally sufficient only for personal web pages. A complex site calls for a more comprehensive package that provides database support and application development platforms (e.g., PHP, Java, Ruby on Rails, ColdFusion, and ASP.Net). These facilities allow the customers to write or install scripts for applications like forums and content management. For e-commerce, SSL is also highly recommended to guarantee website interaction privacy and security.

The host may also provide an interface or control panel for managing the web server and installing scripts as well as other services like e-mail.

Some hosts specialize in certain software or services (e.g., e-commerce). They are commonly used by larger companies to outsource parts of their network infrastructure.

A common claim from the popular hosting providers is "99% or 99.9% server uptime" but this often refers only to a server being powered on and does not account for network downtime. Real downtime can potentially be larger than the percentage guaranteed by the provider. Many providers tie uptime and accessibility into their own service level agreement (SLA). Hosting services can take multiple shapes:

- *Free web hosting service*: Free, (sometimes) advertisement-supported web hosting, often limited when compared to paid hosting
- *Shared web hosting service*: One's website is placed on the same server as many other sites, ranging from a few to hundreds or thousands. Typically, all domains may share a common pool of server resources, such as RAM and the CPU. A shared website may be hosted with a reseller.
- *Reseller web hosting*: Allows clients to become web hosts themselves; resellers could function for individual domains, under any combination of these listed types of hosting, depending on who they are affiliated with as a provider. Resellers' accounts may vary tremendously in size: they may have their own virtual dedicated server to a collocated server.
- *Virtual dedicated server*: Dividing a server into virtual servers, where each user feels like he is on his own dedicated server, but the use is actually sharing a server with many other users; the users may have root access to their own virtual space. This is also known as a virtual private server or VPS.
- *Dedicated hosting service*: The user gets his or her own web server and gains full control over it (root access for Linux/administrator access for Windows); however, the user typically does not own the server. Another type of dedicated hosting is self-managed or unmanaged. This is usually the least expensive for dedicated plans. The user has full administrative access to the box, which means the client is responsible for the security and maintenance of his own dedicated box.
- *Managed hosting service*: The user gets his or her own web server but is not allowed full control over it, however, the user is allowed to manage data via FTP or other remote management tools. The user is disallowed full control so that the provider can guarantee quality of service by not allowing the user to modify the server or potentially create configuration problems. The user typically does not own the server. The server is leased to the client.
- *Collocation web hosting service*: Similar to the dedicated web hosting service, but the user owns the collocation server; the hosting

company provides physical space that the server takes up and takes care of the server. This is the most powerful and expensive type of web hosting service. In most cases, the collocation provider may provide little to no support directly for its client's machine, providing only the electrical, Internet access, and storage facilities for the server. In most cases for collocation, the client would have his own administrator visit the data center on site to do any hardware upgrades or changes.

- *Clustered hosting*: Having multiple servers hosting the same content for better resource utilization; clustered servers are a perfect solution for high-availability dedicated hosting, or creating a scalable web hosting solution.
- *Grid hosting*: This form of distributed hosting is when a server cluster acts like a grid and is composed of multiple nodes.
- *Home server*: Usually a single machine placed in a private residence can be used to host one or more websites from a usually consumer-grade broadband connection. These can be purpose-built machines or more commonly old PCs.

Web hosting is often provided as part of a general Internet access plan; there are many free and paid providers offering these services. A customer needs to evaluate the requirements of the application to choose what kind of hosting to use. Such considerations include database server software, scripting software, and operating system.

### 5.4.5 Organizational Arrangements and Procedures: The Nestle Case[8]

*Nestle Waters*

Bottled water from Nestlé Waters is sold in 130 countries with 70 different brands produced in 103 factories in 36 countries, and is the world's leading (mineral) water company. In 2001, in order to improve efficiency of manufacturing operations, Nestlé corporate introduced the Best-in-Class Repositories (BiCR), that should contain best practices in different business processes (e.g., manufacturing, logistics, and product specifications). With the help of BiCR, the top management aimed at collecting, storing, and distributing the best skills of NW for gaining competitive advantage. A NW employee is expected to supply the related Best Practice (BP) content in a standardized template. The submitted BP is reviewed by the Industrial Performance (IP) department manager and afterwards stored in the repository. The server from which the BiCR runs is controlled by the IT department at Nestlé corporate, which also manages access rights for users.

This case was studied when the BiCR had been used for five years, in 2007–2008, and initiated by the managers at NW, who became concerned by a low usage of the repository. And indeed, a document analysis and the analysis of log data (in the period from July 2006 to July 2007) have shown that the repository has an average of 90 hits a month, corresponding to an average of about 1 hit per registered user per month. Furthermore, the content was regarded by the management as of moderate quality, not relevant, and insufficiently up-to-date (which was an opinion shared by the employees as is explained later). Best Practices were supplied only after people were forced by management, but on one instance on 2007 only 10% made a contribution. We agreed with the management to establish a sequential research design. First, aiming at getting an overall picture of usage, we applied structured interviews (June 2007). 169 users received an invitation, while 52 finally participated in interviews. The protocol for structured interviews included questions about relevance of BiCR for the NW Industrial Performance employees, perceived content quality, expectations, and possible improvements. After finalizing preliminary results of the structured interviews, open conversational interviews were conducted aiming at gaining detailed information on user perceptions concerning the usefulness and content characteristics of the repository. Moreover, inputs from the open interviews laid the basis for the re-design solutions. Users of the repository, members from the Product and Technology Center (PTC, which is the central laboratory for quality improvement in Nestle Waters), and people working at NW head office were interviewed to get more information on user perceptions and to collect ideas to improve the BiCR's use and supply.

### *Situation Analysis and Requirements*

The content of the BiCR we met when starting this study is divided into "Water Processes" and "Common Processes." The latter concerns processes applicable to other businesses in Nestlé and is shared with other BiCRs in Nestlé. The content of "Common Processes" is mainly supplied by supportive services (like the quality, environment, and engineering departments). "Water Processes" is divided into "Product Group" (PET, Glass, and HOD), "Overall Factory," and "Good Practices." The content of "Overall Factory" is applicable to all three product groups (PET, Glass, and HOD). The repository was built along the financial structure used in NW. Therefore, the content of "PET," "Glass," and "HOD" is divided by "Variable costs" and "Fixed Cost". Content concerning "Variable costs" is divided by the type of production process. For example, "PET" involved Blowing, Injection, and Filling & Packaging. These processes were further divided into sub-processes.

There is a standard format in which a BP should be supplied and stored in the BiCR. On top of the BP template a supplier fills in the "Area", "Category", "KPA" (Key Performance Area), and "Topi" concerned with the BP. The template further has the following fields: (1) "date" of content supply and "revision date", (2) "Benchmarks" for the Best Practice, a Data Summary, and the Rationale for Best in Class, (3) "Data Summary" presents the Best in Class data, (4) "Best Practices" consists of the drivers with their description, detail, and rationales, (5) "Prerequisites" with hyperlinks for Supporting Documents, (6) "Assessment Process" explains how an assessment of the BP is and should be made, (7) "Resource Network" presents the names and e-mail addresses of the supplier of the practice and other people with knowledge of this BP, and (8) "Improvement Projects" refers to projects done on this particular BP.

Analysis of the structured interviews revealed that users did not know what the BiCR was for. With respect to perceived ease of use, respondents stressed that in their view, BiCR had "Poor search functions", "Poor internet connection", and that it needed to "Add more examples of the BP's". Log data on use and available data on supply suggested low "intention to use" and "intention to supply", but the structured interviews showed opposite results: 72.5% of the users indicated that they were willing "to supply information to the BiCR". Only 2.0% of the interviewees gave negative answers, and 3.9% did not intend to use a BP.

Users' intentions to supply best practices were characterized by the following statements: (1) "We should exchange information to learn

*Table 5.7* Requirements for the Nestlé Waters Best-in-Class Repository Service

Content:

C1. Good level of content quality; C2 All useful information should be present in the repository (not only BP); C3 Match between what users need and actual content supplied after search; C4 Practices should be applicable in different contexts

Use:

Uv1 Information searched for should be easy to find; Uv2 The knowledge repository should be easily accessible; Uv3 Location of the repository should be known to users; Uv4 Consistency in content location; Uv5 Friendly user interface; Uv6 Information should be presented in an understandable template; Uv7 It should be easy for suppliers to supply a practice; Uv8 Users should be kept aware of the repository.

Revenue:

R1 Stimulate use by incentives; R2 Stimulate supply by incentives.

from each other", (2) "We should use a mandatory update after target setting projects", (3) "Provide training on how to supply information to the BiCR", (4) "It is difficult to say if our way of doing is a Best Practice or not", (5) "We do not have time to supply", (6) "BiCR is not suitable to our situation", and (7) "I never found anything useful in BiCR". Such statements show that users were indeed willing to work with the BiCR and submit best practices to the repository. However, they felt different barriers were disturbing their intentions: no special time allocated for the use of BiCR, or not enough training on the use of the repository, or finally, no clear policies on what should be regarded as "best practices". Interviewees stated that much useful knowledge is available in several factories, which probably does not qualify as best practice. Finding this knowledge is difficult and thus the BiCR should be extended by good practices as well. GPs are successful methods and examples that can be applied to increase efficiency and to develop a mindset for continuous improvement. GPs mostly concern softer, non-technical issues, which makes the practices more applicable to different contexts—for instance, "energy", "environment", "hygiene", "logistics", "maintenance", "management", "manufacturing", "purchasing", "quality", and "raw material". The new template for good practices is designed and presented here. The GPs were considered before by the IP department manager, because they recognized that useful knowledge was going around that did not qualify as a BP (for instance, on safety issues and workplace organization). She also recognized that it takes quite some time and effort to validate a BP and that lower-performing factories' practices often are still quite useful for others to share (although it mostly does not qualify as BP). A BP is also regarded as context-specific. What turns out to be a BP for one region may not be a BP in another region or factory, because of local issues like labor cost and legal differences.

### *Suggestions for Improvement*

Requirements for content, use-value, and revenue can be satisfied by socio-technical means, at two levels: the process design and the infrastructure design. The process design integrates the recognized processes in one coherent process model. Figure 5.11 gives an improved process design, i.e., including a submission and review process for good practices and more feedback and communication options.

To select appropriate design components for each requirement, interviews and brainstorms were held with owners of other BiCRs within Nestlé, repository users, IP management, and the IT department.

"Good level of content quality" (C1) is met by using a template that is understandable for users and by having all content reviewed for its

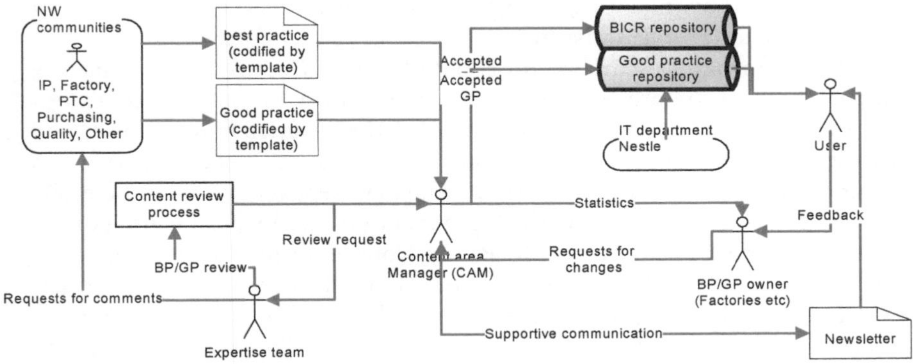


*Figure 5.11* The new Nestlé Waters information process structure.

relevance, usefulness, and up-to-dateness. A constant level of content quality is sustained by assigning responsibilities for content quality and consistency processes. Good practices (GP) were added to the BiCR and are divided in more general topics.

The submission template for good practices is given in Figure 5.12. On top of the template a supplier fills in the "Topi", "Title", "Factory" in which the practice is developed and "Ref", which refers to keywords or issues the practice involves. This helps the owner to store the GP in the right location in the BiCR and to add relevant keywords to the search function. The information in the template is divided into Why? (referring to the objective, rationale, and drivers), What? (referring to key success factors and results), How? (describing the implementation steps), and Who? (referring to prerequisites, necessary resources and tools, and supporting documents). Especially the description of implementation steps is put forward in the GP template. "All useful information should be present in the BiCR" (C2) is met by establishing links to information in other repositories (IT5), and by having all content reviewed for its relevance, usefulness, and up-to-dateness. Ensuring that all useful information is present in the repository is sustained by assigning responsibilities for the content quality and consistency processes. "The match between content needs and the content supplied (levels of conceptualization and representation) (C3)" is met by implementing a new repository structure (to be described later) and by using templates that are understandable for users. Direct links from other files to the concerned practice (IT3) also help in ensuring the right match. This requires assigning responsibilities for content quality and consistency processes. "Practices should be applicable in different contexts" (C4) is met by renovating the repository structure and adding the good practices, by using appropriate and understandable templates, and by including an expert list in the repository for consulting experts when needing assistance.

"The information searched for should be easy to find" (UV1) is met by implementing a comprehensible repository structure, by including an expert list in the repository, which can be used if the practice is not found, and by establishing direct links from other files to the concerned practice and to information in other repositories. "The NW repository should be easily accessible" is met by skipping the login for users and by establishing direct links from other places to the BiCR and from other files to the concerned practice. "Location of the NW repository should be known to users" (UV3) is met by establishing direct links from other places to the NW repository and from other files to the concerned practice. This requires assigning responsibilities for the promotion processes. "Consistency in content and content location" (UV4) is met by the new repository structure and the constant content review. "Friendly and easy to use interface" (UV5) is met by implementing a comprehensible repository structure, by having practices opened in a new window, instead of in the main repository window, and by assigning responsibilities and implementing processes for content quality and consistency. "Information should be represented in an understandable

| | GOOD PRACTICE DESCRIPTION | |
|---|---|---|
| | **Category/Topic:** | |
| | **Factory**: | **Contact**: |
| | **Ref.:** | **Date:** |
| | **Title:** | |
| | | |
| WHY | **Objective:** | |
| WHY | **Rationale / Drivers:** | |
| | **Key success factors/Results:** | |
| | | |
| HOW | **Description of implementation steps:** | |
| | | |
| WHO | **Prerequisites:** | |
| WHO | **Resources / Tools needed:** | |
| | **Supporting documents:** | |

*Figure 5.12* The Nestlé Waters good practice template.

template" (UV6) is met by using appropriate and understandable templates and assigning responsibilities for the content quality and consistency process. "It should be easy for suppliers to supply a practice" (UV7) is met by using easy-to-fill-in templates and providing instructions for suppliers. "Users should be kept aware of the existence of the NW repository" (UV8) is met by establishing direct links from other places to the BiCR and from other files to the concerned practice and by assigning responsibilities for promotion.

"Stimulate use by incentives" (R1) and "Stimulate supply by incentives" (R2) are met by assigning responsibilities for promotion and rewarding especially suppliers.

### *Implementation of Suggestions*

The new repository consists of two parts: "Best in Class Data" and "Nestlé Waters Repository." The first part contains operational details and specifications. The content is divided in "benchmark files" and "product specifications." Figure 5.13 also shows likely suppliers of different types of content, likely the PTC, who deliver new products specifications, people involved in benchmark projects, the procurement department, which also works with product specifications and related material costs, and the suppliers of NW who provide their product specifications. Likely suppliers for the technical and management issues in the NW repository are the factories themselves, who supply their GPs, and people from the IP department who apply GPs in factories. The GP template, with a detailed description of how to fill it in, can be found in the repository. This should make it easier for suppliers to fill in the template. A manual for suppliers is included in the repository, along with instructions on how to fill in the template. A list with contact data of experts and their area of expertise is included in the repository. Contact data of content area managers and the content area they are responsible for are also included in the repository.

The repository will have a prominent place on the IP intranet website. A desktop item to the repository is created on the desktops of all PCs and laptops. The repository newsletter, distributed twice a year, contains direct links to the repository. An introduction with hyperlinks to the repository will be included in the NW e-learning modules. These modules are used by new employees to gain better understanding about the water business and production processes. Links will be created in other repositories and tools used at NW as well. Hyperlinks to corresponding content in the repository are created in files that are often used (for instance, benchmark files and the repository for Safety, Health, and Environment and the Supply Chain repository). Users who find a gap with benchmark data can instantly go to the appropriate practices.

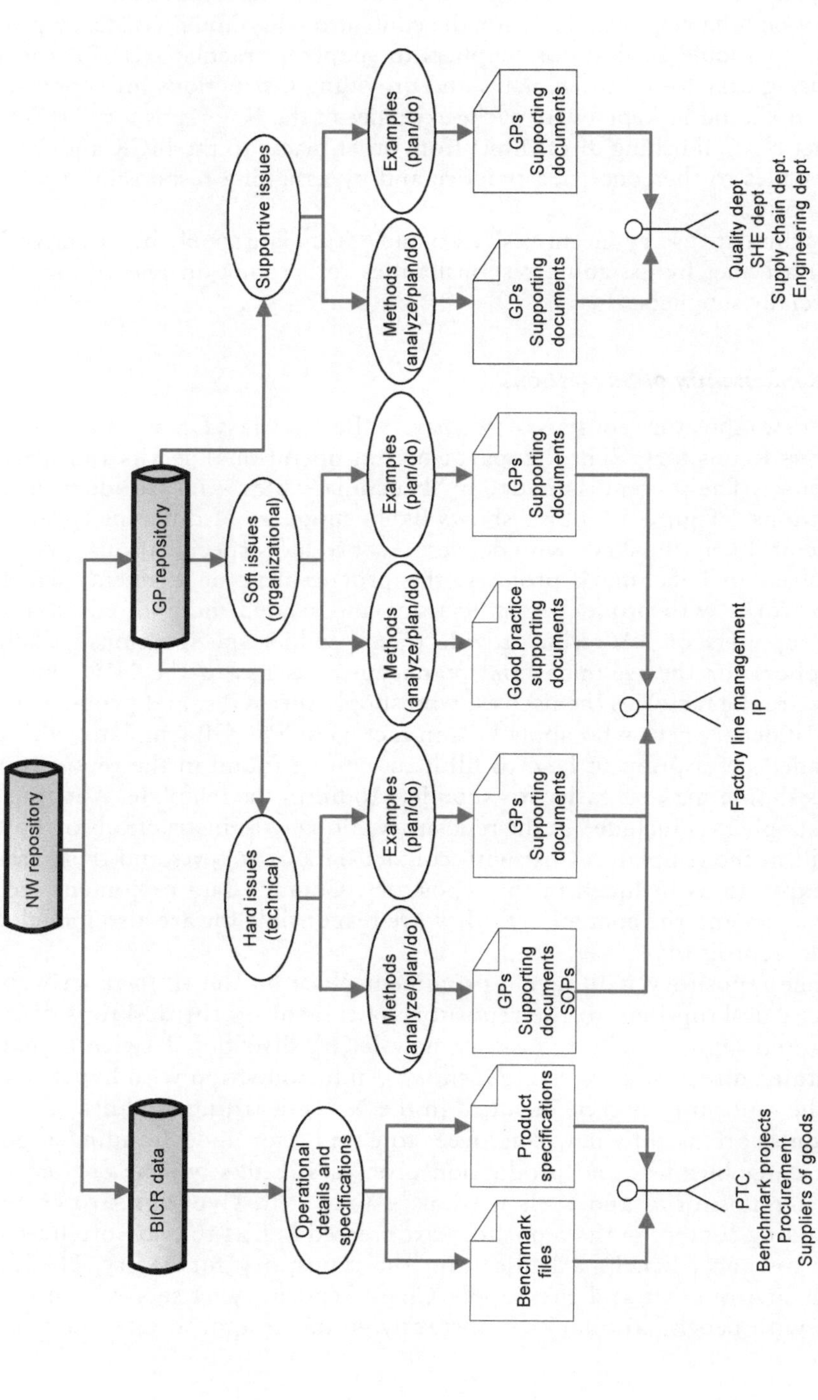


*Figure 5.13* Nestlé Waters's new content structure.

Users have the option of receiving automatically generated e-mails about topics of interest in the repository. These e-mails are sent after content on this topic has been reviewed or new content has been supplied. The e-mails contain direct links to the practices concerned.

To ensure the content in the repository is up-to-date, relevant, complete, and useful, all content in the NW repository was sent out to appropriate experts for review. Missing content was defined and supplied by experts and the IP department. Up until October 2007 about 200 new files were added to the content in the repository and all relevant and useful content from the NW repository (about 140 files) was uploaded in the NW repository. The repository now contains 530 files, with a total size of 300 Mb, and is still growing. The owner of the repository (a member of the IP department) can monitor levels of content quality by checking dates on documents and by communication with the content area managers (CAM) and users of the repository. Users have the option of providing feedback to the owner about all aspects involved with the repository.

The CAM is responsible for ensuring content quality and consistency for a specific content area. She or he is responsible for reviewing this content on a regular basis to ensure it is up-to-date, relevant, and consistent. The supplier sends the GP in the template and the CAM reviews and may approve the GP. He or she can ask for additional information and modifications from the supplier or others in the Nestlé Waters community. The CAM has the help of an expert team and is responsible for maintaining this team. The CAM stores supplied GPs in the repository ensuring consistency in the content and repository structure. The owner can monitor if the search function delivers the desired content and if he can easily find the content through the repository structure.

The repository owner, CAMs, expert teams, and the IP network have a responsibility concerning promotion. The owner is responsible for the newsletter. Furthermore he or she provides statistical information to users to promote the repository and content. So-called one-point lessons will be used in the newsletters, which tell success stories of applied practices. Statistics on most-viewed practices will be used to promote these practices. Furthermore practices recommended by IP will be promoted and made visible on the front page of the repository. The owner can monitor repository promotion by communicating with CAMs and the IP network. Log data can be used to assess whether promotion helps in increasing use and supply. The repository owner is responsible for tracking people who are considered for some kind of revenue—for instance, frequent suppliers and suppliers of frequently used practices. Suppliers will be informed when their practice has proven to be very useful or has been viewed frequently. One-point lessons will be used in the newsletters, which tell success stories of applied practices.

## 5.5 CREATING SERVICE ARCHITECTURES

The scope of information services design stretches from enterprise architecture to IT architecture. Within this scope, different enterprise architecture frameworks take on a different place, and have a different set of methods and techniques (see Lankhorst et al., 2009 for an overview). This section focuses on the ArchiMate method because this method covers both the technical and organizational means of an information service. The ArchiMate 1.0 release has also been accepted by the The Open Group as an enterprise modeling standard (see http://www.opengroup.org/archimate/doc/ts_archimate/).

Figure 5.14 shows the ArchiMate language framework. This framework identifies three design layers (Lankhorst et al., 2009):

- The business layer offers products and services to external customers, which are realized in the organization by business processes (performed by business actors or roles).
- The application layer supports the business layer with application services, which are realized by (software) application components.
- The technology layer offers infrastructural services (e.g., processing, storage, and communication services) needed to run applications, realized by computer and communication devices and system software.

Jonkers et al. (2004) distinguish the following domains within the three layers:

- The information domain holds all information that is relevant for the enterprise architecture from a business perspective.
- The product domain describes the products or services that are offered by an organization to its customers.
- The process domain describes the business functions and their process.
- The organization domain describes the actors and the roles they have in the business processes.
- The data domain describes what type of data can be automatically processed.
- The application domain describes the software applications that enable the business functions and processes.
- The technical infrastructure domain describes the technical hardware platforms and the communication they have with the supported applications.

The identified domains in the ArchiMate language framework are also abstracted to general domain concepts. The domains are categorized in three columns; the passive structure (information aspect), behavior (behavior aspect), and the active structure (structure aspect).

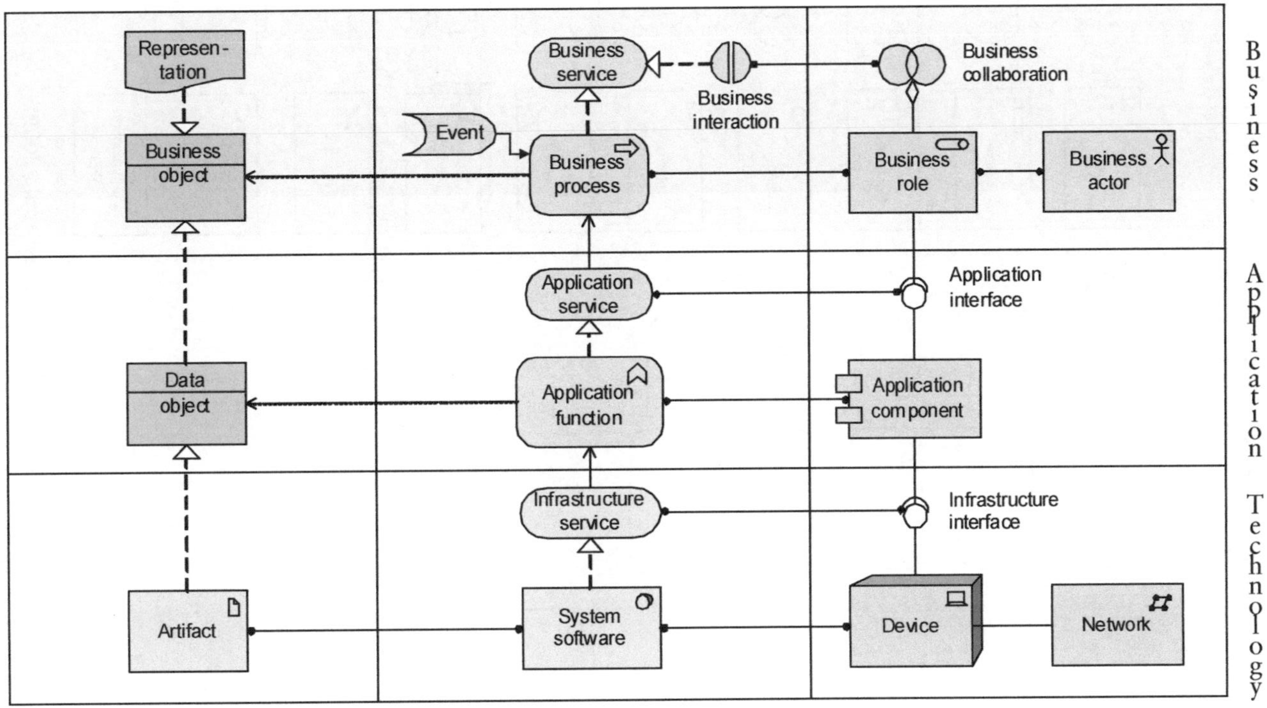


*Figure 5.14* ArchiMate language framework (Lankhorst et al., 2009: 91).

With these layers and domain-specific descriptions, a set of concepts has been made that forms the basis of the ArchiMate language. A detailed overview of the concepts is given in the ArchiMate quick reference (see Figure 5.15).

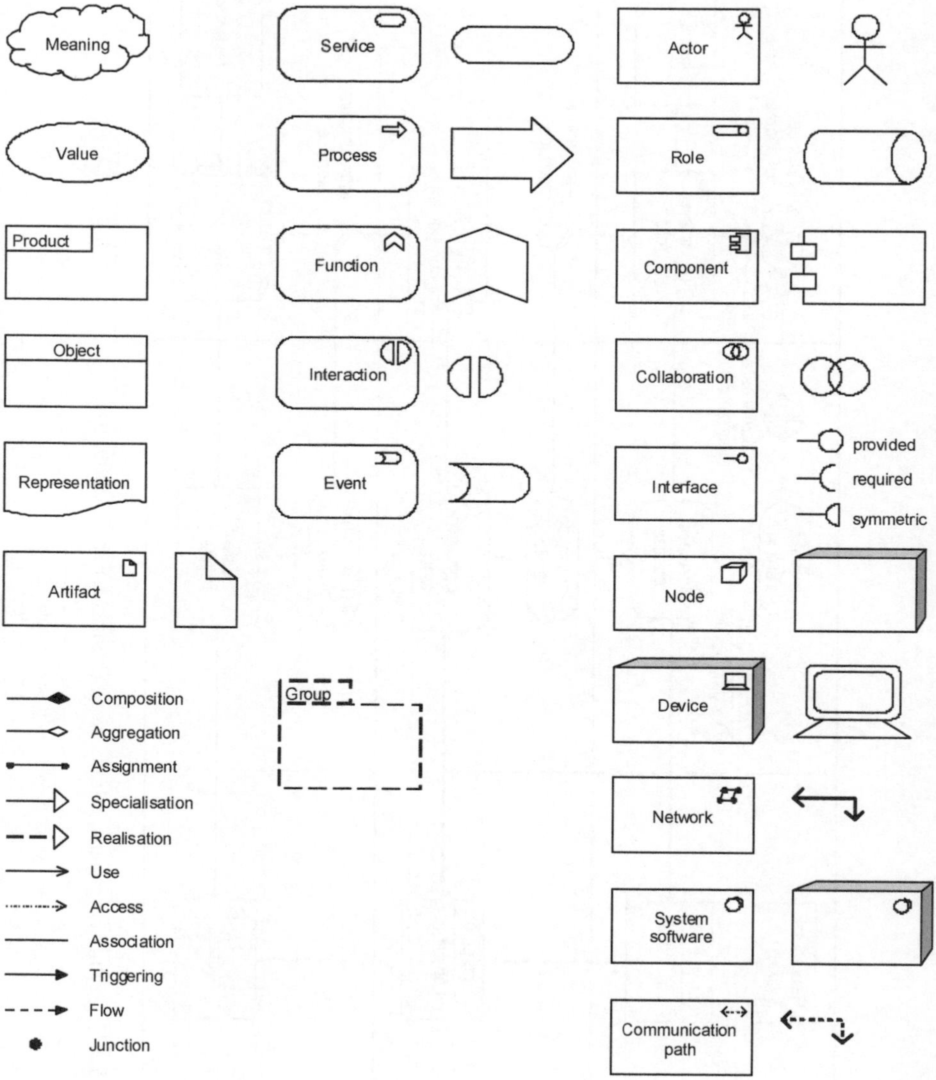


*Figure 5.15* The ArchiMate quick reference (Lankhorst et al., 2009)

*Note*: For the downloadable ArchiMate tool go to http://archi.cetis.ac.uk/download.html (accessed October 26, 2010).

ArchiMate has a top-down structure: on top the business layer, next the application layer, and finally the technology layer. On each layer, the concepts of a general enterprise architecture are depicted. Between the different concepts and layers, relationships are identified. This brings the advantage of being able to see, for example, which application components are linked to what processes or network nodes. For different stakeholders, different views can be identified that show only the relevant information. It can be seen that all components in the enterprise and IT architecture are related. This enables quick impact analyses of changes and migrations in IT integration projects. The concepts in the ArchiMate view are chosen on such a generic level that processes and IT components are visible and linked with the front-end of an organization, the customer and the products of the organization.

The strength of ArchiMate is to model the business, application, and infrastructure aspects of an information system. Because all these layers can be modeled in a single diagram, the diagram shows how the business and processes are supported by the applications and which infrastructure components are required for running the applications. The business aspects are modeled using actors, roles, and processes. The application is modeled by external application services and application components and services. The infrastructure is modeled using external infrastructure services and infrastructure components.

An example of an information service architecture modeled in ArchiMate has been made for the vtsPN case (which was introduced in section 5.3)—see Figure 5.16.

The top of the diagram includes the actors, the third layer is about the processes, the application components are modeled in the fifth layer, and the infrastructure components are modeled in the bottom layer.

## 5.6 CONCLUSIONS

### 5.6.1 Summarizing Conclusions

Chapter 2 described the following Leibnizian aspects of process-oriented theories: construction of causal models for explanation or prediction; testing of these models on logical consistency; and application of these models as means (causes) and goals (effects) relations in designs and architectures of services. We used the Leibnizian inquiring system to explain methods for designing the infrastructure of an information service. These methods and techniques are expected to deliver logically consistent analysis and design products on the basis of elementary kernel theories and business and process requirements. Two groups of methods and techniques were identified:

1. *Analysis* techniques, which describe and model business goals, service boundaries, business models, content models, service models, domain-level requirements, and critical quality requirements; together the analysis techniques describe the context in which an information service will operate and a specification of requirements for its means.

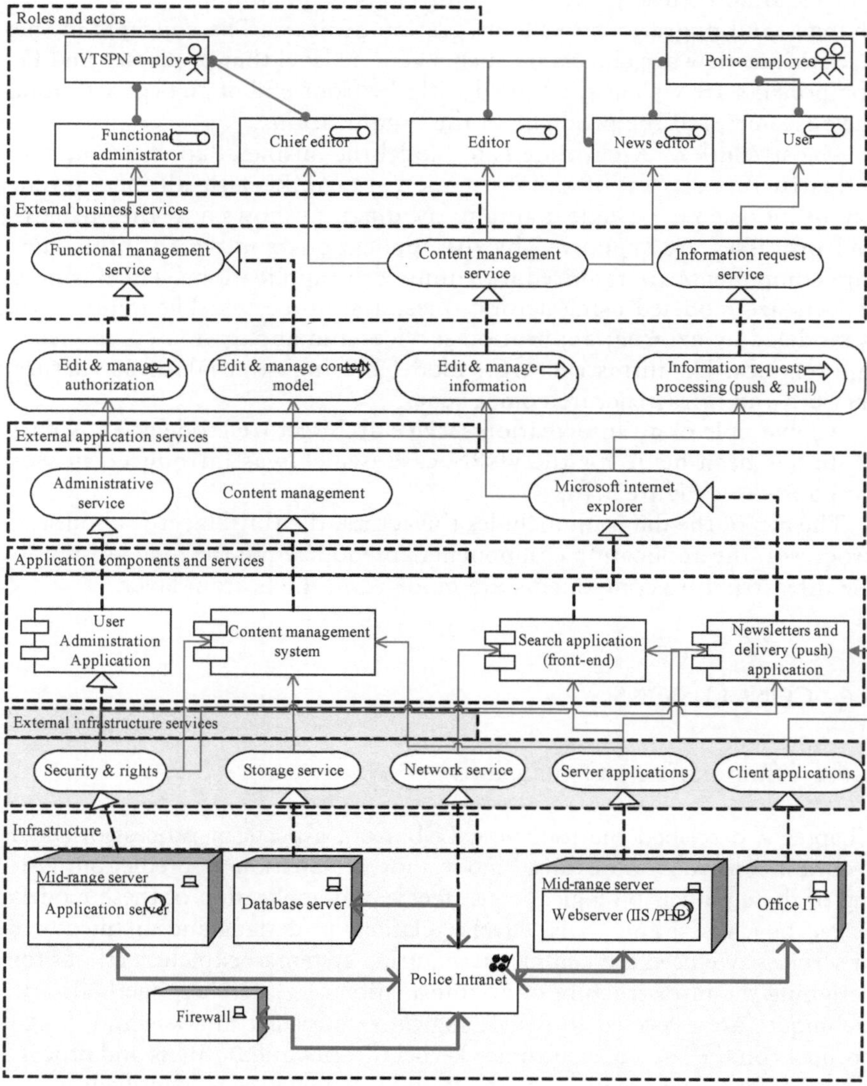


*Figure 5.16* vtsPN information service ArchiMate model.

2. *Design* techniques, which involve the selection of solution components per aspect, such as the application and IT-infrastructure components and organizational structure; for design the following techniques were suggested: data model diagram, navigational map, application objects—UML WAE—web application navigation map/navigational map with screen attributes, role-and-activity diagram and organization charts, and system architecture diagram. After this design effort, a critical step can be taken: the selection of means for the information service. These means can be grouped around the three aspects—content, use and revenue—and the human-organizational means were added for all these aspects. ArchiMate was proposed as a language to integrate these means in a Leibnizian goal-directed logical model.

### 5.6.2 Discussion

This chapter gave several differences between an information service and an Internet project. This distinction is suggested before as a distinction between websites and web-based systems projects (Kautz et al., 2007). A key difference is the importance of *content*. In contrast to many Internet projects, content acquisition, representation, and use in information services are more difficult than in web-based systems projects (like e-commerce projects). In the last, the most challenging aspect is not content but actual use and revenue. It also involves more design and organizational activities than what is suggested by the term "website development", and consequently, the term information service design seems to be more appropriate. We lack data for an empirical generalization over all types of information services. But, the recognition of this limitation points to several interesting potential differences with information service projects in other contexts. The exchange governance structure may result in substantial differences in the content, use, and revenue aspects.

### 5.6.3 Reflective Exercise

The challenge in designing is not the reading and seeing of the results, but the decision-making among alternatives. To get a feeling of the complexity here, consider the following two design assignments.

- A local newspaper is losing subscribers and advertisers and thinks about meeting these challenges by increasing the level of customization and personalization of the delivery of high-quality news via the Internet and e-readers. Consider what this implies for its business processes and make an analysis and design of innovative means needed. Finally, make an ArchiMate diagram of the new situation.
- A large globally operating trades firm wants to change its management reporting services by increasing the level of personalization of its

deliveries. It recognizes that this does not only involve new management reporting systems, but also requires other ways of information goods production and deliveries that are supported by computer and human explanation and discussion facilities. What are the implications for the set of means and the information service architecture?

- Compare both cases, and draw the implications of both contexts for how the project will have to be managed and equipped.

## 5.7 FURTHER READING

Bourhis, A., Dubé, L., & Jacob, R. (2005). The success of virtual communities of practice. The leadership factor. *Electronic Journal of Knowledge Management, 3*(1), 23–34.

Kim, J., Lee, J., Han, K., & Lee, M. (2002). Business as buildings: Metrics for the architectural quality of internet business. *Information Systems Research, 13*(3), 239–254.

Lankhorst, M. et al. (2009). *Enterprise architecture at work* (2nd ed.). Berlin: Springer.

Larsen, G., & Conallen, J. (2002). Engineering web-based systems with UML assets. *Annals of Software Engineering, 13*, 203–230.

Sowa, J., & Zachman, J. (1992). Extending and formalizing the framework for information systems architecture. *IBM Systems Journal, 31*(3), 590–616.

Vossen, G., & Hagemann, S. (2007). *Unleashing Web 2.0: From concepts to creativity.* Burlington, MA: Morgan Kaufmann.

# 6 Information Service Exploitation

## 6.1 THE LOCKEAN INQUIRING SYSTEM AND INFORMATION SERVICES EXPLOITATION

This chapter discusses the *empirical* (i.e., Lockean) aspects of information services. The empirical approach measures and analyzes data of an information service and its stakeholders and context. Such data are important for revenue collection (e.g., showing evidence for a bill) and for generating insights to improve the service. This chapter focuses on the latter, because improvement is the final step in design science. The type of data needed for improvement differs for the diverse levels of management decision-making. The empirical analysis can be done at the strategic level by measuring site-access, and influencing the audience to increase these numbers by "search engine optimization". At the operational level web analytics can be used to improve insights in the performance of certain parts of information services. Finally, we discuss user questionnaires as a means of finding improvement suggestions. Topics in this chapter are:

- Supplier-oriented performance indicators
- Search engine optimization (SEO) and web analytics
- User evaluation questionnaires

## 6.2 THE CONCEPT OF SERVICE EXPLOITATION

This chapter approaches service exploitation from a management control perspective, in which an information service manager collects data to be compared with the goals and objectives of the service (which should have been defined during business modeling). For this the manager can apply a black box and a white box model. In the black box model, the manager compares his or her objectives with data from the inflow and outflow. These data may be about how people can find the service and from where they enter the service, which is largely serviced by search engine optimization tools. The outflow data check the satisfaction of the users with the service, e.g., by user questionnaires. In the white box

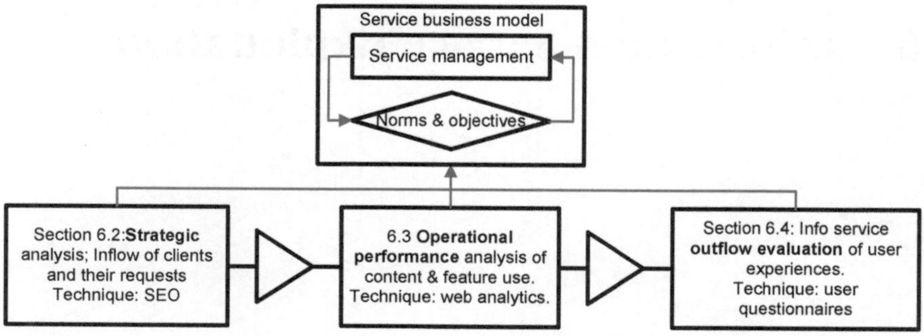


*Figure 6.1* A management control model for information services.

model, the manager checks data internal to the operation of the service with the objectives of the service. This can be done by tracing the user's path in the service by web analytics, and by a more in-depth analysis of the service's internal organization and operations. These methods are presented in Figure 6.1.

This chapter first continues with a strategic perspective by discussing measures of hits and visits to learn to better position an information service on the market. At the operational level web analytics are discussed for improving certain parts of the information services. There are several methodological and ethical issues related to web analytics that need attention as well. Finally, user questionnaires are discussed as a method for letting the experienced information consumer speak.

## 6.3 STRATEGIC INFORMATION SERVICE PERFORMANCE AND SEARCH ENGINE OPTIMIZATION[1]

### 6.3.1 Strategic Performance of an Information Service

Several performance indicators for information services and websites exist and a discussion of them reveals that the choice for only one of them results in a biased view. Additionally, the indicators are not always easy to interpret. Consequently, I list and discuss the most frequently mentioned ones here.

- *Hit*: A request for a file from the web server; the web server is the technical platform of the information service. The number of hits received by a website is frequently cited to assert its popularity, but this number can dramatically over-estimate popularity. A single web page typically consists of multiple (often dozens of) discrete files, each of which are counted as a hit as the page is downloaded, so the number of hits is more reflective of the complexity of individual pages on the website than the website's actual popularity. The total number of visitors or page views provides a more realistic and accurate assessment of popularity.

- *Page view*: A request for a file whose type is defined as a page in log analysis; in log analysis, a single page view may generate multiple hits as all the resources required to view the page (images, .js and .css files) are also requested from the web server.
- *Visit/session*: A series of requests from the same uniquely identified client; this client is the technical platform of the information service consumer. A visit or session is supposed to end after several minutes (especially for public parts of sites) of inactivity or after a log out (especially for private parts of sites). A visit is expected to contain multiple hits and page views.
- *First visit/first session*: A visit from a new visitor who has not made any previous visits
- *Visitor/unique visitor/unique user*: The uniquely identified client generating requests on the web server (so-called logs) or a page (identified by page tags) within a defined time period (i.e., day, week, or month); a unique visitor counts once within the timescale. A visitor can make multiple visits within such a timescale. The unique user is a single instance of the set of users of a site or service, independent of the number of visitors, identified by an IP address. Note, however, that organizational users mostly share an IP address, which makes unique identification of users difficult.
- *Repeat visitor*: A visitor that has made at least one previous visit. The period between the last and current visit is called visitor recency and can be measured in hours, days, or whatever other timescale applicable. The repeat visitor number is important because it partially excludes the visitors that "accidentally" accessed the site and preferred never to come back. The unique visitor/repeat visitor ratio may indicate how well the service attracts the target population and how much it convinces visitors to revisit and rebuy (if the site aims at selling something).
- *Percentage first visits*: This is the percentage of visits that have been made by new visitors within a certain timescale. If this percentage is very small this indicates a very loyal clientele, but it also may indicate lack of growth and a possible need for substantial innovation of the site. If this percentage is very large, it could indicate disappointment of first visitors, who seem not to come back again.
- *Impression*: An impression is each time that an advertisement loads on a user's screen. This indicates presence of a single visitor which is an important indicator for the value of advertising.

- *Singletons*: The number of visits where only a single page is viewed; the number of singletons is indicative of various forms of "click fraud" and is used to calculate bounce rate and in some cases identifies automatons ("bots").
- *Bounce rate*: The percentage of visits where the visitor enters and exits at the same page without visiting any other pages on the site in between; it also could indicate the low level of effectiveness of a home page to get visitors interested in the rest of the site's content, but only when the number of click frauds and bot activity can be identified in the total number of singletons.
- *% exit*: The percentage of users who exit from a page.
- *Visibility time*: The time a single page, blog, ad, or banner is viewed.
- *Session duration*: Average time that visitors spend on the site they visit; this metric is impractical because analytics programs cannot measure the length of the final page view, unless an explicit log out is implemented or a rather ad hoc number of passive minutes is taken as an end of a page view. Also, if a visitor comes back to the site within a short period of time, it may probably be measured as a continuation of the first session.
- *Page view duration*: Average time that visitors spend on each page of the site; as with session duration, this metric is complicated, but in commercial settings sometimes duration metrics are implemented for billing purposes.
- *Depth/page views per session*: Depth is the average number of page views that a visitor consumes before ending the session. This is calculated by dividing the total number of page views by the total number of sessions and is also called page views per session or PV/session. Although the number if pages viewed per session is highly dependent on the site's structure (there can be more or less content on one page or more pages being used for the same content), the fact that visitors explicitly move to multiple pages to know more of the site's topic indicates their level of interest in the topic and thus the level of depth they reached. When knowing some visitor information (e.g., IP address location of some key data from a filled-out form), the site may be able to customize the level of abstraction and representation (as mentioned in Chapter 3) for different target audiences.
- *Frequency/session per unique visitor*: Frequency measures how often visitors come to a website. It is calculated by dividing the total number of sessions (or visits) by the total number of unique visitors and thus gives an indication of a site's consumer loyalty.
- *Conversion*: Most information service managers want the highest performance on each (or at least one) of these criteria, because such performance indicators could indicate the value of the site and could predict conversion rates. Conversion rates are the percentage

of visits that end up in the private area of a site and get engaged in a legal transaction of some kind, like the placement of an order, a payment, submission of content, or subscription to some kind of service, or a click-through to another affiliated site as part of a click-through program.

### 6.3.2 Search Engine Optimization

To receive a high score on the previously mentioned criteria, the site needs to be well indexed. Search engine optimization (SEO) is the process of improving the volume and quality of traffic to a website via targeted keywords. Usually, the earlier a site is presented in the search engine results pages or the higher it "ranks", the more searchers will visit that site.

As a marketing strategy for increasing a site's relevance, SEO considers how search algorithms work and what people search for. SEO efforts may involve a site's coding, presentation, and structure, as well as fixing problems that could prevent search engine indexing programs from fully spidering a site. For example, pictures and video and audio material are hard to find directly because they are non-textual and thus will not correspond directly to a query statement. Annotating such material is therefore important to direct searchers to them.

The term "SEO" can also refer to "search engine optimizers", terms adopted by an industry of consultants who carry out optimization projects on behalf of clients, and by employees who perform SEO services in-house. Search engine optimizers may offer SEO as a stand-alone service or as a part of a broader marketing campaign. Because effective SEO may require changes to the HTML source code of a site, SEO tactics may be incorporated into website development and design projects. The term "search engine friendly" may be used to describe website designs, menus, content management systems, URLs, and shopping carts that are easy to optimize.

Webmasters and content providers began optimizing sites for search engines in the mid-1990s, as the first search engines were cataloging the early Web. Initially, all a webmaster needed to do was submit a page, or URL, to the various engines, which would send a spider to "crawl" that page, extract links to other pages from it, and return information found on the page to be indexed. The process involves a search engine spider downloading a page and storing it on the search engine's own server, where a second program, known as an indexer, extracts various information about the page, such as the words it contains and where these are located, as well as any weight for specific words and all links the page contains.

Site owners started to recognize the value of having their sites highly ranked and visible in search engine results. They also recognized that the higher their site ranking, the more people would click on the website. Early versions of search algorithms relied on webmaster-provided information such as the keyword metatag or index file. Metatags provided a guide to each page's content. But using metadata to index pages was found to be less than reliable because the webmaster's accounts of keywords in the metatag were often not truly relevant to the site's actual keywords. Inaccurate, incomplete, and inconsistent data in metatags caused pages to rank for irrelevant searches. Web content providers also manipulated a number of attributes within the HTML source of a page in an attempt to rank well in search engines (Brin & Page, 1998).

By relying so much on factors exclusively within a webmaster's control, early search engines suffered from abuse and ranking manipulation. To provide better results to their users, search engines had to adapt to ensure their results pages showed the most relevant search results, rather than unrelated pages stuffed with numerous keywords by unscrupulous webmasters. For this, search engine suppliers responded by developing more complex ranking algorithms that were more difficult for webmasters to manipulate.

As graduate students, Larry Page and Sergey Brin, the founders of Google, developed a search engine that relied on a mathematical algorithm to rate the prominence of web pages. The number calculated by the PageRank algorithm is a function of the quantity and strength of inbound links. PageRank estimates the likelihood that a given page will be reached by a web user who randomly surfs the Web, and follows links from one page to another. In effect, this means that some links are stronger than others, as a higher PageRank is more likely to be reached by the random surfer. Off-page factors (such as PageRank and hyperlink analysis) as well as on-page factors (such as keyword frequency, metatags, headings, links, and site structure) enable Google to avoid the kind of manipulation seen in search engines that considered only on-page factors for their rankings. Many sites focused on exchanging, buying, and selling links, often on a massive scale. Some of these schemes, or link farms, involved the creation of thousands of sites for the sole purpose of link spamming. In recent years major search engines have begun to rely more heavily on off-web factors such as the age, sex, location, and search history of people conducting searches in order to further refine results.

By 2007, search engines had incorporated a wide range of undisclosed factors in their ranking algorithms to reduce the impact of link manipulation. Google says it ranks sites using more than 200 different signals. The three leading search engines, Google, Yahoo, and Microsoft's Live Search, do not disclose the algorithms they use to rank pages. Notable SEOs have published their opinions in online forums and blogs (searchenginewatch.com; SEOmoz.org, 2007).

Google, Yahoo!, and Microsoft use crawlers to find pages for their algorithmic search results. Some search engines, notably Yahoo!, operate a paid submission service that guarantees crawling for either a set fee or cost per click. Such programs usually guarantee inclusion in the database, but do not guarantee specific rankings within the search results. Yahoo's paid inclusion program has drawn criticism from advertisers and competitors (searchenginewatch.com, 2007). Two major directories, the Yahoo Directory and the Open Directory Project, both require manual submission and human editorial review. Google offers Google Webmaster Tools, for which an XML Sitemap feed can be created and submitted for free to ensure that all pages are found, especially pages that are not discoverable by automatically following links.

Due to the high marketing value of targeted search results, there is potential for an adversarial relationship between search engines and SEOs. In 2005, an annual conference, AIRWeb (Adversarial Information Retrieval on the Web), was created to discuss and minimize the damaging effects of aggressive web content providers. One outcome was that SEO companies that employ overly aggressive techniques can get their client websites banned from the search results. Some search engines have also reached out to the SEO industry, and are frequent sponsors and guests at SEO conferences, chats, and seminars. In fact, with the advent of paid inclusion, some search engines now have a vested interest in the health of the optimization community. Major search engines provide information and guidelines to help with site optimization. Google has a Sitemaps program to help webmasters learn if Google is having any problems indexing their website and also provides data on Google traffic to the website. Yahoo! Site Explorer provides a way for webmasters to submit URLs, determine how many pages are in the Yahoo! index and view link information (Searchenginewatch.com, 2007).

Placement at or near the top of the rankings increases the number of searchers who will visit a site. However, more search engine referrals do not guarantee more sales. SEO is not necessarily an appropriate strategy for every website, and other Internet marketing strategies can be much more effective, depending on the site operator's goals. SEO may generate a return on investment; however, search engines are not paid for organic search traffic, their algorithms change, and there are no guarantees of continued referrals. Due to this lack of guarantees and certainty, a business that relies heavily on search engine traffic can suffer major losses if the search engines stop sending visitors. It is considered wise business practice for website operators to liberate themselves from dependence on search engine traffic. A top-ranked SEO blog, Seomoz.org, has reported that search marketers receive a very small share of their traffic from search engines. Instead, their main sources of traffic are links from other websites.

## 6.4 OPERATIONAL INFORMATION SERVICE PERFORMANCE AND WEB ANALYTICS

Web analytics is the study of online behavior in order to improve it. There are two categories: *off-site* and *on-site* web analytics.

Off-site web analytics refers to web measurement and analysis irrespective of whether you own or maintain a website. It includes the measurement of a website's *potential* audience, share of voice on the information market and the Internet (visibility), and comments on what is happening on the Internet as a whole.

On-site web analytics measure a visitor's journey once *on your website*. This includes its drivers and conversions—for example, which landing pages encourage people to make a purchase. On-site web analytics measure the performance of your website in a commercial context. This data is typically compared against key performance indicators, and used to improve a website or marketing campaign's audience response.

Many different vendors provide on-site web analytics software and services. There are two main technological approaches to collecting the data. The first method, *logfile analysis*, reads the logfiles in which the web server records all its transactions. The second method, *page tagging*, uses JavaScript on each page to notify a third-party server when a page is rendered by a web browser. Both collect data that can be processed to produce web traffic reports.

In the early 1990s, website statistics consisted primarily of counting the number of client requests (or *hits*) made to the web server. This was a reasonable method initially, since each website often consisted of a single HTML file. However, with the introduction of images in HTML, and websites that spanned multiple HTML files, this count became less useful. Two units of measurement were introduced in the mid-1990s to gauge more accurately the amount of human activity on web servers. These were *page views* and *visits* (or *sessions*). A *page view* is a request made to the web server for a page, as opposed to a graphic, while a *visit* is a sequence of requests from a uniquely identified client that expired after a certain amount of inactivity, usually 30 minutes. The page views and visits are still commonly displayed metrics, but are now considered rather unsophisticated measurements.

The emergence of search engine spiders and bots in the late 1990s, along with web proxies and dynamically assigned IP addresses for large companies and ISPs, made it more difficult to identify unique human visitors to a website. Log analyzers responded by tracking visits by cookies, and by ignoring requests from known spiders.

The extensive use of web caches also presented a problem for logfile analysis. If a person revisits a page, the second request will often be retrieved from the browser's cache, and so no request will be received by the web server. This means that the person's path through the site is lost. Caching can be defeated by configuring the web server, but this can result in degraded performance for the visitor to the website.

Concerns about the accuracy of logfile analysis in the presence of caching, and the desire to be able to perform web analytics, led to the development of page tagging or "web bugs".

In the mid-1990s, web counters were commonly seen—these were images included in a web page that showed the number of times the image had been requested, which was an estimate of the number of visits to that page. In the late 1990s this concept evolved to include a small, invisible image instead of a visible one, and, by using JavaScript, to pass along with the image request certain information about the page and the visitor. This information can then be processed remotely by a web analytics company to generate statistics. The web analytics service also manages the process of assigning a cookie to the user, which can uniquely identify them during their visit and in subsequent visits.

Logfile analysis is almost always performed in-house. Page tagging can be performed in-house, but it is more often provided as a third-party service. For logfile analysis you have to store and archive your own data, which often quickly grows very large. Although the cost of hardware to do this is minimal, the overhead for an IT department can be considerable. For example, if you run out of disk space your database will start overwriting and this can often be irreparable. For logfile analysis you need to maintain the software, including updates and security patches. Complex page tagging vendors charge a monthly fee based on volume i.e., number of page views per month collected. However, some vendors now offer page tagging solutions for free, like Google Analytics, Microsoft Analytics, and Yahoo IndexTools.

Integrating web analytics into the server is gaining popularity due to increases in computing power, parallel processing, and the need for real-time web analytics that are enriched with business context such as orders, products, and customers.

Google has a special program of services to help you analyze the operational nature of your service. See Figure 6.2.

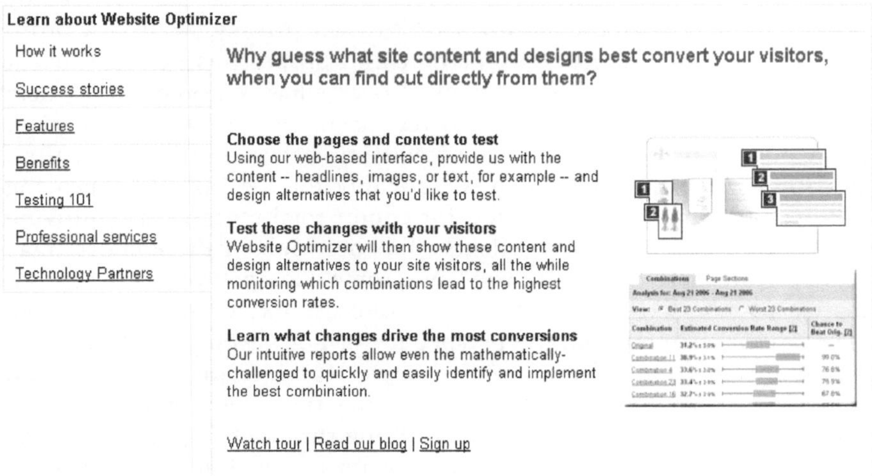


*Figure 6.2* Google's analytics page (Google Corporation, 2010, https://www.google.com).

Historically, vendors of page-tagging analytics solutions have used third-party cookies sent from the vendor's domain instead of the domain of the website being browsed. Third-party cookies can handle visitors who cross multiple unrelated domains within the company's site, since the cookie is always handled by the vendor's servers. However, third-party cookies in principle allow tracking an individual user across the sites of different companies, allowing the analytics vendor to collate the user's activity on sites where s/he provided personal information with activity on other sites where the user thought s/he was anonymous. Although web analytics companies deny doing this, other companies such as those supplying banner ads have done so. Privacy concerns about cookies have therefore led a noticeable minority of users to block or delete third-party cookies (for an instruction of why and how to do this see http://www.brighthub.com/computing/windows-platform/articles/7054.aspx; accessed September 28, 2010).

Most vendors of page-tagging solutions have now moved to provide at least the option of using first-party cookies (cookies assigned from the client subdomain). When web analytics depend on cookies to identify unique visitors, the statistics are dependent on a persistent cookie to hold a unique visitor ID. When users delete cookies, they usually delete both first- and third-party cookies. If this is done between interactions with the site, the user will appear as a first-time visitor at their next interaction point. Without a persistent and unique visitor ID, conversions, click-stream analysis, and other metrics dependent on the activities of a unique visitor over time cannot be accurate.

Many ethical issues exist with web analytics, which information services share with most databases. These issues have been summarized by Mason (1986) under the acronym PAPA, i.e., privacy, accuracy, property, and access. It is not only privacy and property issues that are at stake, but also people's loss of control over what is stored about them (access) and how they can get a correction in case of error (accuracy). The Google Corporation has been frequently accused of interfering too much into people's personal lives, probably for the sake of improving its understanding of its users and for commercial reasons of improving commercial messages for its clients. But the result of these efforts may be a "big brother is watching you" syndrome. Competitors in the search engine market, like Microsoft and its Internet Explorer, now promote their search engines from the perspective of not keeping and collecting private information. Alternatively, though, search engine services could easily give consumers information on what they know about individual clients (access) and tools for controlling this content (e.g., removing when needed; property). Some services want to give Internet consumers back control by a deletion tool like the "suicide machine" (see http://suidemachine.org/).

## 6.5 OUTFLOW ANALYSIS BY USER QUESTIONNAIRES

The literature on information systems quality has frequently discussed information systems' substantive and technical quality, especially with respects to their impact on use intension and user satisfaction. For a good overview of this literature, the reader is referred to Delone and McLean (2003). This discussion on information systems quality has appeared in the website and information service literature as well. The issue is especially acute, because many information services have non-compulsory use and the service owners are dependent for some level on the information service client's user satisfaction for revenues or conversion rates.

With respect to content quality, it is many times stated that content is more difficult to control and assess for services on the Internet than on regular information systems. Therefore, several rating mechanisms have been developed to score the content quality of information services, but the effectiveness of these rating mechanisms is largely dependent on the credibility of these ratings, which are often supposed to be influenced by the number of raters, the rater's expertise level, and collaborative filtering mechanisms (Poston & Speier, 2005).

With respect to technical quality and use-features, an over-abundance of use-features may easily result in perceived website complexity, when the user is not very familiar with the website. A perceived high complexity may result in low user satisfaction when people want to straightforwardly find answers to their questions. This may be less the case when they have more experiential use purposes (Nadkarni & Gupta, 2007) (see Figure 6.3).

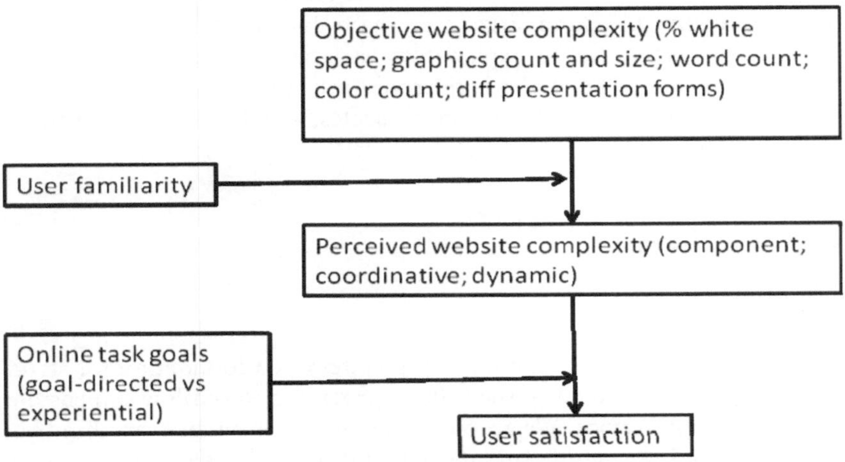


*Figure 6.3* Nadkarni and Gupta's propositions about the impact of website complexity on user satisfaction

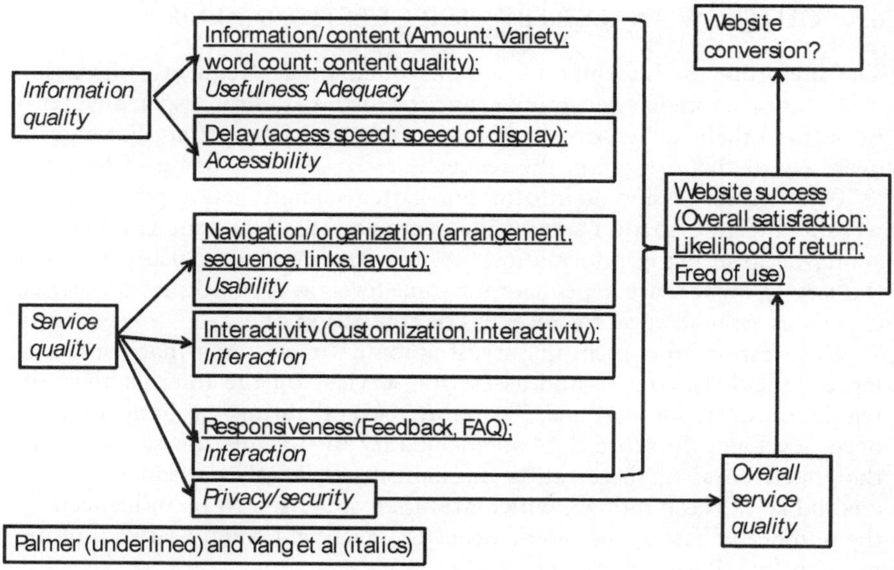


*Figure 6.4* A summary of user questionnaire indicators for information service quality.

*Note*: Underlined constructs refer to Palmer's scales; italics refer to Yang et al.

Summarizing the discussion on website and information service quality, Palmer (2002) and Yang et al. (2004) have developed and validated several measures to assess content and information service quality by user questionnaires. Figure 6.4 summarizes the main constructs that Palmer and Yang et al. have identified as explanatory variables for website success and website conversion . The reader is referred to the original papers of Palmer and Yang et al. for finding details on the scales, which Palmer and Yang et al. have validated.

## 6.6 CONCLUSION

### 6.6.1 Summarizing Conclusions

This chapter used the Lockean inquiring system as a foundation for structured exploitation via data of the inflow, process, and outflow dimensions of an information service. We absolutely do not believe that everything has been said about information service exploitation in this chapter and therefore have referred to Internet resources, which give sometimes excellent up-to-date and practical insights.

### 6.6.2 Discussion

After writing this chapter, I recognize that the empirical dimension has only been used as part of exploitation. The empirical dimension, though, also should have a role in the process of developing business ideas and validating these ideas. This approach is also important for the validation of designs and process models. It is my experience, however, that designers are much more Leibnizian thinkers than Lockean thinkers, i.e., they aim at nice, rational systems, without knowing if they can really work in practice. Market research and empirical testing of designs should fill in this gap, but they are often regarded as expensive and time-consuming. This may be true to some extent, but there is need for some careful empirical inputs in the early phases of service development as well. The opportunities of information services in collecting all kinds of data and analyzing them may allow for more empirical insights as part of the earlier design stages of an information service. The design science literature, however, is making much progress in constructively using empirical evidence (of any kind, not just figures or statistics) in developing new artifacts and learning about reality via these development projects (see Hevner & Chatterjee, 2008).

### 6.6.3 Reflective Exercise

We have found that Google analytics and other log file analysis tools are useful but treacherous. Make an analysis of the following:

1. Professor Marks from the Faculty of Economics was informed by public relations officials that his web page in the last month had more hits than the rest of the pages of the whole faculty. Make a systematic analysis so that Professor Marks has a realistic view of what this message could mean.
2. The New Technology University (which is just an imaginary name) has started to use Google Scholar to find indicators of the performance of its faculty. What data does Google Scholar provide? What are the pros and cons of such an effort and are there any alternatives?
3. Car dealer Johnson wants to use his website to increase the number of conversions. What would you advise him to do? What do you not recommend?

## 6.7 FURTHER READING

Clifton, B. (2010). *Advanced web metrics with Google analytics* (2nd ed.). Indianapolis, IN: Wiley.

Nadkarni, S., & Gupta, R. (2007). A task-based model of perceived website complexity. *Management Information Systems Quarterly, 31*(3), 501–524.

Palmer, J. (2002). Web site usability, design, and performance metrics. *Information Systems Research, 13*(2), 151–167.
Poston, R., & Speier, C. (2005). Effective use of knowledge management systems: a process model of content ratings and credibility indicators. *Management Information Systems Quarterly, 29*(2), 221–244.
Yang, Z., Cai, S., Zhou, Z., & Zhou, N. (2005). Development and validation of an instrument to measure user perceived service quality of information presenting Web portals. *Information & Management, 42*, 575–589.

# 7 Information Service Integrative Problem-Solving Cases

## 7.1 THE SINGERIAN INQUIRING SYSTEM AND THE DESIGN SCIENCE APPROACH TO INFORMATION SERVICES

This book started with the introduction of three aspects (content, use-value, and revenue) and five layers (problem definition, business modeling, process modeling, architecture design, and exploitation) as a framework for the design and exploitation of information services. Information services can have many shapes depending on their context (market, hierarchies, and networks) and content (more or less abstract and more or less complete or codified).

Chapters 3–6 have each discussed items per design layer, but no holistic and integrated account of designing information services has been given yet. This is unsatisfactory from a pragmatic (Singerian) and design science perspective, which both aim at solving real problems from problem understanding till the assessment of the progress that has been achieved both in everyday life and in science. Consequently, the next sections discuss information services design and exploitation as real-life problem-solving through cases. Of course, the cases given are *examples*, and no full overview of all the possible types of information service design and exploitation studies can be given here. Each case also has some more focus on certain aspects or layers, but together they do give a complete description. The cases may be particularly instructive, because they are the end result of a short 140-hour course for master's students at a business and IT university program. Most important, the cases cover the different contexts (market, network, and hierarchy) of information services. A discussion of the pragmatic perspective, however, is not complete without a description of possible future research work, which completes this chapter and book.

## 7.2 THE CASE OF GBA[1]

### 7.2.1 Introduction

The GBA service is a nation-wide citizen administration service used in the Netherlands to create, read, update, and delete citizen data. It is an acronym for "Gemeentelijke Basis Administratie", which can be translated as basic citizen administration. In 2001, modernization of the service was proposed by the national government as part of the development towards new and modern e-government services.

GBA centralizes registrations by municipalities via one central service as an aggregator and integrator of information from different (local) sources. This brings us to the main question: *How does the centralized GBA perform as an information service?* To answer this question the following subquestions related to information service development are raised:

- What problem does the GBA project solve?
- What is a valid business model for GBA?
- What is an effective process model for GBA?
- What infrastructure does the GBA need?
- How should the GBA exploitation be set up?

### 7.2.2 Problem Definition

Before the introduction of the GBA service, each municipality used its own service. With over 400 different municipalities in the Netherlands one can imagine that this caused a lot of difficulties. For example, the exchange of citizen data in the case of a person moving to another town was done manually. Besides the municipalities, there are more parties that need citizen data, in several forms. All those external parties also use their own service with their own data. Obviously, because of this decentralization, data exchange is very labor-intensive.

We thus assume that the overall problem is inefficient use of governmental resources. This is a very broad and non-specific description of the problem, but if we trace back in the causal chain, we eventually land at "different information needs" as the main cause of the problem. Because each stakeholder uses its own service, decentralized storage and low integration are the result. The GBA project committee identified over ten parties that are affected by the project. With the help of Spoelman et al., (2008) we identify the following stakeholders:

- *Municipalities of the Netherlands*: This is where citizen data comes from. When a citizen registers as an inhabitant of a municipality, it is the responsibility of the municipality to update the GBA.
- *National government*: The national government strives for smoothly functioning government processes. The GBA project is expected to greatly contribute to this. Also, municipalities receive a lot of funding from the government so it is important that this funding is used well.
- *Governmental organizations*: Here, several governmental service delivering agencies can be recognized, like the tax offices, IB-Groep

(office that handles student grants), the SVB (provider of social assistance and welfare), and personal ID card providers.

Municipalities need the most detailed data; besides obtaining information, municipalities are the most important suppliers of the information. Governmental organizations need to be able to execute queries in order to gain the right information for delivering the right kinds of services (e.g., providing study allowances). The national government is interested in management information: statistics about citizens, moving numbers, demographics, and other reports. The GBA stores information and, for each information need, specified modules are developed. The service support role, the "OverheidsServiceBus" (OSB),[2] provides the infrastructure on which the service is built.

### 7.2.3 Business Modeling

The GBA project had several goals, which together constitute its value proposition. Initially these goals were specified by a government advice committee (Adviescommissie, 2010):

- GBA should have a central role in the identity structure of citizens.
- Improved speed and accessibility of data
- 24/7 online access
- More flexibility and lower costs for changes to the system
- Improved data quality and reduced complexity
- Improved market mechanisms for ICT packages for municipalities

The following goals were later added:

- Real-time access
- Location-independent operation
- Use of shared service centers
- Explicit utilization of OSB e-governance standards

The GBA project strived to migrate from a spaghetti-like structure to a structure with centralized storage. In the "as-is" situation every stakeholder directly communicates with the stakeholder who owns the needed information. In the to-be situation, every stakeholder retrieves the needed information from a centralized repository, if necessary through a specified module. This centralization process has a huge impact on the actor web, also called the Baligh-Richartz effect (Rose, 1999), by reducing search and transaction costs substantially.

All municipalities enter their data in a central system, which makes it easily available to external parties for reuse. Of course, communication policies and priorities have to be set so that each stakeholder uses the service ethically.

Municipalities are mainly responsible for supplying and requesting citizen data. Other parties profit from the service because they can reuse the data for other purposes. The municipalities must be aware of the importance of their content delivery processes in the integrated system, while the content consumers need to be made aware that their content acquisition processes depend on an integrated system. There is mutual process dependency between the different parties in the information service's network and consequently processes must be tuned to one another.

Chapter 3 discussed four domains of an information service's value architecture: service, technology, organization, and finance. Each domain specifies the service as follows:

- The GBA service offers centralized services to create, read, and update citizen data. All stakeholders benefit from the system, but the municipalities are the target group of the GBA in the first place. Value is created by dramatically increasing the efficiency of the citizen data manipulation process, thus reducing costs and decreasing overhead.
- The OSB is the messenger infrastructure of the service. It enables efficient transportation and delivering of all data. The OSB is based on well-known standards (XML, WSDL, and SOAP) to ensure reliable message and data transfer.
- With the new, centralized GBA, stakeholders do not need to communicate that intensively anymore. They can access and manipulate the needed data independently from each other. Only in the beginning, when filling the new centralized GBA, stakeholders need to closely cooperate to ensure that the data in the GBA is correct, complete, and reliable.
- The finance domain is rather unique in this case. Because the GBA is used for government purposes, development of the service is funded by the national government. Therefore, no commercial prices are used. The project needs an initial investment, which will be earned back by the value creation and cost reduction characteristics of the GBA.

An e3value model (as described in Chapter 3) aims at modeling required value transfers between the stakeholders (Gordijn & Akkermans, 2004). Figure 7.1 shows the e3value business model for the GBA.

The GBA service is placed centrally as the core of the model. According to e3value, the system needs a sponsor—in this case, the national government. The value for the government is that the whole GBA provides more efficient use of governmental resources—optimal tax processes and less search and transaction costs because of integrated systems. Furthermore, they can retrieve management information from the GBA if needed. The Overheids-ServiceBus (OSB) is the infrastructure provider in the business model. The OSB provides the technical platform on which the system is built.

*Figure 7.1* e3value business model for GBA.

*Note*: BPR is an acronym for *Basisadministratie Persoonsgegevens en Reisdocumenten*, (Basic citizen registration and travel documents), which is the national office that is responsible for the GBA.

A business model is valid if the expected resulting profit of each business actor is (1) higher than zero, and (2) higher compared to the expected profit when remaining with the current business model (see Chapter 3). So in order to validate the business model, we have to evaluate the expected profit concerning the two proposed conditions.

In the business case "Modernization of the GBA" (Spoelman et al., 2008), the research team describes the main revenue of the system as *efficiency profits*. They underline this statement by giving an example about time savings in registering, copying, and archiving. These time savings are measurable in FTEs (full-time equivalent) and savings can be calculated. These FTEs then can be used to work on other things, which indirectly return profit.

Analogous to this method, "profits" in the other involved areas can be explained. The GBA project introduces lots of benefits that are summed up as follows:

- *National government*: Less maintenance; a more comprehensive design of the service; phase out current infrastructure; use of e-government standards
- *Municipalities*: Less maintenance; improved service provision; improved fraud protection; improved image towards citizens; trustful government; location-independent working; cost savings on system integration; cost savings because of specialized modules; lower trainee costs

- *Other governmental organizations*: Less query processing time; easier selections; less maintenance; improved service provision; improved fraud protection; trustful government

### 7.2.4 Process Modeling

Information services have three process purposes: content delivery, use-feature facilitation, and revenue collection. For these three purposes we identify the main process requirements and the processes interlinking the activities of the actors. For the GBA information service the ordering and delivering process of content should be content transformation. For different customers of the service (e.g., tax office, IB-Groep[3]), different versions of original information goods need to be offered. For example, municipalities need the full original data resources, while IB-Groep needs only address information and does not need information on marital status. Account creation, subscribing, and customer relationship management (CRM) are all important for content delivery.

For the GBA service format variation is an important requirement, since there need to be some standard reports with customized formats, but also opportunities for analyzing data by data mining tools to generate management information for the national government. Operational use is important since many organizations using the information from the GBA will require different methods of accessing the data. Wrappers need to be created to make the information service accessible from legacy systems of the consumers.

For the GBA service, meta-information may be delivered consisting of the right to use or the right to change form and structure. Depending on the user who retrieves the information, these rights may vary. Semantic-web and ontologies help to standardize and integrate data from different sources in one database.

For this case, the *value network process* type is the best fitting option to model the activities and processes of the GBA project. Firms that can be modeled as value networks rely on a mediating technology (Thompson, 1967) to link clients and customers who are interdependent. The mediating technology facilitates exchange relationships among customers distributed in time and space. Primary activity categories of these firms consist of network promotion and contract management, service provisioning and infrastructure operations. These are concurrent activities across primary activity categories. The value network process diagram for GBA is shown in Figure 7.2.

We did, however, use a slightly different notation than the notation for process models as prescribed by the e3value modeling technique of Chapter 4. Instead of showing all the value exchanges between processes of actors—which would lead to an unreadable chaos of crossing lines—we show only between which actors value is exchanged and add processes in the actor

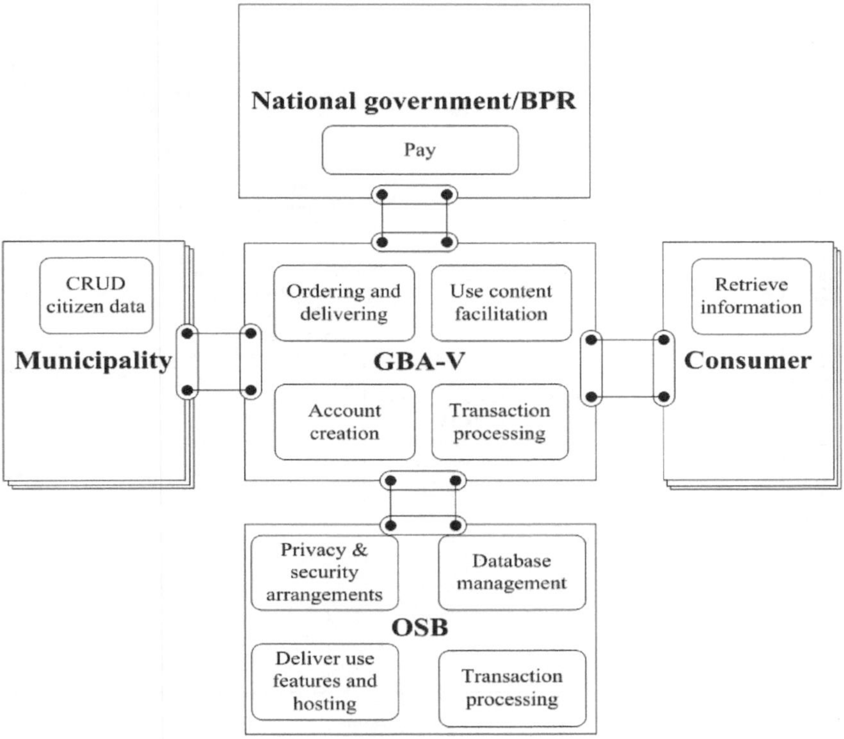


*Figure 7.2* GBA network process model.

objects. Note that in the new situation municipalities remain responsible for their own infrastructure, but they have to connect to the central GBA information service.

### 7.2.5 Infrastructure and Architecture Design

Layne and Lee (2001) identify different stages of e-government development and propose a "stages of growth" model for fully functional e-government. The model is depicted in Figure 7.3 and the stages outline the multi-perspective transformation within government structures and functions as they make transitions to e-government through each stage.

The GBA case illustrates the transition from the Transaction stage to the Vertical Integration stage. In the Transaction stage the government has databases supporting online transactions, whereas in the Vertical Integration stage local services are linked to higher-level services. In stage three, communication and integration-oriented technologies

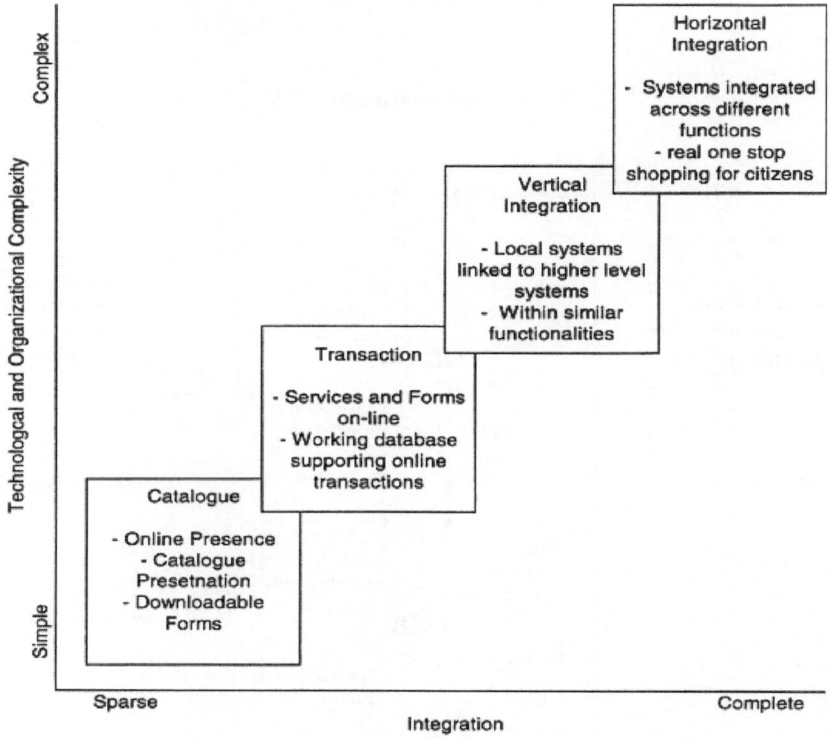


*Figure 7.3* Dimensions and stages of e-government development (Layne & Lee, 2001: 124).

*Note*: Reprinted with permission from Elsevier.

become more important. In the remote connection and virtual transactions, several technological issues emerge, like signal authentication, format compatibility of electronic data interchange, and exposure level of internal legacy systems to the outside. Even though stage three may provide improved efficiencies, privacy and confidentiality issues must first be considered.

We used ArchiMate to design the architecture of the GBA service. ArchiMate models a service in different layers. The architecture is shown in Figure 7.4. We can see in the ArchiMate diagram that the municipalities can update data and retrieve data. The information consumers consist of, among others, the government and tax organizations. The national government is also included in the diagram as the sponsor and by its influence on the knowledge model of the service, by which it can influence how data are stored.

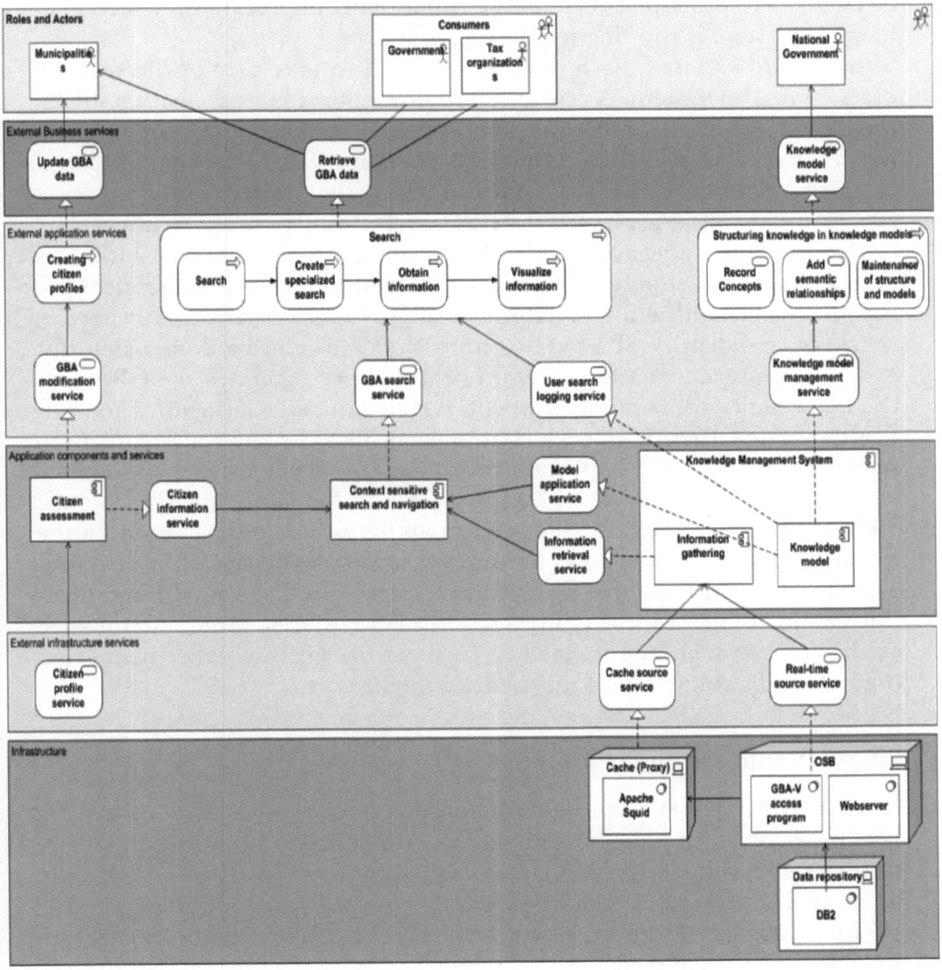


*Figure 7.4* ArchiMate diagram for GBA.

In the external business services layer we see the services the systems offer. These are services for updating data, retrieving data, and changing the system. These services are further implemented in the external application services layer. In the application components and services layer the services are again linked to deeper functions of the system. It is this layer where the knowledge model runs and where is defined in which format all data are stored. This system is running on the external infrastructure services layer. For the infrastructure we identify the existing OSB. This is running on a DB2 database server and Apache Squid. These platforms can be changed to other platforms and it is not really important on which platform the system is running for the layers above.

In the old situation each municipality had to take care of the security of its own GBA system. A central office now coordinates security policies, but the disadvantage is that the central system will become more interesting for hackers and more people are accessing the same system. There are several technical security issues to which the service should be resistant. Among these are issues like SQL-injection, buffer overflows, and DOS-attacks (Kanneganti & Chodavarapu, 2008). The security foundation of the system should consist of three key mechanisms: authentication, authorization, and audit (Ghafoor et al., 2001). Authentication implies checking the identity of a user or an entity. This can be done using, for example, a username and password or a security token. In the GBA case there is a multi-domain environment, which can make authentication difficult, because each user organization may have its own authentication policies. Therefore it is important that a meta-policy is created with which all policies of organizations have to comply. If the authentication is done and the user is verified, the service can apply access control based on the authorizations of a user to determine which actions a user can perform. This access control is done by a central system. Each connected organization can introduce a security breach in the system, so in large systems such as the GBA system audits have to be done to check whether connected organizations comply with the security requirements.

### 7.2.6 Exploitation

For the GBA there is no profit based on the number of accesses or queries on the service. For maintenance purposes it can be interesting to collect statistics about the usage, but it does not make sense to try to increase the usage of the service. The most important value is the continuous availability of the service and the up-to-dateness of its data. For access to the service, no fee is charged.

## 7.3 WIKIPEDIA AS AN INFORMATION SERVICE[4]

### 7.3.1 Introduction

A wiki is a virtual workspace that allows members to create, edit, organize, structure, link, and read web pages that contain content considered to be useful. All wiki functions are accessible through a web browser. Wagner defines a wiki as a set of linked web pages, created through incremental development by a group of collaborating users, and the software used to manage the web pages (Wagner, 2004). The term wiki is an abbreviation from the Hawaiian WikiWiki, meaning fast, which refers to the speed by which content can be created, searched, and edited (Wagner, 2004).

Wikipedia (www.wikipedia.org) is an online encyclopedia in which the articles are created and edited by volunteers. These volunteers can be everyone who feels that he or she can contribute to the encyclopedia. Wikipedia was launched in January 2001 and since that date the number of articles has grown to about 14.4 million in October 2009 (For more up-to-date statistics go to www.WikiMedia.org). In 2010, Wikipedia was rated sixth of the top 500 of popular sites on the web by the website www.alex.com. To maintain the required level of information quality, Wikipedia is monitored by readers and dedicated moderators.

O'Leary (2008) states that wikis satisfy four key knowledge management needs:

- Capturing knowledge from those who have it (contributors share personal knowledge)
- Converting knowledge into an explicitly available format (wiki markup language)
- Connecting those who want knowledge with those who have it (contributors and consumer matching)
- Linking knowledge to knowledge (by using hyperlinks in the text to other articles)

## 7.3.2 Kernel Theory and Problem Statement

We think Wikipedia is a value-adding intermediary between suppliers and consumers of Internet information, and, more precisely, a tool for knowledge sharing. Since wikis are openly editable, widely spread, and used as a data source for many, the possible lack of quality is a serious issue. Users may often trust the information they find but they do not really know if the information on the wiki page is correct. This subsection will focus on the problem of assessing the quality of a wiki, and how this quality can be maintained despite open editing. In the first subsection, we describe the business architecture, the business model, and the factors that encourage the users to participate in Wikipedia pages with different intensions. The second subsection describes the process model of Wikipedia, including possibilities of quality management. The third subsection describes the service architecture of Wikipedia and in the fourth subsection we describe the service construction principles. In the fifth subsection we describe the information service exploitation and our findings. Finally a conclusion is presented, which gives more insight into the problem and future work.

### 7.3.3 Business Modeling

We used the four generic value architecture components defined by Bouwman et al. (2008) to describe the business architecture of Wikipedia. The components of the business architecture are the service concept, the technological concept, the organizational concept, and the financial arrangements that create value for clients and revenue for providers.

The service concept answers the question of what wiki users can do with the information good or service offered, and includes the value proposition, which answers the question of why somebody should use it. For Wikipedia, value is created by adding and linking content across multiple pages. By adding content, the value of the existing content improves. This means that people would not only want content to inform others but also explicitly ask others to provide the knowledge they need for free, which is thus as much beneficial for the information consumer as the information supplier. There is no altruism here.

The technological architecture of Wikipedia consists of web pages with specific content distributed via a web server. The contribution of content is decentralized; it can be edited by anyone from anywhere at any time. Content retrieval is done through the central website.

The organizational arrangements of a wiki rely on a community of contributors. The wiki therefore has a strong user focus. The audience has the role of both contributor and user and therefore cooperates to gather knowledge.

The financial arrangements component of Wikipedia relies fully on donations; there seem to be no other cash inflows because Wikipedia is free to use and there are no advertisements.

The main goal of a business model is to answer the question, "Who is offering what to whom and expects what in return?" (Akkermans et al., 2004). Therefore, Chapter 3 states that the central notions in any business model should be value and revenue, in order to explain the creation and additions of value in a multi-party stakeholder network, as well as the exchange of value between stakeholders. We use the e3value modeling technique to conceptually represent stakeholders and their value and revenue activities. Figure 7.5 shows the value model of Wikipedia, detailing the value of the exchanged value objects.

Groupware systems such as wikis are great tools in a knowledge sharing process. All those involved in knowledge sharing can benefit from an effective sharing process. People gather their knowledge on various subjects through experience, studies, and from mistakes. When that knowledge is shared (e.g., by creating an article about it on Wikipedia), it will become easier for others to get the information faster. At the moment of writing, Wikipedia has about 1,000,000 unique voluntary contributors per year. But why should contributors share

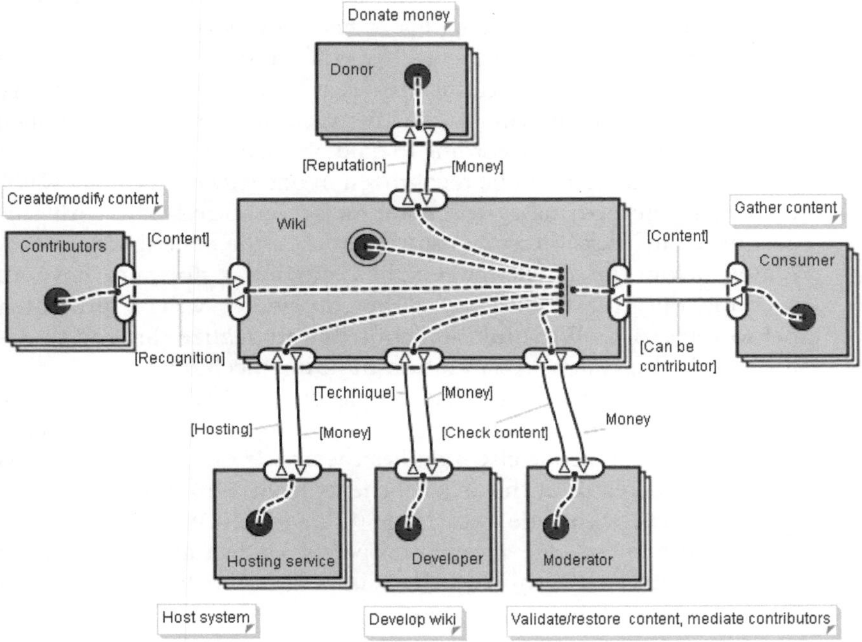


*Figure 7.5* e3value model of Wikipedia.

their knowledge with Wikipedia and what is their revenue? We will describe some of the most important reasons here.

1. Developing the appropriate technology for information interchange is vital for the improvement of communication and knowledge sharing. The technology needs to have the right span of use-features and needs to be flexible enough to support the evolving needs for knowledge creation in various forms. This technology is encouraging consumers to add or modify content without going through a barrier, such as creating an account. With this ease of editing, consumers are driven to correct little typos or grammar mistakes or create/modify articles with their knowledge, making them contributors too. The only thing contributors need for sharing their knowledge is a well working web browser where they can access the wiki via a URL, like http://www.wikipedia.org/ (Wei et al., 2005). Its availability and ease of use from any location can turn everybody with a web browser into productive participants. This openness of Wikipedia as a publicly editable website is a motivating factor for people to work together and share their knowledge to teach the world (Pfaff & Hasan, 2007).

2. When people see interesting articles on Wikipedia they get the feeling that somebody is providing his or her knowledge and expertise to them. When they see this benefit, they will become motivated to share their own knowledge by creating articles as well. According to O'Leary (2008), wikis facilitate connections between interested parties, which motivate them to share according to quid pro quo logic.
3. Furthermore people can be recognized in one way or another. Wikipedia has the possibility to create an account and edit with this account. The nickname or original name of the contributor is presented below the article. When the contributor does not have an account, only the IP address of the contributor will be presented below the article. We think that contributors realize this and therefore use Wikipedia as a reputation-building mechanism.
4. There is also a possibility that people do not know quite enough about a specific topic. They then put their knowledge on Wikipedia and hope that someone else modifies the article or extends it. In this way the first creator of the article benefits from the fact that s/he created an article with little knowledge (O'Leary, 2008). Now s/he can gather more knowledge about that specific subject as it is added by other contributors. Consequently, Wikipedia contributions are used to let others work for you for free.

In the following subsection we focus on information process models in a wiki-based information service. These models contain services that make it possible for consumers, contributors, moderators, and donors to use the wiki.

### 7.3.4 Information Process Models in a Wiki-Based Information Service

The actors involved in the wiki information service are, among others, contributors, consumers, donors, moderators, and hosting services. The first three can share a role; they can both be supplier (adding and editing content, thus creating value), consumer (searching and retrieving content), and donor (donate money when they like the information service). These roles can be dynamically interchanged. This means an individual can change roles during a single session, first searching content (consumer role), later editing content (contributor role), and moments later donating money (donor). In this subsection, the emphasis on these shared roles. Each actor can have a contributor-relation with several consumers and a consumer-relation with several contributors. This matches the value net process model. A value net process defines actors in a network and their interlinking process. Figure 7.6 gives it for Wikipedia.

In these networks, information services manage the interlinking processes. For a wiki, we can define at least four core processes:

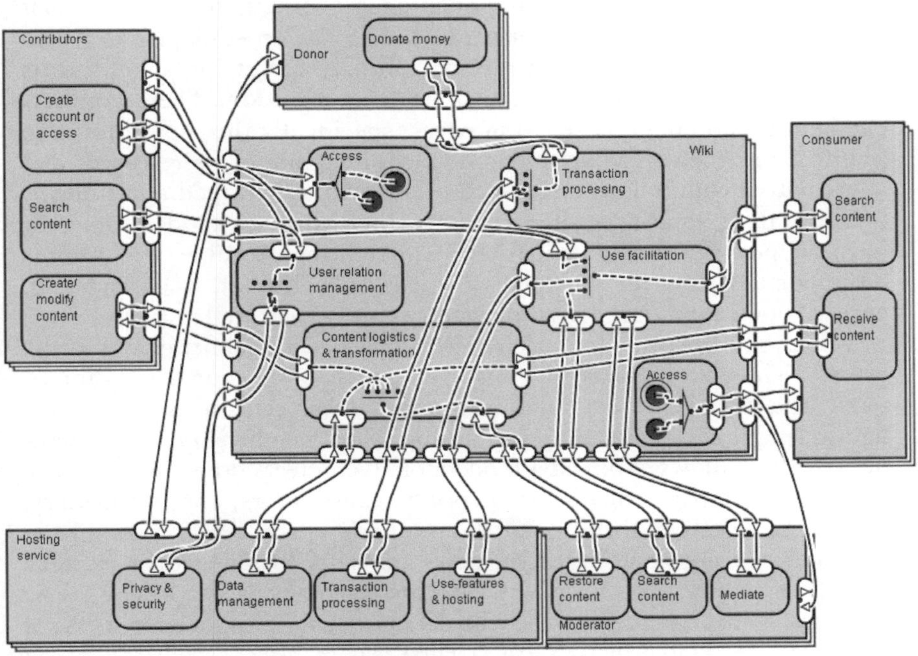


*Figure 7.6* The value net process model for Wikipedia.

- *Network membership management processes consisting of user relationship management*: It also provides arrangements for user privacy, security, and property rights.
- *Logistics and transformation*: This process acquires, store, distributes, and transforms content to a specific format. This increases the value by delivering the proper kind of representation and the proper kind of conceptualization.
- *Use facilitation*: This process provides content-interaction and meta-information, like search options.
- *Transaction processing*: This process compensates the hosting service by collecting money from donors, which is the only money source for Wikipedia.

Yet a critical factor to bear in mind is that Wikipedia is a public online wiki. One vandal can be enough to adapt an article with wrong content or misuse it. This is different compared to a corporate wiki of an organization. Employees who make contributions to the corporate wiki are employed by the organization as specialists whose opinions will be highly regarded by their organizations as trusted and authoritative (Wei et al., 2005).

Another major issue involving open page editing is the conflicts that may arise. Contributors do not necessarily agree on edits made by others. A contributor could, for instance, simply revert the article to its previous form, thus deleting the others' contribution. These conflicts can be found on many discussion pages, specifically those pertaining to political or other sensitive topics. If a conflict cannot be resolved, and contributors continue to undo each other's work, Wikipedia has means of arbitrating such a conflict. This is done through moderators that have the power to ban a contributor from editing. Conflict resolution is an important issue for Wikipedia, as it is only through well-discussed, agreed, open edits that a certain quality can be achieved.

There are some other tools that increase the overall quality of Wikipedia articles. These tools protect articles from misuse or deletion. For example, many pages that contain vandalism-sensitive subjects, such as political figures, require a Wikipedia membership. This membership comes without cost, but allows Wikipedia moderators (volunteers doing maintenance work) to trace page edits back to specific contributors, and if necessary, take action (e.g., ban them).

Moderators are allowed to delete pages and block IP addresses or accounts (membered users). Also, they have the right to revert any page to older versions (backups), which can preserve the wiki database against loss of data in case of system failures (Pfaff & Hasan, 2007). Furthermore they can mediate between discussing contributors. At the moment of writing there are 1,707 moderators, who all maintain the wiki for free (for more information on moderation of Wikipedia pages, see the website www.WikiMedia.org).

Of course, these moderators cannot operate without the help of the information consumers and information contributors (due to the number of articles), who are reporting the moderators of vandalism, misuse, or wrong content. We think that it should become easier for contributors to check articles and to contact moderators by tools that can check articles on content (e.g., specific words) and markup and can contact moderators. Nowadays there are some tools available for this, but they can only compare the new edited article with the old one. Furthermore this checking functionality is available only for registered users. Wikipedia could design such a feature and make it available for every user who wants to contribute to an article. This feature could consist of a button to contact moderators. The button should motivate wiki users to contact the moderator so they can hasten the process of restoring the article, which finally improves the quality of it.

### 7.3.5 Information Service Architecture

From the content aspect, there are two types of information service architectures: centralized website architecture and the aggregator architecture (see Chapter 5). In a centralized website architecture, the information service provider takes responsibility for providing its target clients with the right kind of information. In the aggregator architecture, the information provider gives the client the opportunity to compose his or her own information goods from different sources.

From the use-value aspect two other information service architectures exist (see Chapter 5). These services are the community building and the data integration information service architeture. The community architecture aims at providing ways of interacting with content in a way that enables community building. The integrated data architecture aims at the combination and integration of data from different data sources.

An architecture design of Wikipedia is depicted in Figure 7.7. The design was made using ArchiMate. This ArchiMate diagram has seven seven

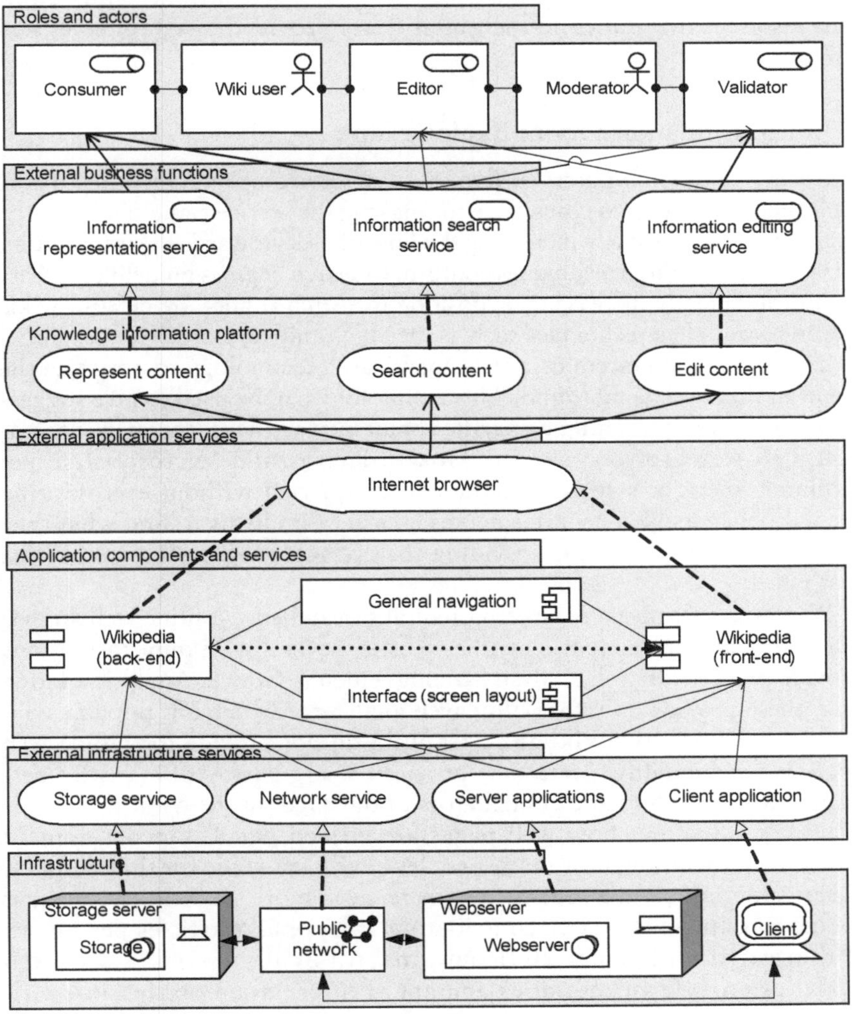


*Figure 7.7* The service architecture of Wikipedia.

layers. The roles and actors layer can be seen as the business layer, because this layer consists of the external customers and their roles. The next four layers belong to the application layer, because these layers are needed to support the business layer and they consist of applications and services. The final two layers describe technology infrastructure that is needed to run the applications. Due to the use of the ArchiMate diagram it is easy to see which infrastructure is needed for the business layers.

The Wikipedia architecture has a centralized website architecture in the three bottom layers. This due to the fact that only one central storage is used. By looking at the top layers and especially the roles and actors layer, one can recognize the community architecture. In the community architecture users can have multiple roles, such as consumer and editor. One also sees that data and their quality are provided by editor roles and validator roles.

### 7.3.6 Information Service Exploitation

The basic condition for users surfing to a web service is that they can find it. A multitude of techniques is available for making the service stand out in search engine results, thus likely increasing the flow of users towards the information service. Some of these techniques conform to search engines guidelines; others try to fraudulently increase their position in search results. By default, wikis use non-fraudulent techniques such as metatags and keyword systems.

The MetaWiki system uses the OpenSearch technology to optimize the pages in the wiki being found. This technology can be used to give suggestions to visitors searching a specific topic. Furthermore, through integration with web browsers such as Mozilla Firefox and Microsoft Internet Explorer, the wiki's search engine can be queried without even visiting the wiki page itself. The latter makes it easier for clients to find what they are looking for on a wiki, providing they stumbled upon the wiki in the first place.

Web analytics measure either potential site audience (offline web analytics) or actual visits to (parts of) the website. Several wiki implementations provide plugins for web analysis, among which is Google Analytics. However, these provide only for online web analytics. By default, popular wiki systems such as DokuWiki and MetaWiki do not provide for offline web analysis functionality. MetaWiki provides a large array of statistics pertaining to the visitors and contributors of the pages in the wiki.

Figure 7.8 shows how well pages are viewed per Wikipedia domain (language), including how many articles have been made for that domain. When zooming in on a specific language, even more statistics are present concerning the most active contributors and popular articles per month of the year from January 2001 onwards. All in all, the wiki's own web analytics provide an enormous amount of information on the site's visitors and contributors.

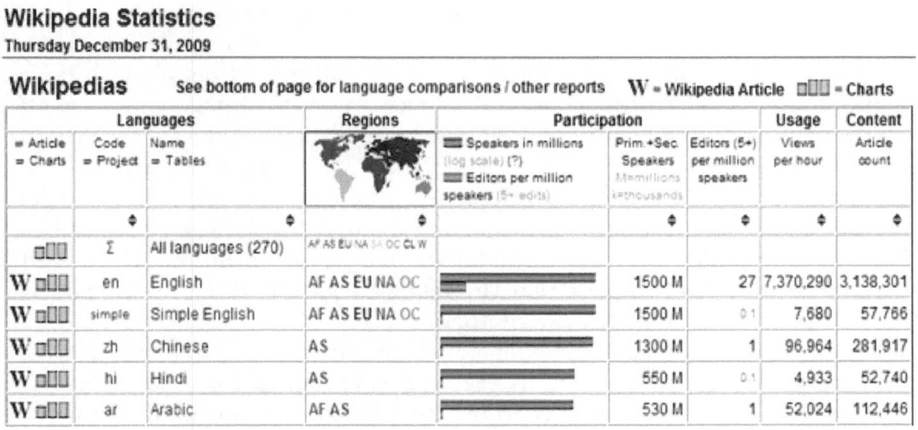

**Wikipedia Statistics**
Thursday December 31, 2009

**Wikipedias** See bottom of page for language comparisons / other reports W = Wikipedia Article □□□ = Charts

| Languages | | | Regions | Participation | | | Usage | Content |
|---|---|---|---|---|---|---|---|---|
| = Article = Charts | Code = Project | Name = Tables | | Speakers in millions (log scale) (?) Editors per million speakers (5+ edits) | Prim.+Sec. Speakers M=millions k=thousands | Editors (5+) per million speakers | Views per hour | Article count |
| □□□ | Σ | All languages (270) | AF AS EU NA SA OC CL W | | | | | |
| W □□□ | en | English | AF AS EU NA OC | | 1500 M | 27 | 7,370,290 | 3,138,301 |
| W □□□ | simple | Simple English | AF AS EU NA OC | | 1500 M | 0.1 | 7,680 | 57,766 |
| W □□□ | zh | Chinese | AS | | 1300 M | 1 | 96,964 | 281,917 |
| W □□□ | hi | Hindi | AS | | 550 M | 0.1 | 4,933 | 52,740 |
| W □□□ | ar | Arabic | AF AS | | 530 M | 1 | 52,024 | 112,446 |

*Figure 7.8* Wikipedia statistics for pages in some languages.

What is still left for consideration is how the information in web analytics can be qualified. Figure 7.8 does not say anything about how this should be interpreted—in other words, are these numbers good or bad? Chapter 6 described several quality indicators related to web statistics, which are discussed in relation to wiki information systems in Table 7.1.

*Table 7.1* Performance Indicators for Wikipedia

| *Performance indicator* | *Relation to wiki information service* |
|---|---|
| Page views | A server request for a complete page; the top 1,000 articles (most hits) have a combined 180,000,000 hits per day (WikiMedia.org). |
| Page views per session | Wikipedia has an average of four unique page visits per session. |
| Unique visitor | WikiMedia site analytics contain the unique visitors for Wikipedia per month in millions. |
| Impression | As Wikipedia does not use advertising on its pages, this indicator is not relevant. |
| Singletons/bounce rate | The percentage of visitors that visits only a single page is, according to Alexa.com, around 45% for the last three months. |
| Session duration | Alex.com states that the average session length for Wikipedia visitors is around five minutes. |

Table 7.1 shows that the Wikipedia information service does well for every indicator. But it is unsure of there is any correlation between the quality of information on a website and the number of people visiting it (Keen, 2007). Wikipedia's top 1,000 pages in terms of page views are all articles with a long history of contributions. The fact that they are visited often suggests that this editing process has led to many improvements. However, pages can still be vandalized when the editing process lacks accountability. Although one might assume that this lack of accountability would result in rampant vandalism and poor quality content, Pfaff and Hasan (2007) suggest that the main allegation about Wikipedia is that the information *varies* in quality.

One metric for encyclopedic article quality is a comparison with existing encyclopedias, such as the world-renowned *Encyclopedia Britannica*. This encyclopedia is edited by a board of experts on the fields they write about. Theoretically, this would lead to the highest quality of articles, as it resembles the academic standard of peer reviewing. Giles (2005) made a comparison of scientific Wikipedia and *Encyclopedia Britannica* articles. His conclusion was that Wikipedia articles have on average of four errors (factual mistakes) whereas *Encyclopedia Britannica* articles have three. This at least gives some indication of the quality achieved by Wikipedia's open editing.

## 7.4 DESIGNING A MOBILE APPLICATION FOR TRAVELERS ONCE THEY HAVE BOOKED[5]

### 7.4.1 Introduction

Information services help people understand the world by delivering, making accessible, or sharing relevant and useful information. Such services can be developed for different platforms and one still growing platform is smartphones. Mobile applications enable improved accessibility of services, i.e., 24/7 access at nearly all places in western countries. A well-developed and well-marketed application can enhance customer loyalty or even generate customer lock-in.

TSi Solutions creates solutions for automation processes in the tourism industry (www.tsi-solutions.nl/en). These solutions include service customization. When TSi develops a website for a tour operator or a trip reseller, many extra services for customers can be added to the website. Examples of these services are information supply about weather, accommodations, or reviews by travelers. This is possible because next to developing tourist software applications and web services, TSi also collects, structures, evaluates, and distributes travel content. But despite all this travel content, TSi's data indicate that once a trip is booked, the customer engagement is low. So, how can mobile applications be used to improve customer loyalty? For this design project, the focus is on supporting a customer by providing (personalized) information between the moment of booking and the moment of departure. TSi has two main questions:

- What information is relevant for a traveler who booked a trip?
- What would be the source of this information?

Next to these questions defined by TSi, we also identified the following questions related to each information service design step:

- How can the application provide value to all stakeholders?
- What business processes are involved in the application?
- How should the service be structured?
- What should the interface look like?
- How can this product be exploited successfully?

The conclusion and recommendations are given at the end.

### 7.4.2 Problem Identification

In order to gain insights about the challenges and the possible solutions we have created a mind map. A mind map is an outline based on organizing information via hierarchies, categories, and their associations (see Mindjet MindManager at www.mindjet.com). We structured the mind map around a central goal. The goal of this research is to develop a mobile application to support customers *once they have booked* a holiday, with the underlying idea that this will increase engagement and customer loyalty. Ideally the application will improve the customer experience such that he or she will book the next holiday with the same reseller. The associations flowing from the central goal depict the questions, or knowledge problems, that have to be answered. Related to these questions are assumptions and ideas that we thought of as possible answers during a brainstorming session.

This project wants to contribute to resellers in the travel industry by increasing their number of returning customers after their customers have completed a holiday with them.

### 7.4.3 Business Model

Al-Debei and Avison (2010) mention that business requirements can be represented in a business model, which they view as a (explicit or tacit) business proposal for all actors involved in a business. Teece (2010) mentions that the essence of a business model is in defining the manner by which the enterprise delivers value to customers, entices customers to pay for value, and converts those payments to profit. A good business model is essential in order to capitalize on new developments, because the same idea or technology with different business models will yield different economic outcomes (Chessbrough, 2010).

According to Osterwalder and Pigneur (2009) a business model has nine building blocks. These building blocks show the logic behind how the company will achieve making money, and cover four main areas of the business: customers, offer, infrastructure, and financial viability. The nine building blocks are: customer segments, value propositions, channels, customer relationships, revenue streams, resources, activities, partnerships, and cost structure.

The *customer* segment consists of resellers. These resellers for TSi can be travel agencies or booking websites. These companies will use the application to increase engagement and customer loyalty. The value proposition is that this application will deliver all relevant trip information in one application. In between booking and going on holiday, the user can find all necessary information in the application.

The *distribution channels* are the resellers, confirmation e-mails, and marketplaces. The resellers give their customers the opportunity to use the application by providing them with an activation code. With this code the customer can activate the application and become a user. Booking websites can provide this code through a confirmation e-mail, which is sent after a trip is booked. The customer can download the app through the platform-specific marketplaces.

The *customer relationship* has a focus on loyalty. By providing all necessary trip information to the user, the user (customer) is expected to be more loyal to the reseller, and even customer lock-in may be achieved.

The *revenue* is generated by a subscription fee, which will be paid by the reseller. The reseller could, for example, pay a fixed amount for providing the application to its customers, or it might have to pay per user of the application.

The *resources* are data and people. The data are an important resource because they are the basis of the actual information service: the data are the information that is offered to the customers of the resellers, and thus the users of the application. People are an important resource because the application will have to be created and it has to be configured for each reseller, by bundling the desired data.

The *activity* is information gathering, structuring, and distribution. The information that is offered to the users of the application has to be gathered from different sources and then structured, to be able to be bundled when configuring the application for a specific reseller.

The *strategic partners* are the smartphone producers, the resellers, and information providers. The smartphone producers offer the devices and platforms on which the application is offered. The resellers are the main source of income for TSi, since they will pay a subscription fee to TSi in exchange for offering the application to their customers. The information providers are strategic partners because these parties provide the information that TSi bundles into the application, and this information is then offered to the users of the application.

The costs are generated by people, hosting, and information. The people are the employees of TSi, who will have to be paid in exchange for their efforts. The hosting costs consist of the costs for hosting all the information that TSi offers through the application, and the information costs consist of fees that are paid to information providers in exchange for using their information in the application.

The resulting actor web can be represented by the e3value technique, which describes the actors and their value exchanges. In e3value, value objects are exchanged via value interfaces, which have value ports that offer or request value objects (Gordijn, 2004). A requirement for the business model to work is that each actor benefits. In other words, the incoming value objects should have greater value for the actor than the outgoing value objects, or effort. Figure 7.9 shows the value web for this

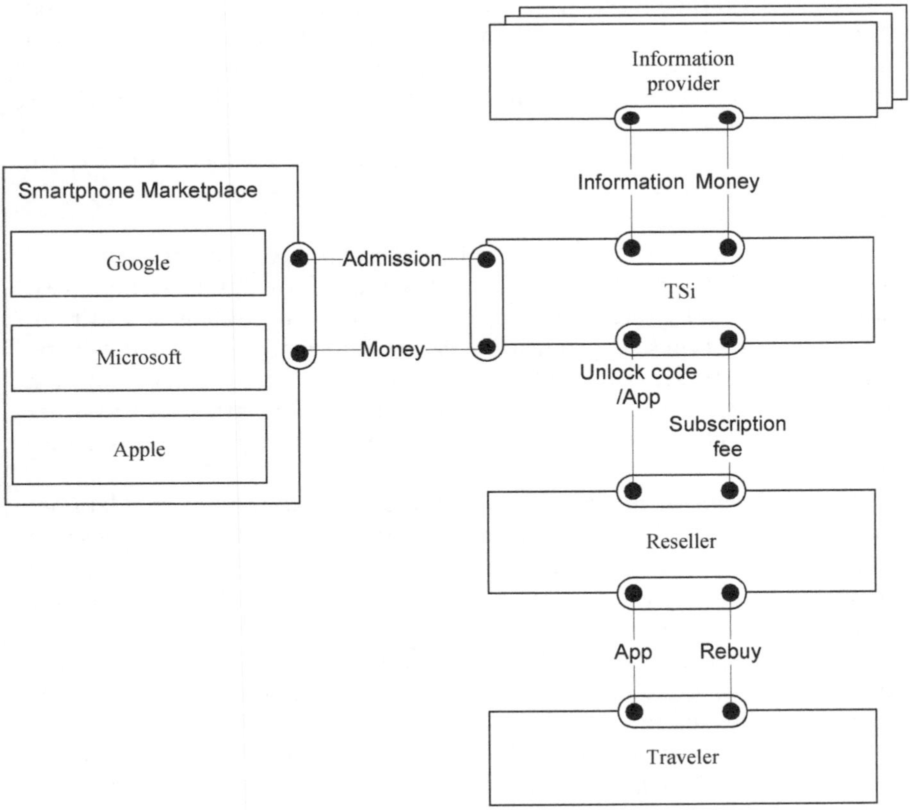


*Figure 7.9* Value web of the mobile application service using the e3value method.

case. TSi is the central actor and the initiator of this business model. It creates the application for the different mobile operating systems, pulls the information from the different information providers, and takes care that it is put in the different app marketplaces. The reseller pays a subscription fee to have the app tailor-made and available to the resellers' customers. The customer of the travel reseller gets the app for free, since the reseller thinks it has a greater chance that the traveler will book again at its organization because it increased the customer experience.

### 7.4.4 Process Model

In order to get a better idea of how the mobile application functions we need to focus on the different processes that are involved in this mobile application. The specification of a process model deals with more fine-grained views of business transactions, their relationships, and choreography in business collaborations.

Since the main idea of this application is to improve customer loyalty by providing all relevant trip information in one mobile application, the focus is on the information goods management process. Information goods management consists of information creation, distribution, and activation of the application. The stakeholders that we refer to in this model are the travelers who have already booked their holiday with the customer of TSi.

Since the abstraction level of the information good is low, a value chain process model is most appropriate (see Chapter 4). For the mobile app, we define the following core processes:

*Acquisition*: All the data related to the trip has to be acquired and stored from different resources. The data acquisition can be done in two ways: 1) internal content creation and 2) external content acquisition. TSi uses both types of acquisition. Some information is created internally, e.g., destination-related information, and some other information is acquired from external resources, e.g., trip information and weather information. The contract support activity is used to manage this acquisition process.

*Data refinement, integration, and standardization*: Once the data are acquired it is refined and integrated. Data are also standardized and saved in the database. TSi has "batch data set importer" and "incremental data importer" activities for data refinement and standardization. TSi already has data acquisition and data standardization services.

*Bundling and versioning*: Once the data are refined and standardized they have to be bundled. The data are categorized according to country, region, and destination.

*Distribution of apps*: Depending on the subscription of the reseller and the destination, the trip information is filtered and assigned to a certain trip. If the reseller wants more information, then s/he has to pay more for his or

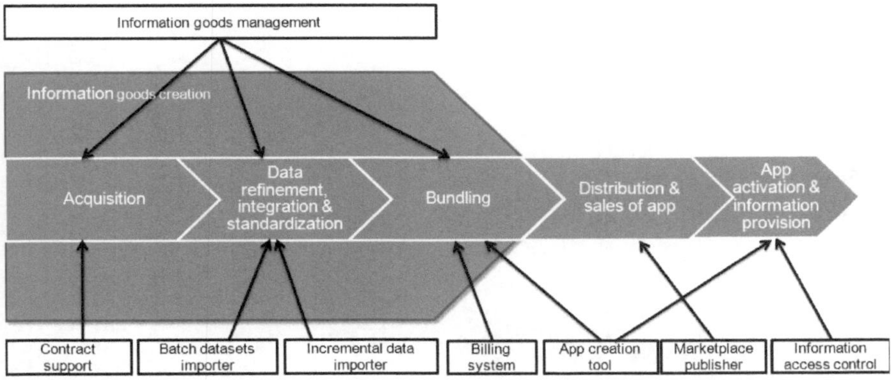


*Figure 7.10* Process model of mobile application.

her bundle. Since TSi already has a bundling process in place in the framework for normal websites, this information selection is done in the distribution process and a separate tool. The selected information is coupled to a certain trip, and is made available in the application via a unique unlock code. The mobile application is published and distributed via the resellers, but in the future the application could also be directly sold to travelers via app stores. In that case, TSi might have to promote the application.

*App activation and information provision*: The buyer will be sent a confirmation e-mail along with the booking code and a link to download this application. The app user has to enter the booking code in order to get complete access to this app. If the booking code is valid and authorized the app is accessible and the user can use the app. The complete process model for the mobile application can be found in Figure 7.10.

### 7.4.5 Service Architecture

The architecture for the information service for TSi is shown in Figure 7.11. This architecture was created in ArchiMate and consists of three layers: business, application, and technology. The three processes can be recognized from the business process model: information goods creation, app distribution, and service application provision. The first two steps of the information goods creation are ignored in this architecture, since these processes already exist within TSi and are not changed by the designed information service.

The important parts of the architecture cope with which information is needed, and how it will be structured. The delivery focus is thus very much on the use-value, because the information service is aimed at a group of users with similar interests (travelers) and data from different sources is consolidated. The information offered is supplied by TSi and users cannot compose their own information good.

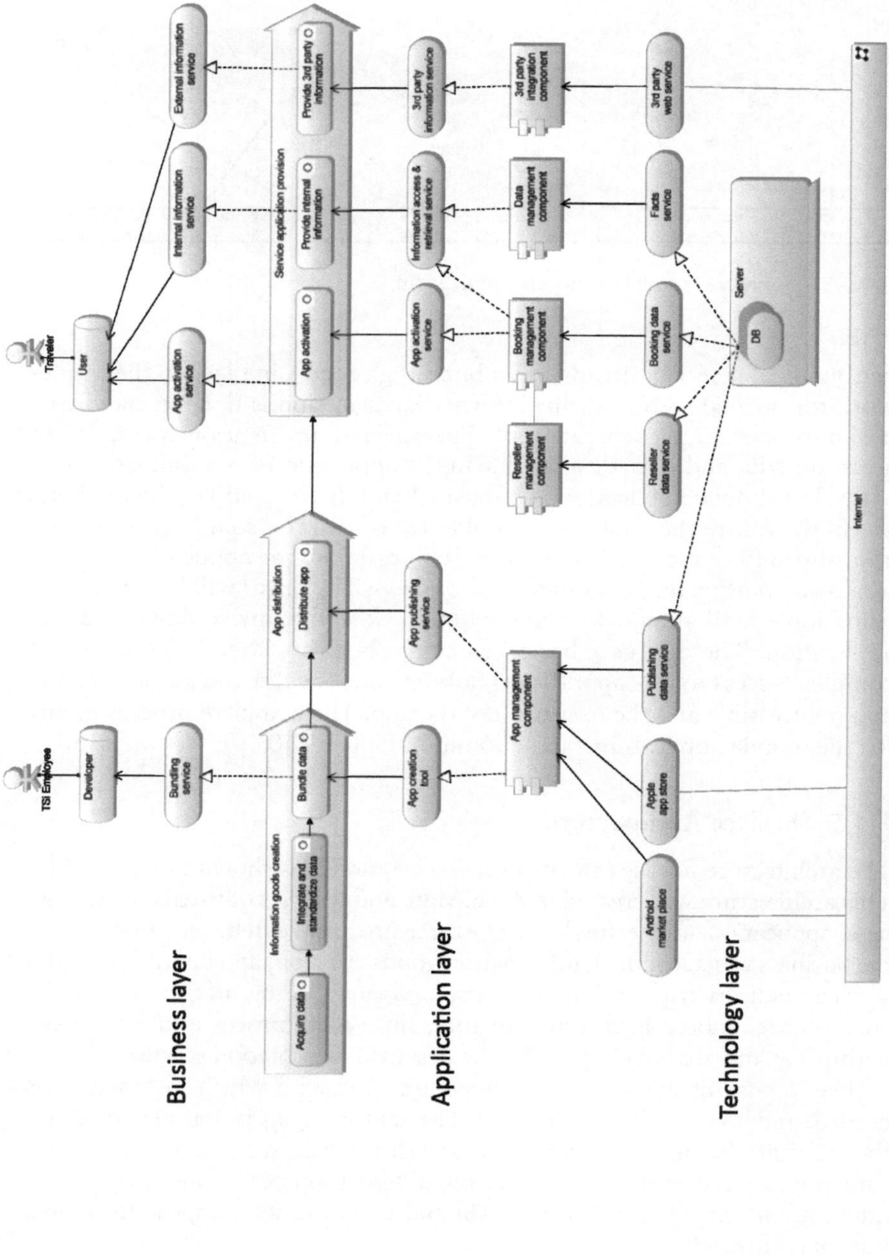


*Figure 7.11* Service architecture for TSi.

*Table 7.2* TSi Information Service Content and Sources

| *Content* | *Source of content* |
|---|---|
| Weather information | Weerplaza.nl |
| Checklist of insurance; passport; medication/ medical passport; fill out emergency information | New Toeristiek database; user (adding new items to checklist) |
| Contact info of tour operator; airline company; Dutch embassy | Tour operator; Toeristiek |
| Travel plan | TSi |
| Group composition | Reseller/tour operator |
| Language module with common words in foreign language | Google Translate |
| Flight info, like flight number, departure time, and gate | TSi; airline companies (dynamic update) |
| Destination info like country; area; city; time difference; upcoming holidays and events; Dutch embassy; currency rate | Toeristiek |
| User-generated multimedia about destination | Twitter; Flickr; YouTube |
| Warning in case of negative travel advice | Toeristiek |
| Agenda items like time till departure, travel plan, activities by tour operator, flight info, upcoming holidays | TSi |
| Emergency information like booking number, insurance policy number (health, trip, cancellation) insurance, contact information insurance (healthcare, travel insurance), contact information credit card company, contact information mobile phone service supplier, personal contact information (family), contact information embassy | Tour operator; user; Toeristiek (Dutch embassy information) |

We have also created a list of information that should be available to the users, which is shown in Table 7.2. For each type of content the source is described. A source can be either internal or external. Toeristiek is a brand of TSi and is thus treated as an internal source.

### 7.4.6 Prototype and Implementation

This section describes the use-features of the infrastructure by paper prototyping. Paper prototyping is a method of usability testing that is useful for websites, web applications, and conventional software. Instead of coding a prototype, the needed screens are hand-sketched. Paper prototyping is useful for presenting ideas about problems, concepts and terminology, navigation and workflow, content, page layout, and functionality. A polished-looking design can actually encourage the wrong kind of feedback, like "I don't like that color" or "I don't like that font". In paper prototypes it is obvious to users that you have not specified the look yet. This encourages users to focus on the concepts and functionality, and avoids nit-picky feedback. Also it encourages creativity and makes non-technical users more comfortable giving ideas for improvement. With minimum effort you find significant problems early in the design process, so you can experiment to find the best solution before investing in its implementation.

For this project we used Balsamiq Mockups, a rapid wireframing tool that reproduces the experience of sketching and uses a small library of sketched buttons (www.balsamiq.com). Following the information service content and sources table (Table 7.2), nine screens are defined and for each screen a drawing is made. The designs were discussed within the group and with the supervisors from TSi. After some regrouping, this resulted in a home screen and the use-features listed in Figure 7.12.

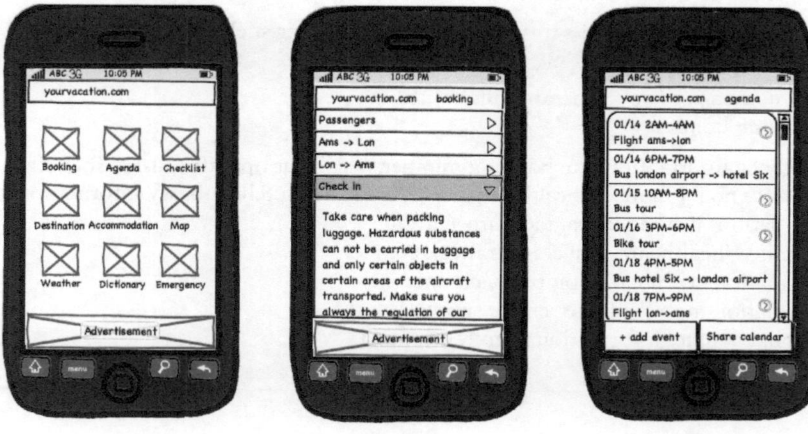


This is the home screen of the app. Pressing the back button (bottom right) redirects the user to another screen. The top shows the reseller's logo. Pushing this redirects to the home screen. The bottom shows relevant advertisements, like train tickets and car rental.

This screen shows all booking information, and is a copy of the booking confirmation mail.

This screen shows the agenda of the trip. Next to transport and planned events by the tour operator, the user can add events.

*(continued)*

*Figure 7.12* Paper prototype for TSi.

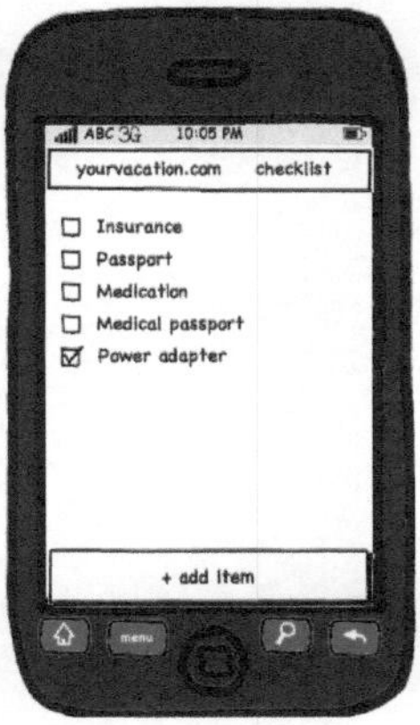


TSi has an extensive checklist available depending on both destination and traveling party (for example: children yes/no, babies yes/no). The user can add his own checklist items.

This screen displays TSi information on the country, region, and city. The user can unfold an information block by clicking on the header.

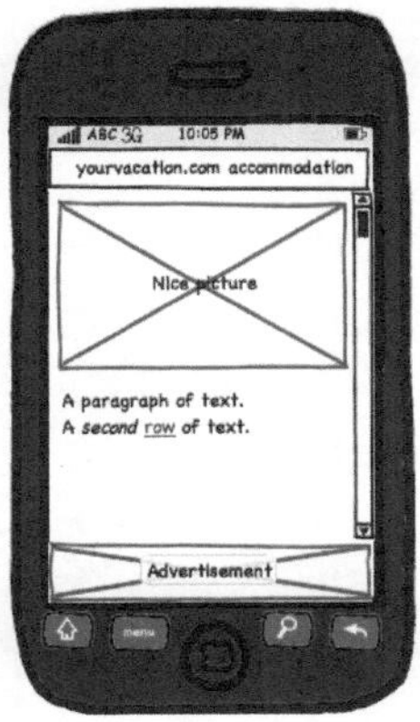


This screen displays the accommodation information from the booking site, including pictures. This also enables the traveler to show his trip to friends.

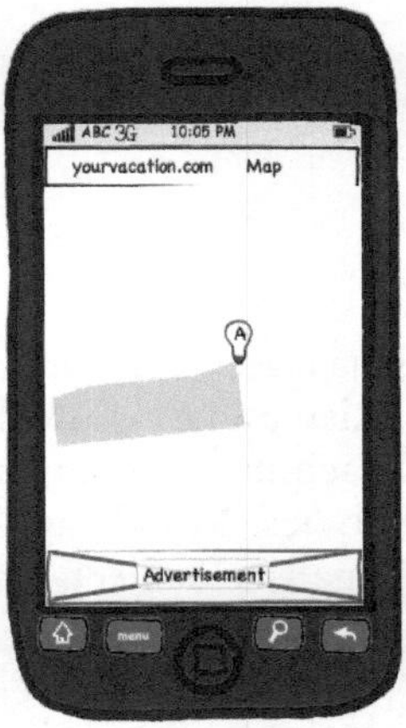


This is an offline map of the destination. The map also shows other points of interest (POI) in the accommodation area. If the user has an Internet connection the user can use Google's Street View here.

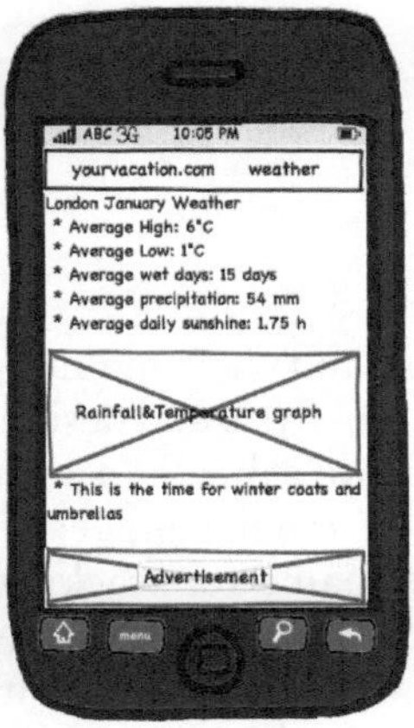


This screen shows average weather information in the month of the trip. This includes average temperature, rainfall, and clothing information.

The dictionary gives common words and expressions. By clicking on a row, the word or sentence will be pronounced.

*(continued)*

*Figure 7.12* (continued)

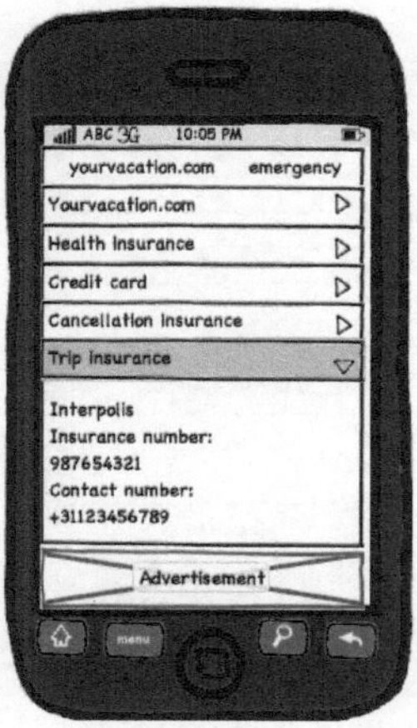


This shows emergency information. The user can fill in his credit card, insurance card, and customer number. When there is an emergency all contact information is in one app.

*Figure 7.12* (continued)

### 7.4.7 Exploitation

Understanding the end-users and their requirements has been the cornerstone of information systems analysis and design. This demand to know the requirements of end-users and to achieve an advantage against the competitors has created a demand for mobile application analytics. Mobile application analytics is the trade name for tracking systems that collect data regarding the users' behavior in the application (Juhlin, 2010).

The main goal of TSi is to create a better user experience, and hence increase loyalty of travelers to the trip reseller. Therefore, the application should be branded for the trip reseller and should be provided for free to the travelers. This service can be sold to the resellers in different ways: the reseller could pay for a subscription, or could pay a commission per download, or a percentage of bookings. Also TSi can receive (a part of) the revenue generated from the in-app advertisements.

With the present idea, once the customer books a holiday from a reseller, s/he receives a confirmation e-mail with the link to download this mobile application along with the authentication code. Once the mobile application is downloaded it has to be activated using the authentication code (or activation code).

To make sure that this mobile app really helps in improving customer satisfaction and hence customer loyalty, an exploitation plan has to be made. An analysis has to be done for checking the performance and generating insights for improvement of this service. The feedback source can be of two types: communication from users and statistical data. Communication from users is useful but statistical usage data are more helpful.

Statistical data can be obtained from the marketplace. The mobile app actively records usage information and sends it to the service database. Flurry (www.flurry.com) can be used for this purpose and can provide statistical information such as how many people use the app, when, how many times, for how long they use the app, geographical distribution of users, and the hardware they use. It also provides information like how the app is performing across different smartphones. There are several alternatives to Flurry, e.g., Localytics (www.localytics.com) and Appclix (www.mobilytics.net). Google Analytics also provides ways to track user interaction with (parts of) websites and applications accessed from a mobile device.

In order to confirm that this mobile application has improved the customer loyalty of TSi it is necessary to make sure that the person who uses this mobile application rebooks some vacation with a TSi reseller. If the person clicks on the link provided in the confirmation e-mail, it means that the person has downloaded the app and if the same person rebooks with the same reseller, we can assume that this application has improved customer loyalty. Questionnaires should be sent after rebooking or after the trip to find out whether the app has played a part in the decision to book again with the same reseller.

### 7.4.8 Conclusion

This section explained the steps that have to be followed in building an information service that helps improve customer loyalty for TSi. The framework of design science research explained in this book has been used to build the service. This information service (mobile application) makes the best use of the trip-related information that TSi already has in its database and helps improve customer loyalty and revenue generation of TSi. This service provides different trip-related information between the moment of booking and the moment of departure for TSi customers (direct and indirect). At present the focus is just on providing the information between the moment of booking and the moment of departure, but the enhancement would be to provide information even after the departure (e.g., during the vacation).

## 7.5 CONCLUSIONS AND DISCUSSION

### 7.5.1 Conclusions

Chapter 2 identified the following characteristics of the Singerian (pragmatic) process-oriented theory: project management theory, articulating the role of different kernel theories for realizing concrete systems, and prototypes to learn about how to contribute to real human progress. This chapter illustrated by three cases how an information service development project can be run in the different steps of problem articulation, business modeling, process modeling, design, and exploitation. Via these project steps Lockean, Leibnizian, Kantian, and Hegelian ideas are integrated in a solution.

We now can reapply the guidelines for design science as presented in Chapter 2, and summarize the learning in this book along them:

- *Guideline 1 (design as an artifact)*: Each case resulted in a concrete solution; sometimes a prototype and sometimes new constructs and methods were applied.
- *Guideline 2 (problem relevance)*: The cases delivered technology-based solutions to important and relevant business problems (TSi) or relevant analysis of a proposed solution (GBA and Wikipedia).
- *Guideline 3 (design evaluation)*: The utility, quality, and efficacy of a design artifact were demonstrated via the analysis of its business model and via the analysis of its consequence during exploitation.
- *Guideline 4 (research contribution)*: The cases demonstrated the shape and opportunities for information services designs (which are definitely not the same as an information system) on the basis of kernel theoretical design foundations, and related design methodologies.
- *Guideline 5 (research rigor)*: Rigor was applied by grounding the insights in philosophy and by demonstrating insights via cases.
- *Guideline 6 (design as a search process)*: The cases showed that designing is a research effort. Problem understanding and solution do not pop up at once but require substantial debate and possible search and application of existing knowledge in the field.
- *Guideline 7 (communication of research)*: Design science research must be presented effectively both to technology-oriented as well as management-oriented audiences. This book tries to serve both audiences, with a focus on the managerial aspects of information services.

### 7.5.2 Discussion

Has everything been said now about information service design and exploitation? Absolutely not—actually, *we* are just beginning! By "we" I mean practitioners, entrepreneurs, scientists, and educators.

Practitioners and entrepreneurs have been given a systematic account of the layers and aspects of information services in this book. With the delivered concepts, theories, and methods, they should be able to systematically develop information entrepreneurship. They will not have to rely solely on the expertise of information technologists, but will be able to integrate insights from several disciplines (like economics, social science, and computer science) in their efforts to build a service, not only a system.

For educators, this implies that informing is more than only information systems teaching or communication and media science, but the recognition of a new discipline, which needs a position on its own in educational curricula. We have applied a design science approach to learning about this area, which challenges students to become creative problem solvers and developers of new scientific insights at the same time. This is a view of learning that fits very well with the action orientation that many students are searching for.

For scientists, this implies a new program of research on the different layers and aspects of the development and exploitation space. This research can have multiple shapes. As a pragmatist, I believe that any kind of methodology can contribute substantially to this field, but following Churchman (and he followed Spinoza), the ultimate goal of science is ethical, i.e., progress for mankind. I identify two types of ethical issues related to information services:

1. Contributions of information services to important social problems
2. The ethics inside an information service itself

Regarding the first topic, Table 7.3 proposes a list of research areas. Of course, this table presents only a list of example studies, just to help the reader to become creative on his or her own.

*Table 7.3* Example Research Ideas for Studying Information Services

| *Philosopher* | *Subject* |
|---|---|
| Locke (observation and data) | An analysis of the credit crisis using a systematic method to evaluate the correctness of (derivative) decisional data and reports<br>Question: Could Lockean requirements have avoided wrong investment decisions that caused troubles of financial institutions?<br>Deliverable: Method and criteria for data evaluation |
| | Sentiment mining in politics and business<br>Question: What is the added value of sentiment mining compared to alternative sources of strategic information?<br>Deliverables: Review of sentiment mining methods, their strengths and weaknesses against alternative intelligence methods (like polls) |

*(continued)*

*Table 7.3* (continued)

| *Philosopher* | *Subject* |
|---|---|
| Leibniz (causal modeling) | Effectiveness of forecasting systems as an informative tool<br>Question: How useful and misinforming forecasts can be in the political and business context?<br>Deliverable: Theory and methods for evaluating forecasts |
| Kant (perspective-taking and integration) | Ontologies of business processes and the need for new techniques for information services<br>Question: Do current business process ontologies sufficiently cover the nature of information service processes?<br>Deliverable: Information service ontologies and related modeling practices |
| | A method of developing web services using different source systems<br>Question: Does web service development require different modes of working compared to information systems development?<br>Deliverables: Review of systems development practices and their relevance for information services |
| Hegel (dialectic information politics) | Making a software tool for Hegelian dialectics of political topics<br>Question: What is the nature of a software tool that helps information consumers in applying Hegelian dialects?<br>Deliverables: A review of the current Hegelian dialectics method and a software prototype |
| | Applying Hegelian informative dialectics on major political issues<br>Question: Is it possible to generate substantial innovative insights on political issues via the Hegelian informative dialectics method (Wijnhoven & Meertens, 2010)?<br>Deliverable: In-depth case studies |

*(continued)*

*Table 7.3* (continued)

| *Philosopher* | *Subject* |
|---|---|
| Singer (pragmatics) | Singerian principles and open innovation<br>Question: Is it possible to emulate Singerian principles fully by open innovation?<br>Deliverable: Operationalization of Singerian principles to a method for information collection and processing for innovation; comparison of Singerian requirements to existing open innovation platforms |
| | Social media for open innovation<br>Question: What social media tools are used for open innovation?<br>Deliverables: Classification of existing social media tools along key dimensions of open innovation; compare strengths and weaknesses and develop a mechanism for companies to select the best. |

### 7.5.3 Exercise

As a final exercise, I would like the reader to do the following:

1. Students are given the following case from a friend of mine. He has developed a management consulting firm and advises the boardrooms of internationally top companies in diverse sectors. To serve his clients better and maintain relationships, he developed a periodic newsletter, which has been recognized as an extremely valuable informative product, read by over 10,000 CEOs and direct subordinates regularly. Because CEOs have limited time to read and are very demanding regarding the quality and relevance of the information they receive, make an analysis of the business model, processes, and means needed to increase the quality and relevance of this service. Also make a prototype.
2. Entrepreneurs can take the same problem, but in this case for an information service of their own. How does the information service approach actually impact the existing methods of project management?
3. Educators are given the task to design a bachelor's and a master's program on information services. What should be learned in what courses?
4. Scientists are given the task to design a research program in this field for the coming five years. What would be the main subjects, what research questions, and what deliverables should be searched for?

# Notes

## NOTES TO CHAPTER 2

1. This description of John Locke is based on Uzgalis (2007) and Meyers (2006).
2. This description of Leibniz is based on Look (2008) and Churchman (1971).
3. This description of Immanuel Kant is based on Churchman (1971), Mason and Mitroff (1973), and Hartnack (1967).
4. This description of Hegel is mainly based on Churchman's (1971) description. A more detailed account can be found in Redding (2006) and Sinnerbrink (2007).
5. With regard, though, to this "simplistic optimism", Churchman notes that it is doubtful whether Singer himself would so strongly express his hope for mankind.

## NOTES TO CHAPTER 3

1. I appreciate the help of Michel Angelo Meyer in writing parts of this section.
2. Several parts of this section are based on Voermans (2007). I acknowledge the contributions of Koen Voermans, who collected the data, value nets, and calculation mechanisms.

## NOTES TO CHAPTER 4

1. Much of this section is based on Wijnhoven (2002a and b).
2. Much of this section is based on Elorrieta et al. (2005).

## NOTES TO CHAPTER 5

1. Note the distinction between the business architecture (described in Chapter 3) and the service architecture.
2. I appreciate the collaboration with Frank Timmer on developing the ideas and the vtsPN case.

3. This section made extensive use of an internal comparative research note of ZMPX. We thank Richard ten Barge for allowing us to do so.
4. http://www.cmsmatrix.org/
5. Retrieved on June 28, 2007.
6. http://www.cnet.com/
7. For Drupal, please refer to http://drupal.org/project/Modules. For Joomla!, please refer to http://extensions.joomla.org/.
8. I appreciate the collaboration with Tanya Bondarouk and especially the efforts of Wieteke Meijer in collecting the data for this case.

## NOTES TO CHAPTER 6

1. This text is partially based on Wikipedia's text on SEO of November 2010, which has continuous updates of this fast-changing subject. I also refer the reader to Brian Clifton's 2010 book on web analytics, which offers a more specialized and detailed account of web analytics.

## NOTES TO CHAPTER 7

1. The research for this case has been done by my students Arjan Krukkert, Kelvin Divendal, Ronald Damhuis, and Tycho Bom as part of a master's course on information services.
2. OverheidsServiceBus means government service bus. During this study, the OSB was renamed *Digikoppeling,* since January 11, 2010. Despite this, we retain "OSB" in this document. (http://www.logius.nl/producten/gegevensuitwisseling/digikoppeling/naamswijziging).
3. IB-Groep is the Netherlands government agency that provides study allowances on behalf of the ministry of education.
4. Research for this case was done by Koen Klein Tank, Tom Hendrixen and Sjoerd van der Spek.
5. The research for this case was done by Chaithany Karanth, Martin Haitsma, Renske Vermolen, and Laurens Vliegen as part of a master's course on information services. I also thank TSi Travel Service International B.V. for their collaboration on this case. For more information on TSi see http://tsi-solutions.nl/en.

# Bibliography


Adviescommissie Modernisering GBA. (2010). *GBA in de toekomst. Gemeentelijke Basis Administratie persoonsgegevens als spil voor toekomstige identiteitsinfrastructuur.* (In Dutch. Short translation: Citizen data registration in the future). The Hague: Ministry of the Interior.

Akkermans, H., Baida, Z., Gordijn, J., Peña, N., Altuna, A., & Laresgoiti, I. (2004). Value webs: Using ontologies to bundle real-world services. *IEEE Intelligent Systems*, 19, July/August, 57–66.

Alavi, M., & Leidner, D. (2001). Knowledge management and knowledge management systems: Conceptual foundations and research issues. *Management Information Systems Quarterly*, *25*(1), 107–136.

Albert, T., Goes, P., & Gupta, A. (2004). GIST: A model for design and management of content and interactivity of customer-centric web sites. *Management Information Systems Quarterly*, *28*(2), 161–182.

Al-Debei, M., & Avison, D. (2010). Developing a unified framework of the business model concept. *European Journal of Information Systems*, *19*, 359–376.

Alexander, I., & Robertson, S. (2004). Understanding project sociology by modeling stakeholders. *IEEE Software*, *21*(1), 23–27.

Avison, D., & Wood-Harper, A. (1990). *Multiview: An exploration in information systems development.* London: Blackwell.

Avison, D., Wood-Harper, A., Vidgen, R., & Wood, J. (1998). A further exploration into information systems development: The evolution of multiview 2. *Information, Technology and People*, *11*(2), 124–139.

Axelrod, R. (1976). *Structure of decisions: Cognitive maps of political elites.* Princeton, NJ: Princeton University Press.

Baeza-Yates, R., & Ribeiro-Neto, B. (1999). *Modern information retrieval.* New York: Addison-Wesley.

Baskerville, R., & Wood-Harper, A. (1998). Diversity in information systems action research methods. *European Journal of Information Systems*, *7*(2), 90–107.

Becker, J., Knackstedt, R. & Pöppelbuß, J. 2009. Developing maturity models for IT management. *Business & Information Systems Engineering*, 1, 213–222.

Belkin, N. J., & Croft, W. B. (1992). Information filtering and information retrieval: Two sides of the same coin? *Communications of the ACM*, *35*(12), 29–38.

Benbunan-Fich, R. (2001). Using protocol analysis to evaluate the usability of a commercial web site. *Information & Management*, *39*(2), 151–163.

Berners-Lee, T., Hendler, J., & Lassila, O. (2001). The semantic web. *Scientific American*, Retrieved from http://www.sciam.com/

Berners-Lee, T., Hendler, J. & Lassila, O. (2001). A new form of Web content that is meaningful to computers will unleash a revolution of new possibilities. *Scientific American*, 284, 34–43.

Bernstein, R. J. (1976). *The restructuring of social and political theory.* Oxford, UK: Basil Blackwell.
Bhargava, H., & Choudhury, V. (2004). Economics of an information intermediary with aggregation benefits. *Information Systems Research, 15*(1), 22–36.
Bhargava, H. K., & Choudhury, V. (2001). Information goods and vertical differentiation. *Journal of Management Information Systems, 18*(2), 89–106.
Bierman, H. S., & Fernandez, L. (1998). *Game theory with economic applications* (2nd ed.). Reading, MA: Addison-Wesley.
Binney, D. 2001. The knowledge management spectrum–understanding the KM landscape. *Journal of Knowledge Management*, 5, 33–42.
Bohn, R. E. (1994). Measuring and managing technological knowledge. *Sloan Management Review, 36*(1), 61–73.
Boiko, B. (2005). *Content management bible.* Hoboken, NJ: Wiley.
Boisot, M. H. (1998). *Knowledge assets: Securing competitive advantage in the information economy.* Oxford: Oxford University Press.
Bourhis, A., Dubé, L., & Jacob, R. (2005). The success of virtual communities of practice: The leadership factor. *Electronic Journal of Knowledge Management, 3*(1), 23–34.
Bouwman, H., Faber, E., Haaker, T., Kijl, B., & De Reuver, M. (2008). Conceptualizing the STOF model. In H. Bouwman, H. De Vos, & T. Haaker (Eds.), *Mobile service innovation and business models* (pp. 31–70). Berlin: Springer-Verlag.
Brin, S., & Page, L. (1998). The anatomy of a large-scale hypertextual web search engine. *Seventh International World-Wide Web Conference (WWW 1998)*, Brisbane, Australia.
Brin, S. & Page, L. (1998). The anatomy of a large-scale hypertextual Web search engine* 1. *Computer networks and ISDN systems*, 30, 107–117.
Broadbent, M., & Weill, P. (1997). Management by maxim: How business and IT managers can create IT infrastructures. *Sloan Management Review, 38*(3), 77–92.
Brown, J., & Duguid, P. (2000). *The social life of information.* Boston, MA: Harvard Business School Press.
Caillaud, B., & Jullien, B. (2001). Competing cybermediaries. *European Economic Review, 45*(4–6), 797–808.
Carrington, P., Scott, J., & Wasserman, S. (Eds.). (2005). *Models and methods in social network analysis.* New York: Cambridge University Press.
Chen, K., & Yen, D. (2004). Improving the quality of online presence through interactivity. *Information & Management, 42*(1), 217–226.
Chessbrough, H. (2010). Business model innovation: Opportunities and barriers. *Long Range Planning, 43*(40239), 354–363.
Choi, S., Stahl, D., & Whinston, A. (1997). *The economics of electronic commerce.* Indianapolis, IN: MacMillan.
Choo, C., Detlor, W., & Turnbull, D. (2000). *Web work: Information seeking and knowledge work on the World Wide Web.* Dordrecht, Netherlands: Kluwer Academic Publishers.
Churchman, C. (1971). *The design of inquiring systems.* New York: Basic Books.
Chyi, H., & Sylvie, G. (2000). Online newspapers in the US: Perceptions of markets, products, revenue, and competition. *Journal of Media Management, 2*(2), 69–77.
Ciborra, C. (1987). Research agenda for a transaction costs approach to information systems. In R. Boland & R. Hirschheim (Eds.), *Critical issues in information systems research* (pp. 253–274). Chichester, UK: Wiley.
CIO Council, Best Practices Committee. (2002). *Value measuring methodology: How-to-guide.* Washington, DC: Federal CIO Council.

Clemons, E., & Lang, K. (2003). The decoupling of value creation from revenue: A strategic analysis of the markets for pure information goods. *Information Technology and Management, 4*, 259–287.

Clifton, B. (2010). *Advanced web metrics with Google Analytics* (2nd ed.). Indianapolis, IN: Wiley.

Cole, C. (1998). Intelligent information retrieval: Diagnosing information need. Part I. The theoretical framework for developing an intelligent IR tool. *Information Processing & Management, 34*, 709–720.

Courtney, J. (2001). Decision making and knowledge management in inquiring organizations: Toward a new decision-making paradigm for DSS. *Decision Support Systems, 31*, 17–38.

Courtney, J., Haynes, J., & Paradice, D. (Eds.). (2005). *Inquiring organizations: Moving from knowledge management to wisdom*. Hershey, PA: Idea Group.

Cross, R. & Sproull, L. 2004. More than an answer: Information relationships for actionable knowledge. *Organization Science*, 446–462.

Davenport, T., & Prusak, L. (1997). *Information ecology: Mastering the information and knowledge environment*. Oxford: Oxford University Press.

Delone, W., & McLean, E. (2003). The DeLone and McLean model of information systems success: A ten-year update. *Journal of Management Information Systems, 19*(4), 9–30.

Denzin, N. (2009). *The research act: A theoretical introduction into sociological methods*. Chicago: Aldin.

Dewan, R., Freimer, M., & Zhang, J. (2002). Managing web sites for profitability: Balancing content and advertising. *Proceedings of the 35th Hawaii International Conference on Systems Science*. Hawaii: IEEE Computer Society.

Dix, A., Finlay, J., & Abowd, G. (1997). *Human computer interaction*. Harlow: Prentice-Hall.

Dodd, J. (1996). Information brokers. *Special Libraries, 87*(4), 307–317.

Doll, W., & Torkzadeh, G. (1988). The measurement of end-user computing satisfaction. *Management Information Systems Quarterly, 12*(2), 258–275.

Dubé, L., & Paré, G. (2003). Rigor in information systems positivist case research: current practices, trends, and recommendations. *Management Information Systems Quarterly, 27*(4), 597–635.

Earl, M. (1993). Experiences in strategic information systems planning. *Management Information Systems Quarterly, 17*(1), 1–24.

Elorrieta, C., Lopez, J., & Wijnhoven, F. (2005). Supporting knowledge integration at SMEs: The KINX portal. In A. Jetter, J. Kraaijenbrink, H-H. Schröder, & F. Wijnhoven (Eds.), *Knowledge integration* (pp. 143–159). Heidelberg: Springer-Physik Verlag.

European Commission DG XII/E (Ed.). (1996). *Strategic developments for the European publishing industry towards the year 2000: Europe's multimedia challenge*. Brussels/Luxembourg: European Commission.

Faran, D. 2011. A *critical rationalist inquiry of managerial epistemology: toward the confrontation of the unawareness problem*. PhD, University of Twente.

Fetscherin, M., & Knowlmayer, G. (2004). Business models for content delivery: an empirical analysis of the newspaper and magazines industry. *The International Journal of Media Management, 6*(1/2), 4–11.

Fisher III, W. (2004). *Promises to keep: Technology, law, and the future of entertainment*. Palo Alto, CA: Stanford University Press.

Floridi, L. (2005a). Is semantic information meaningful data? *Philosophy and Phenomenological Research, 70*(2), 251–370.

Floridi, L. (2005b). Semantic conceptions of information. In E. N. Zalta (Ed.), *Stanford encyclopedia of philosophy*. Retrieved from http://plato.stanford.edu/archives/spr2011/entries/information-semantic/

Furubotn, E., & Pejovich, S. (1974). *The economics of property rights*. Cambridge, MA: Ballinger.

Gallaugher, J., Auger, P., & BarNir, A. (2001). Revenue streams and digital content providers: an empirical investigation. *Information & Management, 38*(7), 473–485.

Ghafoor, A., Aref, W., Spafford, E., & Joshi, J. (2001). Digital government security infrastructure design challenges. *Computer, 34*(2), 66–72.

Giaglis, G. (2001). A taxonomy of business process modelling and information systems modelling techniques. *International Journal of Flexible Manufacturing Systems, 13*(2), 209–228.

Giles, J. (2005). Internet encyclopaedias go head to head. *Nature, 438*(7070), 900–901. doi:10.1038/438900a

Gordijn, J. (2002). *Value-based requirements engineering: Exploring innovative e-commerce ideas*. Doctoral dissertation, Free University Amsterdam.

Gordijn, J. & Akkermans, H. (2001). Designing and evaluating e-business models. *IEEE Intelligent Systems, 16*(4), 11–17.

Gordijn, J., & Akkermans, J. (2004). Value-based requirements engineering: exploring innovative e-commerce ideas. *Requirements Engineering, 8*(2), 114–134.

Gould, R., & Fernandez, R. (1989). Structures of mediation: A formal approach to brokerage in transaction networks. *Sociological Methodology, 19*, 89–126.

Green, P., & Rosemann, M. (2000). Integrated process modeling: An ontological evaluation. *Information Systems, 25*(2), 73–87.

Gregor, S. (2006). The nature of theory in information systems. *Management Information Systems Quarterly, 30*(3), 611–642.

Grote, B., Rose, T., & Peter, G. (2002). Filter and broker: An integrated architecture for information mediation of dynamic sources. *Journal of Organizational Computing and Electronic Commerce, 12*(2), 133–160.

Gruber, T. (1993). A translation approach to portable ontology specifications. *Knowledge Acquisition, 5*, 199–220.

Guha, R., McCool, R., & Fikes, R. (2004). Contexts for semantic web. In S. McIlraith, D. Plexousakis, & F. van Harmelen, (Eds.), *The semantic Web—ISWC 2004 (Lecture notes in computer science, 3298)* (pp. 32–46). Berlin: Springer.

Gunnlaugsdottir, J. (2003). Seek and you will find, share and you will benefit: organizing knowledge using groupware systems. *International Journal of Information Management, 23*(5), 363–380.

Hall, W., Berners-Lee, T., & Shadbolt, N. (2006). The semantic web revisited. *IEEE Intelligent Systems, 21*(3), 96–101.

Hansen, M. T., Nohria, N. & Tierney, T. (1999). What's your strategy for managing knowledge? *Harvard Business Review*, 77, 106–116.

Hartnack, J. (1967). *Kant's theory of knowledge: An introduction to the critique of pure reason*. New York: Hartcourt, Brace and World.

Herbsleb, J., & Mockus, A. (2003). An empirical study of speed and communication in globally distributed software development. *IEEE Transactions on Software Engineering, 29*(6), 481–494.

Hevner, A., & Chatterjee, S. (2008). *Design research in information systems: Theory and practice*. Berlin/Heidelberg: Springer.

Hevner, A., March, S., Park, J., & Ram, S. (2004). Design science in information systems research. *Management Information Systems Quarterly, 28*(1), 75–105.

Hirschheim, R., Klein, H., & Lyytinen, K. (1996). Exploring the intellectual structures of information systems development: a social action theoretic analysis. *Accounting, Management & Information Technology, 6*(1/2), 1–64.

Hoffer, J. A., Prescott, M. B. & Mcfadden, F. R. (2002). *Modern Database Management*. Upper Saddle Creek, NJ: Prentice Hall.

Hoffman, D. & Novak, T. (2005). A conceptual framework for considering web-based business models and potential revenue streams. International *Journal of Marketing Education*, 1, 7–34.

Hong, J., Suh, E., & Kim, S. (2009). Context-aware systems: A literature review and classification. *Expert Systems with Applications, 36*, 8509–8522.

Hughes, J., & Lang, K. (2006). Transmutability: Digital contextualization, manipulation, and recontextualization as a new source of value in the production and consumption of culture products. *Proceedings of the 39th Hawaii International Conference on System Sciences (HICSS'06)*. IEEE Computer Society.

Iannella, R. (2002). Open digital rights language (ODRL), version 1.1. Retrieved from http://odrl.net/1.1/ODRL-11.pdf

Jansen, B. (2006). Search log analysis: What it is, what's been done, how to do it. *Library & Information Science Research, 28*(3), 407–432.

Johnson, G., Scholes, K. & Whittington, R. (2008). *Exploring corporate strategy: text & cases*. Upper Saddle Creek, NJ: Prentice Hall.

Jonkers, H., Lankhorst, M., Van Buuren, R., Hoppenbrouwers, S., Bonsangue, M., & Van der Torre, L. (2004). Concepts for modelling enterprise architectures. *International Journal of Cooperative Information Systems, 13*(3), 257–287.

Juhlin, D. (2010). *Mobile application analytics—specification for an online analytics tool*. Master's thesis, Division of Engineering Psychology, Luleå University of Technology.

Kambil, A., & Van Heck, E. (1998). Reengineering the Dutch flower auctions: A framework for analyzing exchange organizations. *Information Systems Research, 9*(1), 1–19.

Kankanhalli, A., Tan, B., & Wie, K-K. (2005). Contributing knowledge to electronic knowledge repositories: An empirical investigation. *Management Information Systems Quarterly, 29*(1), 113–143.

Kanneganti, R., & Chodavarapu, P. (2008). *SOA Security*. Greenwich, CT: Manning Publications.

Kaplan, A., & Haenlein, M. (2010). Users of the world, unite! The challenges and opportunities of Social Media. *Business Horizons, 53*(1), 59–68. doi:10.1016/j.bushor.2009.09.003

Karahanna, E., & Straub, D. (1999). The psychological origins of perceived usefulness and ease-of-use. *Information & Management, 35*(4), 237–250.

Kautz, K., Madsen, S. & Nørbjerg, J. (2007). Persistent problems and practices in information systems development. *Information Systems Journal*, 17, 217–239.

Keen, A. (2007). *The cult of the amateur: How the democratization of the digital world is assaulting our economy, our culture, and our values*. New York: Doubleday Currency.

Keinholz, A, Hayes, P. Mishra, R., & Engel, J. (1993). Further validation of the Revised Inquiry Mode Questionnaire. *Psychological Reports, 72*(1), 779–784.

Kim, J., Lee, J., Han, K., & Lee, M. (2002). Business as buildings: Metrics for the architectural quality of internet business. *Information Systems Research, 13*(3), 239–254.

Kimball, R., & Merz, R. (2000). *The data warehouse toolkit: Building the web-enabled data warehouse*. New York: Wiley.

Klein, H., & Myers, M. (1999). A set of principles for conducting and evaluating interpretive field studies in information systems. *Management Information Systems Quarterly, 23*(1), 67–93.

Kotler, P. (1988). *Marketing management*. Englewood Cliffs, NJ: Prentice-Hall.

Kroenke, D. (2008). *Experiencing MIS*. Englewood Cliffs, NJ: Prentice-Hall.

Krueger, C., Swatman, P., & Van der Beek, K. (2004). New and emerging business models for online news: A survey of 10 European Countries. *BLED 2004 Proceedings, paper 28*. http://aisel.aisnet.org/bled2004/28

Laganiere, R. & Lethbridge, T. (2001). Object-Oriented Software Engineering. New York: McGraw-Hill.

Lakatos, I. (1970). Falsification and the methodology of scientific research programmes. In I. Lakatos and A. Musgrave (Eds.), *Criticism and the growth of knowledge* (pp. 91–196). Cambridge: Cambridge University Press.

Landau, M. (1969). Redundancy, rationality, and the problem of duplication and overlap. *Public Administration Review, 29*(4), 346–356.

Lankhorst, M. et al. (2009). *Enterprise architecture at work: Modelling, communication and analysis* (2nd ed.). Berlin: Springer.

Larsen, G., & Conallen, J. (2002). Engineering web-based systems with UML assets. *Annals of Software Engineering, 13*, 203–230.

Lauesen, S. (2002). *Software requirements: styles and techniques*. Reading, MA: Addison-Wesley Professional.

Lawrence, S., & Lee Giles, C. (1999). Accessibility of information on the web. *Nature, 400*, 107–109.

Layne, K., & Lee, J. (2001). Developing fully functional E-government: A four stage model. *Government Information Quarterly, 18*(2), 122–136.

Lei, Y., Motta, E., & Domingue, J. (2004). OntoWeaver-S: Supporting the design of knowledge portals. In E. Motta, N. Shadbolt, & A. Stutt (Eds.), *Engineering knowledge in the age of the semantic Web EKAW, 2004 (Lecture notes in artificial intelligence, 3257)* (pp. 216–230). Berlin: Springer.

Liebeskind, J., Oliver, A., Zucker, L., & Brewer, M. (1996). Social networks, learning, and flexibility: Sourcing scientific knowledge in new biotechnology firms. *Organization Science, 7*(4), 428–443.

Lin, L., Geng, X., & Whinston, A. (2005). A sender-receiver framework for knowledge transfer. *Management Information Systems Quarterly, 29*(2), 197–219.

Lindgren, R., Henfridsson, O., & Schultze, U. (2004). Design principles for competence management systems: A synthesis of an action research study. *Management Information Systems Quarterly, 28*(3), 435–472.

Loebbecke, C. (1999). Electronic trading in on-line delivered content. *Proceedings of the 32nd Hawaii International Conference on Systems Sciences*, http://computer.org/proceedings/hicss/0001/00015/00015009.PDF

Look, B. (2008). Gottfried Wilhelm Leibniz. In E. Zalta (Ed.), *The Stanford encyclopedia of philosophy*. Retrieved from http://plato.stanford.edu/archives/spr2008/entries/leibniz/

Ma, M., & Agarwal, R. (2007). Through a glass darkly: Information technology design, identity verification, and knowledge contribution in online communities. *Information Systems Research, 18*(1), 42–67.

MacKie-Mason, J., Shenker, S., & Varian, H. (1996). Service architecture and content provision: The network provider as editor. *Telecommunications Policy, 20*(3), 203–218.

Maglio, P., & Barret, R. (2000). Intermediaries personalize information systems. *Communications of the ACM, 43*(8), 96–101.

Maloney-Krichmar, D., & Preece, J. (2005). A multilevel analysis of sociability, usability, and community dynamics in an online health community. *ACM Transactions on Computer-Human Interaction, 12*(2), 201–232.

Markus, M. (1983). Power, politics, and MIS implementation. *Communications of the ACM, 26*(6), 430–444.

Markus, M., Majchrzak, A., & Gasser, L. (2002). A design theory for systems that support emergent knowledge processes. *Management Information Systems Quarterly, 26*(3), 179–212.

Martí, R., & Delgado, J. (1998). Definition of service levels for electronic brokerage applications. In S. Trigila, A. Mullery, M. Campolargo, H. Vanderstraeten, & M. Mampaey (Eds.), *Intelligence in services and networks (Lecture notes in computer science, 1430)* (pp. 351–362). Berlin: Springer.

Mason, R. (1986). Four ethical issues of the information age. *Management Information Systems Quarterly, 10*(1), 486–498.

Mason, R., & Mitroff, I. (1973). A program for research on management information systems. *Management Science, 19*(5), 475–487.

McIlraith, S., Plexousakis, D., & van Harmelen, F. (Eds.). (2004). *The semantic Web—ISWC 2004 (Lecture notes on computer science, 3298)*. Berlin: Springer.

McLure-Wasko, M., & Faraj, S. (2005). Why should I share? Examining social capital and knowledge contribution in electronic networks of practice. *Management Information Systems Quarterly, 29*(1), 35–57.

Meyer, M., & Zack, M. (1996). The design and development of information products. *Sloan Management Review, 37*(3), 43–59.

Meyers, R. (2006). *Understanding empiricism*. Chesham, UK: Acumen Publishing.

Mingers, J. (2008). Management knowledge and knowledge management: realism and forms of truth. *Knowledge Management Research & Practice, 6*, 62–76.

Mingers, J. (2001). Combining IS research methods: Towards a pluralist methodology. *Information Systems Research, 12*(3), 240–259.

Moseley, R. (2007). *Developing web applications*. Chichester, UK: Wiley.

Nadkarni, S., & Gupta, R. (2007). A task-based model of perceived website complexity. *MIS Quarterly, 31*(3), 501–524.

Nederlandse Vereniging van Producenten en Importeurs van beeld- en geluidsdragers (NVPI). (2007a). De Entertainmentmarkt in 2006. Retrieved from http://www.nvpi.nl/assets/nvpi/jaarcijfers%202006.pdf

Nederlandse Vereniging van Producenten en Importeurs van beeld- en geluidsdragers (NVPI). (2007b). Onderzoek: Waarom Filesharing Leidt tot Minder Verkopen (In Dutch; title translated as "Why Filesharing Results in Less Sales"). Retrieved from http://www.nvpi.nl/assets/nvpi/onderzoeken%20schade%20_update_.pdf

Nelson, P. (1970). Information and consumer behavior. *Journal of Political Economy, 78*(2), 311–329.

Netanel, N. (2002). Impose a noncommercial use levy to allow free P2P file-swapping and remixing. *Harvard Journal of Law and Technology, 17*(1), 1–82.

Nijssen, G., & Halpin, T. (1989). *Conceptual schema and relational database design: A fact oriented approach*. New York: Prentice-Hall.

Novak, J., & Cañas, A. (2008). The theory underlying concept maps and how to construct and use them. Retrieved from http://cmap.ihmc.us/publications/researchpapers/theorycmaps/theoryunderlyingconceptmaps.htm

Novak, T., & Hoffman, D. (2001). *Profitability on the Web: Business models and revenue streams*. Nashville: Vanderbilt University, eLan, Owen Graduate School of Management.

Nunamaker Jr., J., Chen, M., & Purdin, T. (1991). Systems development in information systems research. *Journal of Management Information Systems, 7*(3), 89–106.

Ogden, C., & Richards, I. (1946). *The meaning of meaning: A study of the influence of language upon thought and of the science of symbolism* (8th ed.). London: Routledge & Kegan Paul.

Oksanen, V., & Välimäki, M. (2005). Copyright levies as an alternative compensation for recording artists and technological development. *Review of Economic Research on Copyright Issues, 2*(2), 25–39

O'Leary, D. (2008). Wikis: From each according to his knowledge. *Computer, 41*, 34–41.

Organisation for Economic Co-operation and Development (OECD). (2006). Broadband statistics to December 2006. Retrieved from http://www.oecd.org/sti/ict/broadband

Organisation for Economic Co-operation and Development (OECD). (2005). Working party on the information economy. Retrieved from www.oecd.org/sti/digitalcontent

Orwant, J. (1996). For want of a bit the user was lost: Cheap user modeling. *IBM Systems Journal, 35*(3–4), 398–416.

Osterwalder, A. (2004). *The business model ontology: A proposition in a design science approach.* Doctoral dissertation, University of Lausanne.

Osterwalder, A., & Pigneur, Y. (2009). *Business model generation.* Amsterdam: Modderman Drukwerk.

Palmer, J. (2002). Web site usability, design, and performance metrics. *Information Systems Research, 13*(2), 151–167.

Pateli, A., & Giaglis, G. (2004). A research framework for analysing eBusiness models. *European Journal of Information Systems, 13*(4), 302–314

Peitz, M., & Waelbroeck, P. (2005). An economist's guide to digital music. *CESifo Economic Studies, 51*(2–3), 359–428.

Pfaff, C., & Hasan, H. (2007). Can Knowledge Management be Open Source? Open source development, adoption and innovation. *Proceedings of the Third International Conference on Open Source Systems.* http://oss2007.dti.unimi.it/index.php?id=acceptedPaper.htm

Picard, R. (2000). Changing business models of online content services: Their implications for multimedia and other content producers. *Journal of Media Management, 2*(2), 60–68.

Picot, A., Bortenlanger, C., & Rohrl, H. (1997). Organization of electronic markets: Contributions from the new institutional economics. *The Information Society, 13*(1), 107–123.

Porter, M. (1985). *Competitive advantage.* New York: The Free Press.

Poston, R., & Speier, C. (2005). Effective use of knowledge management systems: a process model of content ratings and credibility indicators. *Management Information Systems Quarterly, 29*(2), 221–244.

Prahalad, C. K. & Hamel, G. (1994). Competing for the Future. *Harvard Business Review,* 72, 122–128.

Preece, J. (2001). Sociability and usability in online communities: determining and measuring success. *Behavior and Information Technology, 20*(5), 347–356.

Rappa, M. (2007). Managing the digital enterprise: Business models on the Web. Retrieved from http://digitalenterprise.org/models/models.html

Recker, J., Indulska, M., Rosemann, M., & Green, P. (2010). The ontological deficiencies of process modeling practice. *European Journal of Information Systems, 19,* 501–525.

Redding, P. (2006). Georg Friedrich Hegel. In E. Zalta (Ed.), *The Stanford encyclopedia of philosophy.* Retrieved from http://plato.stanford.edu/archives/fall2006/entries/hegel/

Robertson, S., & Reese, K. (1999). A virtual library for building community and sharing knowledge. *International Journal of Human-Computer Studies, 51,* 663–685.

Roll, R. (1984). Orange juice and weather. *The American Economic Review, 74*(5), 861–880.

Rose, F. (1999). *Information age and economy: The economics, concepts, and design of information intermediaries.* Heidelberg: Springer.

Sahlin, D., & Snell, C. (2007). *Building web sites all-in-one desk reference for dummies.* Hoboken, NJ: Wiley.

Scheer, A. (1998). *Aris: Business process frameworks.* Heidelberg: Springer.

Shapiro, C., & Varian, H. (1999). *Information rules: A strategic guide to the network economy.* Boston: Harvard Business School Press.

Sheth, A., Kashyap, V., & Lima, T. (1999). Semantic information brokering: How can a multi-agent approach help? In M. Klusch, O. M. Shehory, & G. Weiss (Eds.), *Cooperative information agents III (Lecture notes in artificial intelligence, 1652)* (pp. 303–322). Heidelberg: Springer.

Sinnerbrink, R. (2007). *Understanding Hegelianism*. Chesham, UK: Acumen Publishing.

Sowa, J. (2004). Laws, facts, and contexts: Foundations for multimodal reasoning. In V. Hendricks, K. Jørgensen, & S. Pedersen (Eds.), *Knowledge contributors* (pp. 145–184). Dordrecht, Netherlands: Kluwer Academic Publishers.

Sowa, J. (2000). Ontology, metadata, and semiotics. In B. Ganter & G. Mineau (Eds.), *Conceptual structures: Logical, linguistic, and computational issues (Lecture notes in artificial intelligence, 1867)* (pp. 55–81). Heidelberg: Springer.

Sowa, J., & Zachman, J. (1992). Extending and formalizing the framework for information systems architecture. *IBM Systems Journal, 31*(3), 590–616.

Spink, A. (1997). A study of interactive feedback during mediated information retrieval. *Journal of the American Society for Information Science, 48*(5), 382–394.

Spoelman, E., Nordhausen, S., Moor, C., & De Wit, C. (2008). *Business case modernisering GBA*. Utrecht: Cap Gemini N.V.

Stabell, C., & Fjeldsted, O. (1998). Configuring value for competitive advantage: On chains, shops, and networks. *Strategic Management Journal, 19*, 413–437.

Stamper, R. (1973). *Information in business and administrative systems*. New York: Wiley.

Stein, E. W. & Zwass, V. 1995. Actualizing organizational memory with information systems. *Information Systems Research*, 6, 85–117.

Strens, R., Martin, M., Dobson, J., & Plagemann, S. (1998). Business and market models of brokerage in network-based commerce. In S. Trigila, A. Mullery, M. Campolargo, H. Vanderstraeten, & M. Mampaey (Eds.), *Intelligence in services and networks (Lecture notes in computer science, 1430)* (pp. 315–326). Heidelberg: Springer.

Swatman, P. Krueger, C., & Van der Beek, K. (2006). The changing digital content landscape: An evaluation of e-business model development in European online news and music. *Internet Research, 16*(1), 53–80.

Tapscott, D., & Lowi, A. (2000). *Digital capital: Harnessing the power of business webs*. Boston: Harvard Business School Press.

Taylor, M., Wade, S., & England, D. (2003). Information IT system web site design through normalization. *Internet Research, 13*(2), 187–204.

Taylor, R. (1968). Question-negotiation and information seeking in libraries. *College and Research Libraries, 29*(3), 178–194.

Teece, D. J. (2010). Business models, business strategy and innovation. *Long Range Planning, 43*(2 & 3), 172–194.

Thompson, J. (1967). *Organizations in action: Social science bases of administrative theory*. New York: McGraw-Hill.

Timmers, P. (1998a). Business models for electronic markets. *Journal on Electronic Markets, 8*(2), 3–8.

Timmers, P. (1998b). *Electronic commerce: Strategies and models for business-to-business trading*. Chichester, UK: Wiley.

Turban, E. (1995). *Decision support systems and expert systems*. Englewood Cliffs, NJ: Prentice-Hall.

Uzgalis, W. (2007). John Locke. In E. Zalta (Ed.), *The Stanford encyclopedia of philosophy*. Retrieved from http://plato.stanford.edu/archives/sum2007/entries/locke/

Van Aken, J. (2004). Management research based on the paradigm of the design sciences: The quest for field-tested and grounded technological rules. *Journal of Management Studies, 41*(2), 219–246.

Van Baalen, P., Bloemhof-Ruwaard, J., & Van Heck, E. (2005). Knowledge sharing in an emerging network of practice: The role of a knowledge portal. *European Management Journal, 23*(3), 300–314.
Van Der Aalst, W., & Van Hee, K. (2004). *Workflow management: Models, methods and systems.* Cambridge, MA: MIT Press.
Van Der Aalst, W., Weijters, A., & Maruster, L. (2004). Workflow mining: Discovering process models from event logs. *IEEE Transactions on Knowledge and Data Engineering, 16*(9), 1128–1142.
Vidgen, R. (2002). Constructing a web information system development methodology. *Information Systems Journal, 12*, 247–261.
Vishik, C., & Whinston, A. (1999). Knowledge sharing, quality, and intermediation. *Software Engineering Notes, 24*(2), 157–166.
Voermans, K. (2007). *Economic validation of a media levy for digital music: Case study in the Dutch download market.* Enschede: University of Twente. http://essay.utwente.nl/57974
Vossen, G., & Hagemann, S. (2007). *Unleashing Web 2.0: From concepts to creativity.* Burlington, MA: Morgan Kaufmann.
Wagner, C. (2004). Wiki: A technology for conversational knowledge management and group collaboration. *Communications of the AIS, 13*, 256–289.
Walls, J., Widmeyer, G., & El Sawy, O. (1992). Building an information system design theory for vigilant EIS. *Information Systems Research, 3*(1), 36–59.
Walsham, G. (2002). Cross-cultural software production and use: A structurational analysis. *Management Information Systems Quarterly, 26*(4), 359–386.
Walsham, G., & Sahay, S. (1999). GIS for district-level administration in India: Problems and opportunities. *Management Information Systems Quarterly, 23*(1), 39–66.
Wand, Y., & Weber, R. (2002). Information systems and conceptual modeling: A research agenda. *Information Systems Research, 13*(4), 363–376.
Warr, K. (1994). *Paying for business information: The role of UK and European information brokers and consultants.* Cleethorpes, UK: Effective Technology Marketing Ltd.
Wei, C., Maust, B., Barrick, J., Cuddihy, E., & Spyridakis, J. (2005). Wikis for supporting distributed collaborative writing. *Proceedings of the 52nd Annual Conference of the Society for Technical Communication.*
Weick, K. (1979). *The social psychology of organizing.* Reading, MA: Addison-Wesley.
Weigand, H., Johannesson, P., Andersson, B., Bergholtz, M., Edirisuriya, A., & Ilayperuma, T. (2007). Strategic analysis using value modeling: The c3-value approach. *Proceedings of the 40th Hawaii International Conference on System Sciences.* Retrieved from http://www.computer.org/portal/web/csdl/doi/10.1109/HICSS.2007.501
Weill, P., & Vitale, R. (2001). *Place to space: Migrating to ebusiness models.* Boston: Harvard Business School Press.
White, S., & Miers, D. (2008). *BPMN modeling and reference guide: Understanding and using BPMN.* Lighthouse Point, FL: Future Strategies Inc.
Wieringa, R. (2003). *Design methods for reactive systems.* San Francisco, CA: Morgan Kaufmann.
Wigand, R. (1997). Electronic commerce: Definition, theory, and context. *The Information Society, 13*(1), 1–16.
Wijnhoven, F. (2002a). Design components for information market services: A framework for research and practice. In J. Monteiro, P. Swatman, & L. Valadares Tavares (Eds.), *Towards the knowledge society: eCommerce, eBusiness and eGovernment* (pp. 49–65). Boston, MA: Kluwer Academic Publishers.

Wijnhoven, F. (2002b). The importance of information goods abstraction levels for information commerce process models. *Journal of Electronic Commerce Research, 3*(2), 40–49.

Wijnhoven, F. (1999). Development scenarios for organizational memory information systems. *Journal of Management Information Systems, 16*(1), 121–146.

Wijnhoven, F., & Kraaijenbrink, J. (2008). Product-oriented design theory for digital information services: A literature review. *Internet Research, 18*(1), 93–120.

Wijnhoven, F., Meertens, L. & Engelse Den, N. 2010. The Hegelian Inquiring System and Critical Triangulation Tools for the Internet Information Slave. *The Ninth Annual Workshop on HCI Research in MIS*. St. Louis, Missouri USA: Association for Information Systems (AIS).

Wijnhoven, F., Timmer, J., & Schuur, P. (2010). The inventor game: Game theoretical analysis of knowledge-sharing between inventors and employers. *Knowledge Management Research & Practice, 8*, 61–75.

Williamson, O. (1992). Comparative economy organization: The analysis of discrete structural alternatives. *Administrative Science Quarterly, 36*, 269–296.

Womack, R. (2002). Information intermediaries and optimal information distribution. *Library & Information Science Research, 24*, 129–155.

Wu, M., Fuller, M., & Wilkinson, R. (2001). Using clustering and classification approaches in interactive retrieval. *Information Processing & Management, 37*, 459–484.

Yang, Z., Cai, S., Zhou, Z., & Zhou, N. (2004). Development and validation of an instrument to measure user perceived service quality of information presenting Web portals. *Information & Management, 42*, 575–589.

Yin, R. (2003). *Case study research: Design and methods* (3rd ed.). London: Sage.

Zott, C. & Amit, R. 2008. The fit between product market strategy and business model: implications for firm performance. *Strategic Management Journal*, 29, 1–26.

# Index